CHINESE-ENGLISH/ENGLISH-CHINESE POCKET LEGAL DICTIONARY

袖珍汉英-英汉法律词典

CHINESE-ENGLISH/ENGLISH-CHINESE POCKET LEGAL DICTIONARY

袖珍汉英-英汉法律词典

YOUNG CHEN

HIPPOCRENE BOOKS, INC.
New York

For information, address:
    Hippocrene Books, Inc.
    171 Madison Ave.
    New York, NY 10016
    www.hippocrenebooks.com

Series Editor: Lynn Visson
Series Consultant: James Nolan

Library of Congress Cataloging-in-Publication Data

    Chen, Young.
        Chinese-English English-Chinese pocket legal dictionary /
        Young Chen.
            p.   cm.
        ISBN 978-0-7818-1215-3 (alk. paper)
            1. Law—Dictionaries—Chinese. 2. Chinese language—
        Dictionaries—English. 3. Law—Dictionaries. 4. English
        language—Dictionaries—Chinese. I. Title.

    K52.C5C425 2008
    340.03—dc22   2007039744

Contents
(目录)

Foreword

This pocket dictionary is designed to help those individuals who need to communicate in real-life situations where it is vital to quickly find an English or Chinese legal term or phrase. The organization of the book is therefore more practical than analytical: entries are not listed strictly according to the conventions of lexicography or grammar; some nouns are listed in the plural if such usage is common. Without attempting to be exhaustive, we have sought to include most of the terms or concepts relevant to everyday legal situations and organized them in seven categories. Terms of a more general character are addressed in a separate category on general and procedural terminology. With a few exceptions, the dictionary does not define the entries. The reader should be aware that legal terms can be specific to a culture and exact equivalents in another language do not always exist.

前言

编纂这本双语双向美国法律词典,是为了给读者提供一本便携便用的工具书,遇有情况打开它就能找到所要的中英文法律词汇。这本词典突出实用性,条目没有严格按照词典学或语法规则编排,有些名词以复数形式列出。编者尽可能多地收录了日常生活中会碰到的法律及与法律有关的词汇,按商业、刑事、家事、健康、住房、移民、交通七类分别排列。程序性词汇以及可同时归入几类或哪类都难以归入的词,收入 "一般和程序性词汇",置于各类之首。因篇幅所限,除个别情况外,本词典不对词条进行释义。法律词汇具有强烈的文化特性,有时在另一种语言中找不到完全对等的词汇,请读者使用时留意。对本词典可能存在的错误,请读者不吝指正。

User Guide
(使用说明)

Notes on parts of speech, pronunciation, and sorting

Parts of speech are given for words, not for phrases. They are designated, where appropriate, by the following abbreviations:

adj   adjective
adv   adverb
n   noun
v   verb

The dictionary uses the simplified form of Chinese characters. Guidance on Chinese pronunciation follows the Basic Rules for Hanyu Pinyin Orthography adopted in China in 1996. Pinyin for all terms is in lower case.

Sorting of Chinese terms is based on the Pinyin alphabetical order. Thus 重组 (chóngzǔ) is grouped under c, while 重罪 (zhòngzuì) is found under z. Characters that share the same sounds are sorted in the order of their tones. Characters that share the same sounds and tones are sorted according to their beginning stroke in the standard stroke order, as follows: dot (丶), horizontal (一), vertical (丨), left-falling (丿), and turning (乛). Exceptions are made in order to keep together terms that begin with the same character.

词类、中文注音和排序说明

本词典只为基本单词标词类, 用下列英文缩略语标注:

adj	形容词
adv	副词
n	名词
v	动词

中文采用简体字, 注音采用汉语拼音。拼音的书写基本采用中国1996年1月颁布的《汉语拼音正词法基本规则》。以词为拼写单位。声调只标原调, 不标变调。音节界线可能混淆的, 用隔音符号 (') 隔开, 如: 投案 tóu'àn。本词典中汉语拼音一律采用小写。

中文词条按汉语拼音字母顺序排列。同音不同调的按声调顺序排列。同音同调的按下列起笔笔形的顺序排列: 点 (丶)、横 (一)、竖 (丨)、撇 (丿)、折 (一)。为便于查阅, 首字相同的词条一般排列在一起。

Chinese-English

（汉英）

一般和程序性词汇
General and Procedural Terms

本节收录了程序性词汇以及可同时收入其他几节或哪节都难以收入的词汇。

安非他明 ānfēitāmíng *n* amphetamine
安乐死 ānlèsǐ *n* euthanasia
安珀警报 ānpò jǐngbào Amber Alert
安全 ānquán *n* safety, security
案件 ànjiàn *n* case
案件重审 ànjiàn chóngshěn new trial of a case
案件流程管理 ànjiàn liúchéng guǎnlǐ caseflow
　　management
案卷 ànjuàn *n* case file
案例 ànlì *n* case
案情 ànqíng *n* facts of a case
暗示 ànshì *adj* implied; *v* imply
败诉 bàisù *v* lose a lawsuit
败诉方 bàisùfāng *n* losing party
办案 bàn'àn *v* handle a case
办案员 bàn'ànyuán *n* caseworker
帮派 bāngpài *n* gang, mob
包庇 bāobì *v* harbor
保安 bǎoān *n* security
保管 bǎoguǎn *n* custody
保护 bǎohù *n* protection; *v* protect
保护令 bǎohùlìng *n* protective order

一般和程序性词汇

保留权利 **bǎoliú quánlì** retain the right, reserve the right

保密 **bǎomì** *adj* secret, confidential

保人 **bǎorén** *n* bail

保释 **bǎoshì** *n/v* bail

保外就医 **bǎowài jiùyī** release on bail for medical treatment (*under Chinese law*)

保证书 **bǎozhèngshū** *n* affidavit

保证信 **bǎozhèngxìn** *n* certified mail

保证邮件 **bǎozhèng yóujiàn** *n* certified mail

报案 **bào'àn** *v* report a case

报复 **bàofù** *v* revenge, avenge

暴力 **bàolì** *n* violence, force

备案律师 **bèi'àn lǜshī** attorney of record

被告 **bèigào** *n* defendant

被告方 **bèigàofāng** *n* defense

被上诉人 **bèi shàngsùrén** *n* appellee, respondent on appeal

苯丙胺 **běnbǐng'àn** *n* amphetamine (又称安非他明 *a.k.a.* **ānfēitāmíng**)

辩护 **biànhù** *n* defense; *v* defend

辩护要点 **biànhù yàodiǎn** brief

辩论 **biànlùn** *n* argument; *v* argue

辩状 **biànzhuàng** *n* pleading

笔迹 **bǐjì** *n* handwriting

冰毒 **bīngdú** *n* methamphetamine

驳回 **bóhuí** *n* dismissal; *v* dismiss

驳回起诉, 不可再诉 **bóhuí qǐsù, bùkě zàisù** dismiss with prejudice

驳回起诉, 但可再诉 **bóhuí qǐsù, dàn kě zàisù** dismiss without prejudice

驳回异议 **bóhuí yìyì** overrule an objection

补偿 **bǔcháng** *n* compensation; *v* compensate

补偿性损害赔偿金 **bǔchángxìng sǔnhài péichángjīn**
  compensatory damages

补充 **bǔchōng** *adj* supplemental, supplementary;
  v supplement

补救 **bǔjiù** *adj* remedial; *n/v* remedy

不诚信 **bùchéngxìn** bad faith

不出庭 **bùchūtíng** failure to appear (FTA)

不当 **bùdàng** *adj* improper, unjust

不当行为 **bùdàng xíngwéi** misconduct, improper act

不法 **bùfǎ** *adj* illegal, unlawful

不可采信的证据 **bùkě cǎixìn de zhèngjù** inadmissible
  evidence

不可反驳的推定 **bùkě fǎnbó de tuīdìng** irrebuttable
  presumption

不可抗力 **bùkěkànglì** act of God

不履行义务 **bùlǚxíng yìwù** breach of duty

不履行债务 **bùlǚxíng zhàiwù** delinquency

不认罪 **bùrènzuì** plead not guilty, enter a not guilty plea

不作为 **bùzuòwéi** omission

财产 **cáichǎn** *n* property

裁定 **cáidìng** *n* adjudication; *v* adjudicate

裁决 **cáijué** *n* ruling, verdict

测谎器 **cèhuǎngqì** *n* polygraph, lie detector

抄袭 **chāoxí** *n* plagiarism; *v* plagiarize

撤回 **chèhuí** *n* withdrawal; *v* withdraw

撤诉 **chèsù** *n* discontinuance

撤销 **chèxiāo** *n* revocation, rescission; *n/v* repeal;
  v rescind, revoke, quash

陈述 **chénshù** *n* declaration, statement; *v* declare, state

陈述人 **chénshùrén** *n* declarant

成年人 **chéngniánrén** *n* adult

呈庭证据 **chéngtíng zhèngjù** exhibit

惩罚性赔偿金 **chéngfáxìng péichángjīn** punitive damages

程序 **chéngxù** *n* procedure

持有人 **chíyǒurén** *n* bearer

重审 **chóngshěn** *n* re-trial

重审理由 **chóngshěnlǐyóu** grounds for re-trial

初审法院 **chūshěn fǎyuàn** trial court

出让人 **chūràngrén** *n* assignor

出庭 **chūtíng** *v* appear in court; *n* court appearance

除非另有约定 **chúfēi lìngyǒu yuēdìng** unless otherwise
    agreed

处罚 **chǔfá** *n* penalty; *v* penalize

传达员 **chuándáyuán** *n* usher

传唤 **chuánhuàn** *v* subpoena, summon

传票 **chuánpiào** *n* subpoena, summons

传闻 **chuánwén** *n* hearsay

传真 **chuánzhēn** *n* facsimile; *v* fax

创伤 **chuāngshāng** *n* trauma

刺伤 **cì shāng** *n* puncture wound, stab wound

篡改 **cuàngǎi** *v* tamper with

错误 **cuòwù** *n* mistake

答辩 **dábiàn** *n* plea

打指印 **dǎ zhǐyìn** *v* fingerprint

大麻 **dàmá** *n* marijuana, cannabis, hemp

大陪审团 **dà péishěntuán** grand jury

大陪审团陪审员 **dà péishěntuán péishěnyuán**
    grand juror

代理 **dàilǐ** *v* represent

代理人 **dàilǐrén** *n* representative

代收公司 **dàishōu gōngsī** collection agency

代言人 **dàiyánrén** *n* spokesman, spokeswoman,
    spokesperson

待审案件目录 **dài shěn ànjiàn mùlù** docket

逮捕 **dàibǔ** *n/v* arrest

逮捕证 **dàibǔzhèng** *n* arrest warrant

担保金 **dānbǎojīn** *n* bond

担任陪审员 **dānrèn péishěnyuán** jury duty

当事人 **dāngshìrén** *n* party

到案 **dào'àn** *v* surrender

到期 **dàoqī** *n* expiration; *v* expire

敌对证人 **díduì zhèngrén** adverse witness

诋毁名誉 **dǐhuǐ míngyù** defamation; defame

抵销 **dǐxiāo** *v* offset

地方法规 **dìfāng fǎguī** ordinance

地方法院 **dìfāng fǎyuàn** district court

地方检察官 **dìfāng jiǎncháguān** district attorney

调查 **diàochá** *n* investigation; *v* investigate

调查记录 **diàochá jìlù** record of investigation

调查结果 **diàochá jiéguǒ** finding

定罪 **dìngzuì** *n* condemnation

动产 **dòngchǎn** *n* chattel, personalty

动机 **dòngjī** *n* motive

动议 **dòngyì** *n* motion

对陪审团的指示 **duì péishěntuán de zhǐshì** charge to the jury

毒品 **dúpǐn** *n* drugs, narcotics

毒瘾 **dúyǐn** *n* drug addiction

渎职 **dúzhí** *n* malfeasance

发回重审 **fāhuí chóngshěn** remand

罚金 **fájīn** *n* fine

法办 **fǎbàn** *v* bring to justice

法定 **fǎdìng** *adj* mandatory, statutory

法官 **fǎguān** *n* judge, justice

一般和程序性词汇

法官对陪审员的指示 **fǎguān duì péishěnyuán de zhǐshì** jury charge

法官审理 **fǎguān shěnlǐ** bench trial

法规 **fǎguī** *n* laws and regulations

法警 **fǎjǐng** *n* bailiff

法令 **fǎlìng** *n* decree

法律 **fǎlǜ** *n* law

法律代理人 **fǎlǜ dàilǐrén** legal representative, attorney, lawyer

法律地位 **fǎlǜ dìwèi** legal status

法律顾问 **fǎlǜ gùwèn** counsel

法律面前人人平等 **fǎlǜ miànqián rénrén píngděng** equality under the law

法庭费用 **fǎtíng fèiyòng** court costs

法院 (庭) **fǎyuàn (tíng)** *n* court

法院 (庭) 书记员 **fǎyuàn (tíng) shūjìyuán** court clerk

法院 (庭) 书记员办公室 **fǎyuàn (tíng) shūjìyuán bàngōngshì** court clerk's office

法院速记员 **fǎyuàn sùjìyuán** court reporter

法院院长 **fǎyuàn yuànzhǎng** presiding judge

翻供 **fāngòng** *v* retract testimony, withdraw confession

翻译 **fānyì** *n* translation, translator (笔头 /written), interpretation, interpreter (口头 /oral)

反驳 **fǎnbó** *n* rebuttal

反对 **fǎnduì** *n* objection

反诉 **fǎnsù** *n/v* counterclaim

犯法 **fànfǎ** *v* break the law

放弃 **fàngqì** *n* waiver; *v* waive

放弃权利 **fàngqì quánlì** waive a right

非法的 **fēifǎ de** *adj* illegal

非法进入 **fēifǎ jìnrù** illegal entry

非故意的 **fēi gùyì de** *adj* involuntary

非自愿的 **fēi zìyuàn de** *adj* involuntary
诽谤罪 **fěibàngzuì** *n* libel
废除 **fèichú** *v* abrogate, annul, repeal
费用 **fèiyòng** *n* cost, fee
分辨是非 **fēnbiàn shìfēi** distinguish between right and
　　wrong
分离诉讼 **fēnlí sùsòng** severance of proceedings
否认 **fǒurèn** *n* denial; *v* deny
服从 **fúcóng** *v* obey
辅助法官 **fǔzhù fǎguān** magistrate judge
副本 **fùběn** *n* copy
附件 **fùjiàn** *n* rider
付款 **fùkuǎn** *n* disbursement, payment
告 **gào** *v* complain, sue, bring a case against
跟踪罪 **gēnzōngzuì** *n* stalking
更改 **gēnggǎi** *v* alter, modify
工伤 **gōngshāng** *n* work-related injury
公司章程 **gōngsī zhāngchéng** bylaws, articles of
　　association
公诉人 **gōngsùrén** *n* public prosecutor
公约 **gōngyuē** *n* convention
公证人 **gōngzhèngrén** *n* notary
供述 **gòngshù** *n* admission
古柯 **gǔkē** *n* coca
故意地 **gùyì de** *adv* knowingly
关税 **guānshuì** *n* customs
管理 **guǎnlǐ** *n* administration; *v* administer
管理人 **guǎnlǐrén** *n* administrator
管辖范围 **guǎnxiá fànwéi** jurisdictional limit
管辖权 **guǎnxiáquán** *n* jurisdiction
惯例 **guànlì** *n* practice, convention
规避 **guībì** *v* circumvent

国籍 **guójí** *n* nationality

国际司法协助 **guójì sīfǎ xiézhù** international judicial assistance

国土安全部 **guótǔ ānquán bù** Department of Homeland Security (DHS)

过失 **guòshī** *adj* negligent; *n* negligence; *v* neglect

过失致死 **guòshī zhìsǐ** wrongful death

海关 **hǎiguān** *n* customs

合并诉讼 **hébìng sùsòng** consolidation of actions

合法 **héfǎ** *adj* legal, lawful, legitimate

合法化 **héfǎhuà** *n* legalization

合理根据 (理由) **hélǐ gēnjù (lǐyóu)** reasonable basis, reasonable ground

合同 **hétong** *n* contract, agreement

合议庭 **héyìtíng** *n* panel of judges

和解 **héjiě** *n* conciliation

后果自负 **hòuguǒ zìfù** at your own risk

护照 **hùzhào** *n* passport

还押候审 **huányā hòushěn** remand

恢复 **huīfù** *v* resume, rehabilitate

回避 **huíbì** *n* recusal; *v* recuse

贿赂 **huìlù** *n* bribe, bribery; *v* bribe

基本权利 **jīběn quánlì** fundamental rights

机密的 **jīmì de** *adj* confidential

激情表述 **jīqíng biǎoshù** excited utterance

缉拿 **jīná** *v* apprehend

缉私 **jīsī** *adj* anti-smuggling; *n* suppression of smuggling

集体诉讼 **jítǐ sùsòng** class action

集体诉讼公平法 **jítǐ sùsòng gōngpíng fǎ** Class Action Fairness Act (CAFA)

继承 **jìchéng** *n* inheritance; *v* inherit

继承人 **jìchéngrén** *n* heir

甲基苯丙胺 **jiǎjī běnbǐng'àn** *n* methamphetamine
　　(俗称冰毒 *a.k.a.* **bīngdú**)
价值 **jiàzhí** *n* value
间接证据 **jiànjiē zhèngjù** circumstantial evidence
监护权 **jiānhùquán** *n* conservatorship, custody
监护人 **jiānhùrén** *n* conservator
减轻的 **jiǎnqīng de** *adj* extenuating, mitigating
检察官 **jiǎncháguān** *n* prosecutor, attorney
简易程序 **jiǎnyì chéngxù** summary proceeding
简易判决 **jiǎnyì pànjué** summary judgment
交叉诘问 **jiāochā jiéwèn** cross-examination; cross-examine
交叉诉讼状 **jiāochā sùsòngzhuàng** cross-complaint
教唆 **jiàosuō** *v* suborn
教唆罪 **jiàosuōzuì** *n* subornation
竭尽救济原则 **jiéjìn jiùjì yuánzé** exhaustion of remedies
诘问 **jiéwèn** *n* question; *v* examine
诘问证人 **jiéwèn zhèngrén** examination of witness
诘问专家 **jiéwèn zhuānjiā** expert examination
解决 **jiějué** *n* settlement
紧迫危险 **jǐnpò wēixiǎn** imminent danger
禁制令 **jìnzhì lìng** *n* injunction
精神病医学鉴定 **jīngshénbìng yīxué jiàndìng**
　　psychiatric evaluation
精神错乱 **jīngshén cuòluàn** insane; insanity
精神分裂症 **jīngshén fēnlièzhèng** *n* schizophrenia
精神缺陷 **jīngshén quēxiàn** mental deficiency
精神失常 **jīngshén shīcháng** mental disorder
精神抑郁症 **jīngshén yìyùzhèng** mental depression
经济担保书 **jīngjì dānbǎoshū** affidavit of support (AOS)
经确证的 **jīng quèzhèng de** *adj* corroborated
警察 **jǐngchá** *n* police, policeman, police officer
警方 **jǐngfāng** *n* police

警告 **jǐnggào** *n* admonition; *v* admonish

警官 **jǐngguān** *n* police officer

警员 **jǐngyuán** *n* policeman

净值 **jìngzhí** *n* net worth

纠纷 **jiūfēn** *n* dispute

酒精 **jiǔjīng** *n* alcohol

酒瘾 **jiǔyǐn** *n* alcohol addiction

拘留 **jūliú** *n* detention; *v* detain

举证责任 **jǔzhèng zérèn** burden of proof

拒绝 **jùjué** *n* denial; *v* deny

开场陈述 **kāichǎng chénshù** opening statement

开庭 **kāitíng** *v* begin a court session

抗辩制 **kàngbiànzhì** *n* adversarial system

可采信的证据 **kě cǎixìn de zhèngjù** admissible evidence

可反驳的 **kě fǎnbó de** rebuttable

可卡因 **kěkǎyīn** *n* cocaine

可信 **kěxìn** *adj* credible; *n* credibility

可支配收入 **kě zhīpèi shōurù** disposable income

恐吓 **kǒnghè** *n* intimidation; *v* intimidate

控告 **kònggào** *n* complaint; *v* complain, sue

控告人 **kònggàorén** *n* complainant

口供 **kǒugòng** *n* verbal confession

口头辩论 **kǒutóu biànlùn** oral argument

口头程序 **kǒutóu chéngxù** oral proceedings

口译 **kǒuyì** *n* interpretation; *v* interpret

口译员 **kǒuyìyuán** *n* interpreter

扣押工资 (财产) 令 **kòuyā gōngzī (cáichǎn) lìng** garnishment

宽限期 **kuānxiànqī** *n* grace period

困窘 **kùnjiǒng** *n* hardship

滥用 **lànyòng** *n/v* abuse

滥用权力 **lànyòng quánlì** abuse of power

滥用信任 **lànyòng xìnrèn** abuse of trust

理算人 **lǐsuànrén** *n* adjuster (*insurance*)

理由 **lǐyóu** *n* ground

连署人 **liánshǔrén** *n* cosigner

联邦调查局 **liánbāng diàochájú** Federal Bureau of Investigation (FBI)

联邦紧急情况管理局 **liánbāng jǐnjí qíngkuàng guǎnlǐ jú** Federal Emergency Management Agency (FEMA)

临床检查 **línchuáng jiǎnchá** clinical examination

流审 **liúshěn** *n* mistrial

履行判决收据 **lǚxíng pànjué shōujù** acknowledgment of satisfaction of judgment

律师 **lǜshī** *n* attorney, lawyer

律师费 **lǜshī fèi** attorney's fee

律师界 **lǜshījiè** *n* bar

麻醉品 **mázuìpǐn** *n* narcotic drugs

美国司法部 **měiguó sīfǎbù** United States Department of Justice (USDOJ)

藐视法庭罪 **miǎoshì fǎtíng zuì** *n* contempt of court

民事控诉 **mínshì kòngsù** civil complaint

命令 **mìnglìng** *n/v* order

没收 **mòshōu** *v* forfeit

脑挫伤 **nǎo cuòshāng** brain contusion

脑损伤 **nǎo sǔnshāng** brain damage

年龄 **niánlíng** *n* age

虐待 **nuèdài** *n/v* abuse

判决 **pànjué** *n* judgment, award, decree; *v* judge

判决摘要 **pànjué zhāiyào** abstract of judgment

判例法 **pànlìfǎ** *n* case law

陪审团 **péishěntuán** *n* jury

陪审团团长 **péishěntuán tuánzhǎng** foreman of jury

陪审员 **péishěnyuán** *n* juror

一般和程序性词汇

披露 **pīlù** *n* disclosure; *v* disclose
平权措施 **píngquán cuòshī** affirmative action
期间 **qījiān** *n* period, term
期满 **qīmǎn** *n* expiration; *v* expire
期限 **qīxiàn** *n* set time, deadline
欺骗 **qīpiàn** *n* deception; *v* deceive
欺诈意图 **qīzhà yìtú** fraudulent intent
起诉 **qǐsù** *v* sue, prosecute
起诉状 **qǐsùzhuàng** *n* indictment, declaration, petition, complaint
契据 **qìjù** *n* deed
契约 **qìyuē** *n* agreement, contract
牵连 **qiānlián** *adj* implicated; *n* implication; *v* implicate
签名 **qiānmíng** *n* signature; *v* sign, affix signature
强制性的 **qiángzhìxìng de** *adj* mandatory
强制执行 **qiángzhì zhíxíng** enforcement (*of judgment*)
窃听 **qiètīng** *n* eavesdropping
侵犯 **qīnfàn** *v* violate, trespass
侵权行为 **qīnquán xíngwéi** tort
侵权行为人 **qīnquán xíngwéirén** tortfeasor
情节证据 **qíngjié zhèngjù** circumstantial evidence
请求 **qǐngqiú** *n/v* claim
请求人 **qǐngqiúrén** *n* claimant
取消 **qǔxiāo** *v* abrogate, annul, cancel
取消资格 **qǔxiāo zīgé** disqualification; disqualify
权利主张 **quánlì zhǔzhāng** claim
权益 **quányì** *n* equity, rights and interests
缺席判决 **quēxí pànjué** default judgment
确认 **quèrèn** *v* affirm
确证 **quèzhèng** *v* corroborate
人身保护令 **rénshēn bǎohù lìng** habeas corpus
认罪 **rènzuì** *v* plead guilty

日期 **rìqī** *n* date

入境 **rùjìng** *n* admission, entry

骚扰 **sāorǎo** *n* harassment

杀人罪 **shārénzuì** *n* manslaughter

煽动 **shāndòng** *n* incitement; *v* incite

伤害 **shānghài** *n* harm, injury; *v* harm, injure

伤口 **shāngkǒu** *n* wound

上诉 **shàngsù** *n/v* appeal

上诉法院 **shàngsù fǎyuàn** court of appeals

上诉人 **shàngsùrén** *n* appellant

上诉通知 **shàngsù tōngzhī** notice of appeal

上诉许可 **shàngsù xǔkě** leave to appeal

社会保障号码 **shèhuì bǎozhàng hàomǎ** Social Security
number (SSN)

社会保障署 **shèhuì bǎozhàng shǔ** Social Security
Administration (SSA)

社会工作者 **shèhuì gōngzuòzhě** social worker

申请 **shēnqǐng** *n* application; *n/v* petition; *v* apply

申诉 **shēnsù** *n/v* petition

身体伤害 **shēntǐ shānghài** bodily injury or harm,
physical injury or harm

审查事实 **shěnchá shìshí** examine the facts

审理程序 **shěnlǐ chéngxù** trial procedure

审理日 **shěnlǐrì** trial date

审判 **shěnpàn** *n* trial; *v* try

审判室 **shěnpànshì** *n* courtroom

生存者 **shēngcúnzhě** *n* survivor

胜诉方 **shèngsùfāng** *n* prevailing party

实施犯罪 **shíshī fànzuì** commission; commit a crime

实质性错误 **shízhìxìng cuòwù** substantial error

适当法律程序 **shìdàng fǎlǜ chéngxù** due process

事件报告 **shìjiàn bàogào** incident report

事实调查 shìshí diàochá fact finding

事先协定的赔偿金 shìxiān xiédìng de péichángjīn
    liquidated damages

事项管辖权 shìxiàng guǎnxiáquán subject-matter
    jurisdiction

誓言 shìyán *n* oath

收集证据 shōují zhèngjù collect evidence

收入 shōurù *n* income

授权书 shòuquánshū *n* power of attorney

受害方 shòuhàifāng *n* injured party

受害人 shòuhàirén *n* victim

受监护人 shòu jiānhùrén *n* conservatee

受让人 shòuràngrén *n* assignee

受损害方 shòu sǔnhài fāng *n* aggrieved party

受托人 shòutuōrén *n* fiduciary, trustee

书面陈述 shūmiàn chénshù written statement

书面回答 shūmiàn huídá written answer

书证 shūzhèng *n* documentary evidence

疏忽 shūhū *adj* negligent; *n* negligence; *v* neglect

属地管辖权 shǔdì guǎnxiáquán territorial jurisdiction

属人管辖权 shǔrén guǎnxiáquán personal jurisdiction

数额 shù'é *n* amount

司法复核 sīfǎ fùhé judicial review

死亡证明书 sǐwáng zhèngmíngshū death certificate

死因调查陪审团 sǐyīn diàochá péishěntuán
    inquest jury

死因审理 sǐyīn shěnlǐ inquest

死者 sǐzhě *n* decedent

死者证言不可采信规则 sǐzhě zhèngyán bùkě cǎixìn
    guīzé dead man's statute

送达 sòngdá *n* service; *v* serve

搜查 sōuchá *n/v* search

搜身 **sōushēn** *n* body search; *n/v* frisk

诉讼 **sùsòng** *n* action, lawsuit, litigation; *v* litigate, take legal action

诉讼程序 **sùsòng chéngxù** proceedings

诉讼待决期间 **sùsòng dàijué qījiān** pendente lite

诉讼代理人 **sùsòng dàilǐrén** attorney, lawyer, legal representative

诉讼当事人 **sùsòng dāngshìrén** *n* litigant

诉讼费用 **sùsòng fèiyòng** litigation cost

诉讼时效法 **sùsòng shíxiàofǎ** statute of limitations

诉讼要点 **sùsòng yàodiǎn** brief

诉状 **sùzhuàng** *n* pleading

损害赔偿金 **sǔnhài péichángjīn** damages

索赔 **suǒpéi** *n/v* claim

索赔人 **suǒpéirén** *n* claimant

贪腐 **tānfǔ** *adj* corrupt; *n* corruption

弹劾 **tánhé** *n* impeachment; *v* impeach

逃庭 **táotíng** failure to appear (FTA)

提供证据的 **tígōng zhèngjù de** evidentiary

替补 **tìbǔ** *adj/n* alternate

天灾 **tiānzāi** *n* act of God

调解 **tiáojiě** *n* mediation; *v* mediate

调解人 **tiáojiěrén** *n* mediator

条款 **tiáokuǎn** *n* clause

条约 **tiáoyuē** *n* treaty

听证会 **tīngzhènghuì** *n* hearing

庭审法官 **tíngshěn fǎguān** trial judge

庭审纪录 **tíngshěn jìlù** transcript, trial record

庭审律师 **tíngshěn lǜshī** trial lawyer

庭外取证 **tíngwài qǔzhèng** deposition

通知 **tōngzhī** *n* notice; *v* notify

同意 **tóngyì** *n* consent

一般和程序性词汇

同意一项动议 **tóngyì yīxiàng dòngyì** grant a motion
投案 **tóu'àn** *v* surrender
团伙 **tuánhuǒ** *n* gang, mob
推迟 **tuīchí** *v* delay
推迟审理 **tuīchí shěnlǐ** continuance
推定 **tuīdìng** *n* presumption; *v* presume
拖欠 **tuōqiàn** *n* arrears
拖欠债务者 **tuōqiàn zhàiwù zhě** delinquent
脱氧核糖核酸 **tuōyǎng hétáng hésuān** DNA
外国的 **wàiguó de** *adj* alien, foreign
外国人 **wàiguórén** *n* alien, foreigner
玩忽职守 **wánhūzhíshǒu** *n* neglect of official duty
威胁 **wēixié** *n* threat; *v* threaten
违法行为 **wéifǎ xíngwéi** offense, violation
违反 **wéifǎn** *n/v* breach
违宪 **wéixiàn** *adj* unconstitutional
维持原判 **wéichí yuánpàn** affirmance of a decision
委托 **wěituō** *n* trust
委托书 **wěituōshū** *n* power of attorney
伪证 **wěizhèng** *n* perjury
猥亵儿童者 **wěixiè értóng zhě** child molester
猥亵行为 **wěixiè xíngwéi** lewd conduct
为诉讼目的 **wèi sùsòng mùdì** ad litem
未成年犯 **wèichéngnián fàn** *n* delinquent
未成年人 **wèichéngniánrén** *n* minor, juvenile
未决诉讼 **wèijué sùsòng** lis pendens
未留遗嘱的 **wèi liú yízhǔ de** intestate
无保留 **wúbǎoliú** *adj* without reservations
无管辖权 **wú guǎnxiáquán** lack of jurisdiction
无条件 **wútiáojiàn** *adj* unconditional
无效 **wúxiào** *adj* invalid, null and void
武器 **wǔqì** *n* weapon

General and Procedural Terms

物证 wùzhèng *n* physical evidence
吸毒 xīdú *n* drug abuse, drug addiction
习惯 xíguàn *n* custom
洗钱 xǐqián *n* money laundering
嫌疑人 xiányírén *n* suspect
宪法 xiànfǎ *n* constitution
享有权利 xiǎngyǒu quánlì enjoyment of rights
消费者 xiāofèizhě *n* consumer
小陪审团 xiǎo péishěntuán petit jury
小陪审团陪审员 xiǎo péishěntuán péishěnyuán
    petit juror
协定 xiédìng *n* agreement
协议 xiéyì *n* agreement
协助 xiézhù *n* assistance, facilitation; *v* assist, facilitate
性别 xìngbié *n* sex
性交 xìngjiāo *n* sexual intercourse
性骚扰 xìngsāorǎo *n* sexual harassment
休庭 xiūtíng *adj* adjourned; *n* adjournment; *v* adjourn
修正 xiūzhèng *v* amend
修正案 xiūzhèng'àn *n* amendment
宣告 xuāngào *n* declaration; *v* declare
宣誓 xuānshì *v* swear, take an oath
宣誓书 xuānshìshū *n* affidavit
宣誓证明 xuānshì zhèngmíng depose
宣誓证人 xuānshì zhèngrén deponent
悬赏 xuánshǎng *v* post a reward
许可证 xǔkězhèng *n* permit
酗酒 xùjiǔ *n* alcoholism
酗酒者 xùjiǔzhě *n* alcoholic, drunk
蓄意 xùyì *adj* deliberate, willful
蓄意作为 xùyì zuòwéi willful commission
询问 xúnwèn *n* inquiry; *v* inquire

一般和程序性词汇

讯问 **xùnwèn** *v* interrogate

押交 **yājiāo** *v* commit (*confine*)

延长延缓期 **yáncháng yánhuǎnqī** extension of period of stay

延期 **yánqī** *v* postpone

验尸官 **yànshǐguān** *n* coroner

要求回避 **yāoqiú huíbì** challenge

要求陪审员回避 **yāoqiú péishěnyuán huíbì** jury challenge

一案不二诉原则 **yī àn bù èr sù yuánzé** res judicata

医疗报告 **yīliáo bàogào** medical report

依据法律 **yījù fǎlǜ** by operation of law

移送联邦法院 **yísòng liánbāng fǎyuàn** removal to federal court

遗产法院 **yíchǎn fǎyuàn** surrogate court

遗弃 **yíqì** *n* abandonment; *v* abandon

遗嘱 **yízhǔ** *n* will

遗嘱检验 **yízhǔ jiǎnyàn** probate

意图 **yìtú** *n* intention; *v* intend

意外 **yìwài** *n* surprise, accident

义务 **yìwù** *n* obligation, duty

异议 **yìyì** *n* objection

淫秽 **yínhuì** *n* obscenity

瘾 **yǐn** *n* addiction

隐藏 **yǐncáng** *v* conceal

隐私 **yǐnsī** *n* privacy

引诱 **yǐnyòu** *v* induce, seduce

印度大麻 **yìndù dàmá** hashish

应负责任的 **yīng fùzérède** *adj* responsible

应受惩罚 **yīngshòu chéngfá** culpable; culpability

英语水平有限 **yīngyǔ shuǐpíng yǒuxiàn** limited English proficiency (LEP)

佣金 **yòngjīn** *n* commission
有保留 **yǒubǎoliú** with reservations
有能力承受审判 **yǒunénglì chéngshòu shěnpàn**
    competent to stand trial
有能力作证 **yǒunénglì zuòzhèng** competent to testify
有条件 **yǒutiáojiàn** *adj* conditional
有条件豁免 **yǒutiáojiàn huòmiǎn** qualified immunity
有效的 **yǒuxiào de** *adj* valid
有形的 **yǒuxíng de** *adj* tangible
诱导性提问 **yòudǎoxìng tíwèn** leading question
预见 **yùjiàn** *v* foresee
冤情 **yuānqíng** *n* grievance
原告 **yuángào** *n* plaintiff, complainant, claimant
再交叉诘问 **zài jiāochā jiéwèn** re-cross examination
责任 **zérèn** *adj* liable; *n* liability, responsibility
摘要 **zhāiyào** *n* abstract
侦探 **zhēntàn** *n* detective
争执 **zhēngzhí** *n/v* dispute
证词 **zhèngcí** *n* testimony
证据 **zhèngjù** *n* evidence, proof
证据保管 **zhèngjù bǎoguǎn** custody of evidence
证据裁定 **zhèngjù cáidìng** evidence ruling
证据开示 **zhèngjù kāishì** discovery
证明 **zhèngmíng** *n* proof; *v* prove
证明价值 **zhèngmíng jiàzhí** probative value
证明书 **zhèngmíngshū** *n* affidavit
证人 **zhèngrén** *n* witness
证书 **zhèngshū** *n* certificate
证言 **zhèngyán** *n* testimony
政府征用权 **zhèngfǔ zhēngyòngquán** eminent domain
正义 **zhèngyì** *n* justice
知情的同意 **zhīqíng de tóngyì** informed consent

执达官 **zhídáguān** *n* bailiff
执行 **zhíxíng** *v* execute, administer
执行人 **zhíxíngrén** *n* executor
执照 **zhízhào** *n* permit
直接代扣收入 **zhíjiē dài kòu shōurù** direct income
     withholding
直接诘问 **zhíjiē jiéwèn** direct examination
指称 **zhǐchēng** *n* allegation; *v* allege
指控 **zhǐkòng** *n/v* charge
指印 **zhǐyìn** *n* fingerprint, fingerprinting
治安法院 **zhì'ān fǎyuàn** justice court
制定法 **zhìdìngfǎ** *n* statute, statutory law
质疑 **zhìyí** *n/v* challenge
中央情报局 **zhōngyāng qíngbàojú** Central Intelligence
     Agency (CIA)
终止 **zhōngzhǐ** *n* discontinuance; *v* discontinue
种族貌相 **zhǒngzú màoxiàng** racial profiling
中毒 **zhòngdú** *n* intoxication; *v* intoxicate
重大过失 **zhòngdà guòshī** gross negligence
逐字纪录 **zhúzì jìlù** verbatim records
主审 **zhǔshěn** *v* preside over
主审法官 **zhǔshěn fǎguān** presiding judge
注意义务 **zhùyì yìwù** duty of care
住所 **zhùsuǒ** *n* domicile
专家 **zhuānjiā** *n* expert
专家意见 **zhuānjiā yìjiàn** expert opinion
专家证人 **zhuānjiā zhèngrén** expert witness
专门知识 **zhuānmén zhīshi** expertise
转让 **zhuǎnràng** *n* assignment; *v* assign
州警 **zhōujǐng** *n* state trooper
资格 **zīgé** *adj* eligible; *n* eligibility
自利交易 **zì lì jiāoyì** self dealing

自杀 **zìshā** *n* suicide; *v* commit suicide
自愿 **zìyuàn** *adj* voluntary; *adv* voluntarily, willingly
总结性陈述 **zǒngjiéxìng chénshù** summation
最后辩论 **zuìhòu biànlùn** closing argument
罪行 **zuìxíng** *n* crime
醉酒 **zuìjiǔ** *adj* drunk; *n* drunkenness
遵守 **zūnshǒu** *v* comply with
作为 **zuòwéi** *n* act
作证 **zuòzhèng** *v* testify, give evidence
作准的 **zuòzhǔn de** *adj* authentic

商法词汇
Commercial Law

商法所涉范围包括合同和商业关系、金融、银行、投资、保险、货物和服务的买卖以及消费者事务等。

401(k) 退休计划 sì líng yī (k) tuìxiū jìhuà 401(k) Plan

W-2 表 w-èr biǎo W-2 Form (**工资和扣税表 gōngzī hé kòushuì biǎo**)

W-4 表 w-sì biǎo W-4 Form (**预扣税减免表 yù kòushuì jiǎnmiǎn biǎo**)

按比例 ànbǐlì pro rata

版权 bǎnquán *n* copyright

半年报告 bànnián bàogào half-year report

保兑银行 bǎoduì yínháng confirming bank

保付支票 bǎofù zhīpiào certified check

保险 bǎoxiǎn *n* insurance

保险费 bǎoxiǎnfèi *n* insurance premium

保用 bǎoyòng *n* warranty

报表 bàobiǎo *n* statement

报税 bàoshuì *v* file a tax return

报税代理人 bàoshuì dàilǐrén return preparer, tax preparer

报销 bàoxiāo *n* reimbursement; *v* reimburse

贝宝 bèibǎo PayPal

被保险人 bèi bǎoxiǎnrén insured

被背书人 bèi bèishūrén endorsee

被担保方 bèi dānbǎofāng secured party

被动经营 bèidòng jīngyíng passive activity

被要约人 bèi yāoyuērén offeree

背书 **bèishū** *n* endorsement; *v* endorse

背书人 **bèishūrén** *n* endorser

本金 **běnjīn** *n* principal

本票 **běnpiào** *n* bank check, cashier's check, teller's check

避税手段 **bìshuì shǒuduàn** tax shelter

边境交货 **biānjìng jiāohuò** delivered at frontier (DAF)

变现 **biànxiàn** *n* liquidation

表 **biǎo** *n* form, table

并购 **bìnggòu** mergers and acquisitions (M&A)

补偿 **bǔcháng** *n* recovery

补充 **bǔchōng** *v* replenish

不公平竞争 **bùgōngpíng jìngzhēng** unfair competition

不记名的 **bùjìmíng de** *adj* bearer

不竞争条款 **bùjìngzhēng tiáokuǎn** no-competition clause

不遵守 **bùzūnshǒu** non-compliance

财务报表 **cáiwù bàobiǎo** financial statement

财务调查员 **cáiwù diàocháyuán** financial investigator

财务交易 **cáiwù jiāoyì** financial transaction

财务义务 **cáiwù yìwù** financial obligation

财政年度 **cáizhèng niándù** fiscal year

采购 **cǎigòu** *n* procurement; *v* procure

查账 **cházhàng** *n/v* audit

查账员 **cházhàngyuán** *n* auditor

产量 **chǎnliàng** *n* production

产品 **chǎnpǐn** *n* product

产品标记 **chǎnpǐn biāojì** product mark

产品责任 **chǎnpǐn zérèn** product liability

长期国库债券 **chángqī guókù zhàiquàn** treasury bill

偿还 **chánghuán** *n* repayment

偿还期 **chánghuánqī** *n* repayment period

超额计费 **chāo'é jìfèi** overbilling

超面值 **chāo miànzhí** above par

超限费 **chāo xiàn fèi** overlimit charge

撤销条款 **chèxiāo tiáokuǎn** cancellation clause

成本, 保险费加运费 **chéngběn bǎoxiǎnfèi jiā yùnfèi** cost, insurance and freight (CIF)

成本加运费 **chéngběn jiā yùnfèi** cost and freight (CFR CF)

承包人 **chéngbāorén** *n* contractor

诚实借贷法 **chéngshí jièdài fǎ** Truth in Lending Act (TILA)

诚信 **chéngxìn** *n* good faith

诚意 **chéngyì** *n* good faith

承保人 **chéngbǎorén** *n* underwriter

承兑 **chéngduì** *n* acceptance

承销人 (货物) **chéngxiāorén (huòwù)** *n* consignee (*for merchandise*)

承销人 (证券) **chéngxiāorén (zhèngquàn)** *n* underwriter (*for stocks and bonds*)

承运人 **chéngyùnrén** *n* carrier

驰名商标 **chímíng shāngbiāo** famous trademark

持票人 **chípiàorén** *n* bearer

冲销帐户 **chōngxiāo zhànghù** write-off account

重复计费 **chóngfù jìfèi** double billing

重复计算 **chóngfù jìsuàn** double counting

重组 **chóngzǔ** *n* restructuring

筹资 **chóuzī** *n/v* finance

初级商品 **chūjí shāngpǐn** *n* commodity

出口 **chūkǒu** *n/v* export

出口商 **chūkǒushāng** *n* exporter

出口退税 **chūkǒu tuìshuì** export drawback

出口许可证 **chūkǒu xǔkězhèng** export permit

出票人 **chūpiàorén** *n* drawer

出让人 **chūràngrén** *n* assignor

出售 **chūshòu** *n* sale; *v* sell
出租 **chūzū** *v* lease, rent, let
储蓄 **chǔxù** *n* savings
储蓄公债 **chǔxù gōngzhài** savings bond
储蓄机构 **chǔxù jīgòu** thrift institution
储蓄账户 **chǔxù zhànghù** savings account
传统个人退休金帐户 **chuántǒng gèrén tuìxiūjīn zhànghu** traditional IRA
船边交货 **chuánbiān jiāohuò** free alongside ship (FAS)
从价 **cóngjià** ad valorem
从价税 **cóngjiàshuì** ad valorem duty
催收公司 **cuīshōu gōngsī** collection agency
存款 **cúnkuǎn** *n/v* deposit
达康公司 **dákāng gōngsī** dot-com company
代表权申明书 **dàibiǎoquán shēnmíngshū** proxy statement
代理 **dàilǐ** *n* agency
代理人 **dàilǐrén** *n* agent
代收行 **dàishōuháng** *n* collecting bank
贷方 **dàifāng** *n* lender, creditor; credit, credit side
贷记 **dàijì** *n* credit
贷款 **dàikuǎn** *n* loan
贷款合并 **dàikuǎn hébìng** loan consolidation
贷款人 **dàikuǎnrén** *n* lender
担保合同 **dānbǎo hétong** contract of guarantee
担保交易 **dānbǎo jiāoyì** secured transactions
担保品 **dānbǎopǐn** *n* collateral
盗版 **dàobǎn** *n* pirated copy, piracy
盗版商品 **dàobǎn shāngpǐn** pirated copyright goods
盗用身份 **dàoyòng shēnfèn** identity theft
到期 **dàoqī** *n* maturity

到期前支取罚金 **dàoqī qián zhīqǔ fájīn** early
　　withdrawal penalty
到期日 **dàoqīrì** due date
登记 **dēngjì** *n* registration; *v* register
抵税 **dǐshuì** *n* tax credit
地方税 **dìfāngshuì** local tax
第七章破产 **dì-qī zhāng pòchǎn** Chapter 7 bankruptcy
第十三章破产 **dì-shísān zhāng pòchǎn** Chapter 13
　　bankruptcy
电汇 **diànhuì** *n* wire transfer
电子商务 **diànzǐ shāngwù** e-business
电子商业 **diànzǐ shāngyè** e-commerce
电子银行 **diànzǐ yínháng** e-banking
电子邮件 **diànzǐ yóujiàn** e-mail
电子资金转帐法 **diànzǐ zījīn zhuǎnzhàng fǎ** Electronic
　　Funds Transfer Act
电子资金转账 **diànzǐ zījīn zhuǎnzhàng** electronic fund
　　transfer (EFT)
订立合同 **dìnglì hétong** conclusion of contract
订约方 **dìngyuēfāng** contracting party
定约人 **dìngyuērén** *n* contractor
定金 **dìngjīn** *n* deposit
定期存单 **dìngqī cúndān** certificate of deposit (CD)
定期存款 **dìngqī cúnkuǎn** time deposit
定期人寿保险 **dìngqī rénshòu bǎoxiǎn** term life
　　insurance
董事 **dǒngshì** *n* director
董事会 **dǒngshìhuì** *n* board of directors
董事会主席 **dǒngshìhuì zhǔxí** chairman
董事长 **dǒngshìzhǎng** *n* chairman
董事总经理 **dǒngshì zǒngjīnglǐ** managing director
冻结 **dòngjié** *v* freeze

独立承包商 **dúlì chéngbāoshāng** independent contractor
对冲基金 **duìchōng jījīn** hedge fund
多样化 **duōyànghuà** n diversification; v diversify
恶意收购 **èyì shōugòu** hostile takeover
发件人 **fājiànrén** n sender
发卡行 **fākǎháng** n issuing bank
发盘 **fāpán** n offer
发票 **fāpiào** n invoice
发生 **fāshēng** v incur
发行 **fāxíng** v float (*loan, bond, etc.*)
发行说明书 **fāxíng shuōmíngshū** offering circular
罚金 **fájīn** n fine, penalty
罚款 **fákuǎn** n fine, penalty
法定货币 **fǎdìng huòbì** legal tender
法人 **fǎrén** n legal person
反诉 **fǎnsù** n/v counterclaim
反索赔 **fǎn suǒpéi** counterclaim
反托拉斯法 **fǎn tuōlāsī fǎ** antitrust law
反要约 **fǎn yāoyuē** counteroffer
放债人 **fàngzhài rén** n moneylender
非法经营 **fēifǎ jīngyíng** illegal business operations
非法收益 **fēifǎ shōuyì** unlawful gains
非工资性支付 **fēi gōngzī xìng zhīfù** nonwage payment
非上市公司 **fēi shàngshì gōngsī** private company
非营利的 **fēi yínglì de** adj nonprofit, not-for-profit
费用 **fèiyòng** n fee, charge, cost
分类账 **fēnlèizhàng** n ledger
分期付款 **fēnqī fùkuǎn** installment
分析报告 **fēnxī bàogào** analyst report
福利 **fúlì** n benefit
福利经理 **fúlì jīnglǐ** benefits manager
服务合同 **fúwù hétong** service contract

附表 **fùbiǎo** *n* schedule
附加福利 **fùjiā fúlì** fringe benefit
附加税 **fùjiāshuì** *n* surcharge
附意合同 **fùyì hétong** contract of adhesion
附属公司 **fùshǔ gōngsī** affiliate
付款 **fùkuǎn** *n* payment
付款到期日 **fùkuǎn dàoqī rì** payment due date
付款人 **fùkuǎnrén** *n* payor, payer
付清 **fùqīng** *v* pay off
复利 **fùlì** *n* compound interest
负债 **fùzhài** *n* liability
高风险投资 **gāo fēngxiǎn tóuzī** high-risk investment
格式合同 **géshì hétong** contract of adhesion
个人识别号 **gèrén shíbié hào** personal identification
　　number (PIN)
个人退休金账户 **gèrén tuìxiūjīn zhànghù** individual
　　retirement account (IRA)
个人支票 **gèrén zhīpiào** personal check
给小费 **gěi xiǎofèi** tip, give a tip
工厂交货 **gōngchǎng jiāohuò** ex works (EXW)
工资支票 **gōngzī zhīpiào** paycheck
公布 **gōngbù** *n* disclosure; *v* disclose
公平市价 **gōngpíng shìjià** fair market value (FMV)
公平信用报告法 **gōngpíng xìnyòng bàogào fǎ** Fair
　　Credit Reporting Act (FCRA)
公平信用结账法 **gōngpíng xìnyòng jiézhàng fǎ** Fair
　　Credit Billing Act (FCBA)
公平债务催收作业法 **gōngpíng zhàiwù cuīshōu zuòyè
　　fǎ** Fair Debt Collection Practices Act (FDCPA)
公司 **gōngsī** *n* company, corporation, firm
公司报告 **gōngsī bàogào** company report
公司标记 **gōngsī biāojì** house mark

公司法 **gōngsīfǎ** company law

公司章程 **gōngsī zhāngchéng** articles of association, bylaws

共同基金 **gòngtóng jījīn** mutual fund

共同签字人 **gòngtóng qiānzìrén** cosigner

供应 **gōngyìng** *n/v* supply

供应商 **gōngyìngshāng** *n* supplier, vendor

购买 **gòumǎi** *n/v* purchase

购买价 **gòumǎijià** purchase price

购者当心 **gòuzhě dāngxīn** caveat emptor, let the buyer beware

估定税额 **gūdìng shuì'é** tax assessment

估计税额 **gūjì shuì'é** estimated tax

估价 **gūjià** *n* assessment; *v* assess

股本 **gǔběn** *n* equity

股东 **gǔdōng** *n* shareholder

股东委托书 **gǔdōng wěituōshū** proxy statement

股份 **gǔfèn** *n* share

股利总额 **gǔlì zǒng'é** gross dividends

股票 **gǔpiào** *n* stock

股市 **gǔshì** *n* stock market

股息 **gǔxī** *n* dividend

雇用税 **gùyòngshuì** *n* employment tax, payroll tax

固定资产 **gùdìng zīchǎn** capital assets

关税 **guānshuì** *n* duties, tariffs

管理 **guǎnlǐ** *n* management; *v* manage

广告 **guǎnggào** *n* advertising, advertisement

国际汇票 **guójì huìpiào** international money order

国内税收法 **guónèi shuìshōu fǎ** Internal Revenue Code (IRC)

国内税收署 **guónèi shuìshōu shǔ** Internal Revenue Service (IRS) (又称国税局 *a.k.a.* **guóshuìjú**)

国税局 **guóshuìjú** Internal Revenue Service (IRS)

合并财务报表 **hébìng cáiwù bàobiǎo** consolidated financial statement

合伙 **héhuǒ** *n* partnership

合伙企业 **héhuǒ qǐyè** partnership business

合伙人 **héhuǒrén** *n* partner

合伙生意 **héhuǒ shēngyì** partnership business

合同 **hétong** *n* contract

合同法 **hétongfǎ** *n* contract law

合同终止 **hétong zhōngzhǐ** termination of contract

合意 **héyì** *n* meeting of the minds

合资企业 **hézī qǐyè** joint venture

合营企业 **héyíng qǐyè** joint venture

黑市 **hēishì** *n* black market

哄抬物价 **hōngtái wùjià** price gouging

红利 **hónglì** *n* dividend, bonus

后备性预扣税 **hòubèixìng yù kòushuì** backup withholding

化作本金的利息 **huàzuò běnjīn de lìxī** capitalized interest

坏账 **huàizhàng** bad debt

回报 **huíbào** *n* return

回报率 **huíbàolǜ** rate of return

回扣 **huíkòu** *n* kickback

回升 **huíshēng** *n* recovery

汇率 **huìlǜ** *n* exchange rate

汇票 **huìpiào** *n* bill of exchange, draft, money order

豁免资产 **huòmiǎn zīchǎn** exempt assets

货币市场 **huòbì shìchǎng** money market

货币市场账户 **huòbì shìchǎng zhànghù** money market account

货交承运人 **huò jiāo chéngyùnrén** free carrier (FCA)

货物 **huòwù** *n* goods, cargo

货运 **huòyùn** *n* shipping
积蓄 **jīxù** *n* savings; *v* save
计划书 **jìhuàshū** *n* prospectus
家庭办公室 **jiātíng bàngōngshì** home office
家庭公司 **jiātíng gōngsī** home-based business
加盟商 **jiāméngshāng** *n* franchisee
加速折旧法 **jiāsù zhéjiùfǎ** accelerated depreciation
假定的 **jiǎdìng de** pro forma
价格 **jiàgé** *n* price
价款 **jiàkuǎn** *n* price
价目表 **jiàmùbiǎo** *n* price catalog
价值 **jiàzhí** *n* value
减税 **jiǎnshuì** *n* tax deduction
见票即付 **jiàn piào jí fù** payable at sight
奖金 **jiǎngjīn** *n* bonus
交付 **jiāofù** *n* delivery; *v* deliver
交货 **jiāohuò** *n* delivery
交易 **jiāoyì** *n* transaction, trades
交易费 **jiāoyì fèi** *n* transaction fee
交易量 **jiāoyì liàng** *n* trading volume
交易人 **jiāoyìrén** *n* trader, dealer
交运 **jiāoyùn** *v* ship
接管 **jiēguǎn** *n* takeover; *v* take over
接受 **jiēshòu** *n* acceptance; *v* accept
节省 **jiéshěng** *n* savings; *v* save
结存 **jiécún** *n* balance
结余 **jiéyú** *n* balance
结账周期 **jiézhàng zhōuqī** billing cycle
结转 **jiézhuǎn** carry over
解除 **jiěchú** *n/v* discharge
解除合同 **jiěchú hétong** discharge of contract
解除债务 **jiěchú zhàiwù** discharge of debt

解约协议 **jiěyuē xiéyì** agreement to discharge a contract

借出 **jièchū** *v* lend

借方 **jièfāng** *n* borrower

借记 **jièjì** *n/v* debit

借记卡 **jièjìkǎ** *n* debit card

借款人 **jièkuǎnrén** *n* borrower

借入 **jièrù** *v* borrow

金降落伞 **jīn jiàngluòsǎn** golden parachute

金牛 **jīnniú** cash cow

金钱赔偿 **jīnqián péicháng** monetary compensation

金融 **jīnróng** *n* finance

金融费用 **jīnróng fèiyòng** finance charge

金融机构 **jīnróng jīgòu** financial institution

进口 **jìnkǒu** *n/v* import

进口商 **jìnkǒushāng** *n* importer

进取型增长基金 **jìnqǔxíng zēngzhǎng jījīn** aggressive growth fund

尽责 **jìnzé** *n* due diligence

尽职 **jìnzhí** *n* due diligence

经纪人 **jīngjìrén** *n* broker

经理 **jīnglǐ** *n* manager

经销权 **jīngxiāoquán** *n* distributorship

净利 **jìnglì** *n* net profit

净收益 **jìngshōuyì** *n* net earnings

净值 **jìngzhí** *n* net worth

竞争 **jìngzhēng** *n* competition; *v* compete

竞争者 **jìngzhēngzhě** *n* competitor

开证行 **kāizhèngháng** issuing bank

开支账户 **kāizhī zhànghù** expense account

可转让票据 **kě zhuǎnràng piàojù** negotiable instrument

客服 **kèfú** *n* customer service

客户 **kèhù** *n* client, customer

客户服务 **kèhù fúwù** customer service
口头合同 **kǒutóu hétong** oral contract, verbal contract
库存 **kùcún** *n* inventory
会计 **kuàijì** *n* accounting
会计年度 **kuàijì niándù** fiscal year
会计师 **kuàijìshī** *n* accountant
宽限期 **kuānxiànqī** grace period
来人 **láirén** *n* bearer
来人支票 **láirén zhīpiào** bearer check
蓝法 **lánfǎ** blue law
累进税 **lěijìnshuì** *n* progressive tax
离岸外包 **lí'àn wàibāo** offshoring
理财 **lǐcái** *n* financial services
理财顾问 **lǐcái gùwèn** financial advisor
利率 **lìlǜ** *n* interest rate
利润 **lìrùn** *n* profit
利润分成 **lìrùn fēnchéng** profit sharing
利润税 **lìrùnshuì** *n* profit tax
利息 **lìxī** *n* interest
利息费用 **lìxī fèiyòng** interest expense
廉价 **liánjià** distressed price
廉价债务 **liánjià zhàiwù** distressed debt
联邦储备银行 **liánbāng chǔbèi yínháng** Federal Reserve Bank (FRB)
联邦储蓄保险公司 **liánbāng chǔxù bǎoxiǎn gōngsī** Federal Deposit Insurance Corporation (FDIC)
联邦贸易委员会 **liánbāng màoyì wěiyuánhuì** Federal Trade Commission (FTC)
联邦税 **liánbāngshuì** *n* federal tax
联名账户 **liánmíng zhànghù** joint account
了解客户 **liǎojiě kèhù** know your client (KYC)
零售 **língshòu** *n* retail

领取 lǐngqǔ *v* collect
流动性 liúdòngxìng *n* liquidity
流动资产 liúdòng zīchǎn liquid asset
流通票据 liútōng piàojù negotiable instrument
留置权 liúzhìquán *n* lien
留置权持有人 liúzhìquán chíyǒurén lien holder
垄断市场 lǒngduàn shìchǎng corner the market
旅行支票 lǚxíng zhīpiào traveler's check
伦敦银行同业拆放利率 lúndūn yínháng tóngyè
　　chāifàng lìlǜ London Interbank Offered Rate (LIBOR)
罗斯个人退休金账户 luósī gèrén tuìxiūjīn zhànghù
　　Roth IRA
买方 mǎifāng *n* buyer
买卖合同 mǎimài hétong agreement for sale and
　　purchase, buy-sell agreement
买卖协议 mǎimài xiéyì agreement for sale and purchase,
　　buy-sell agreement
卖方 màifāng *n* seller, vendor
卖空 màikōng *n* short selling, shorting
毛所得 máo suǒdé gross income
美国税务法院 měiguó shuìwù fǎyuàn United States Tax
　　Court
密码 mìmǎ *n* password
免费 miǎnfèi free of charge
免税 miǎnshuì tax exempt, tax exemption
免息期 miǎnxīqī grace period
面值 miànzhí *n* par value
母公司 mǔgōngsī parent company
目的港船上交货 mùdì gǎng chuánshàng jiāohuò
　　delivered ex ship (DES)
目的港码头交货 mùdì gǎng mǎtóu jiāohuò delivered
　　ex quay (DEQ)

纳税人 **nàshuìrén** *n* taxpayer

纳税申报表 **nàshuì shēnbàobiǎo** tax return

内线交易 **nèixiàn jiāoyì** insider trading

年费 **niánfèi** annual fee

年利率 **niánlìlǜ** annual percentage rate (APR)

年收益率 **niánshōuyìlǜ** annual percentage yield (APY)

扭转 **niǔzhuǎn** *n* turnaround

农产品 **nóngchǎnpǐn** *n* produce

拍卖 **pāimài** *n/v* auction

牌照 **páizhào** *n* license

泡沫公司 **pàomò gōngsī** bubble company

赔偿 **péicháng** *n* compensation, indemnification

赔偿合同 **péicháng hétong** contract of indemnity

批发 **pīfā** *n* wholesale

披露 **pīlù** *n* disclosure; *v* disclose

票据 **piàojù** *n* note

票面价值 **piàomiàn jiàzhí** par value

评估 **pínggū** *v* assess

评估员 **pínggūyuán** *n* assessor

平等信用机会法 **píngděng xìnyòng jīhuì fǎ** Equal
      Credit Opportunity Act (ECOA)

破产 **pòchǎn** *adj* bankrupt; *n* bankruptcy, insolvency

破产法 **pòchǎnfǎ** Bankruptcy Code

破产法院 **pòchǎn fǎyuàn** bankruptcy court

破产人 **pòchǎnrén** *n* bankrupt

普通合伙人 **pǔtōng héhuǒrén** general partner

普通红利 **pǔtōng hónglì** ordinary dividends

期满前提款 **qīmǎn qián tíkuǎn** premature withdrawal

期票 **qīpiào** *n* promissory note

欺骗 **qīpiàn** *adj* deceptive; *n* deception; *v* deceive

欺诈 **qīzhà** *adj* fraudulent; *n* fraud

欺诈性财产转让 **qīzhàxìng cáichǎn zhuǎnràng**
    fraudulent conveyance
欺诈性索赔 **qīzhàxìng suǒpéi** fraudulent claim
企业 **qǐyè** *n* enterprise, business
企业注册 **qǐyè zhùcè** business registration
气球式偿还 **qìqiúshì chánghuán** balloon payment
欠 **qiàn** *v* owe
欠款 **qiànkuǎn** *n* arrears
清偿 **qīngcháng** *n* liquidation
清偿债务 **qīngcháng zhàiwù** liquidate a debt, retire
    a debt
清盘 **qīngpán** *n* winding up
清算 **qīngsuàn** *n* liquidation
取消债务 **qǔxiāo zhàiwù** cancellation of debt
全美消费金融委员会 **quánměi xiāofèi jīnróng
    wěiyuánhuì** National Commission on Consumer
    Finance
权益 **quányì** *n* equity
权责发生制 **quánzé fāshēngzhì** accrual basis
人寿保险 **rénshòu bǎoxiǎn** life insurance
日历季度 **rìlì jìdù** calendar quarter
日历年度 **rìlì niándù** calendar year
日利率 **rìlìlǜ** daily periodic rate
日平均余额 **rì píngjūn yú'é** average daily balance
日余额 **rìyú'é** daily balance
融资 **róngzī** *v* finance
善意 **shànyì** *n* good faith, bona fide
商标 **shāngbiāo** *n* trademark
商标名称 **shāngbiāo míngchēng** brand name
商标注册 **shāngbiāo zhùcè** trademark registration
商会 **shānghuì** *n* chamber of commerce
商品 **shāngpǐn** *n* merchandise

Commercial Law

商品交易所 **shāngpǐn jiāoyìsuǒ** commodity exchange
商人 **shāngrén** *n* businessman, merchant
商人银行 **shāngrén yínháng** merchant bank
商业 **shāngyè** *n* commerce
商业法 **shāngyèfǎ** commercial law
商业合同 **shāngyè hétong** business contract
商业机密 **shāngyè jīmì** trade secret
商业纠纷 **shāngyè jiūfēn** commercial dispute
商业秘密 **shāngyè mìmì** business secret
商业侵权行为 **shāngyè qīnquán xíngwéi** business torts
商业诉讼 **shāngyè sùsòng** commercial litigation
商业银行 **shāngyè yínháng** commercial bank
上期结余 **shàngqī jiéyú** previous balance
上市公司 **shàngshì gōngsī** listed company, public
  company
奢侈品 **shēchǐpǐn** luxury goods
社会保障金 **shèhuì bǎozhàngjīn** Social Security benefits
社会保障收入 **shèhuì bǎozhàng shōurù** Social Security
  income
社会保障税 **shèhuì bǎozhàngshuì** Social Security tax
审计 **shěnjì** *n/v* audit
审计意见 **shěnjì yìjiàn** audit opinion
审计员 **shěnjìyuán** *n* auditor
生产 **shēngchǎn** *n* production
生产力 **shēngchǎnlì** *n* productivity
生产率 **shēngchǎnlǜ** *n* productivity
生意 **shēngyì** *n* business
升值 **shēngzhí** *n* appreciation in value
市场 **shìchǎng** *n* market
市场汇率 **shìchǎng huìlǜ** market rate
市场利率 **shìchǎng lìlǜ** market rate
市政债券 **shìzhèng zhàiquàn** municipal bond

适合销售的 shìhé xiāoshòu de *adj* merchantable
收费 shōufèi *n* fee; *n/v* charge
收购 shōugòu *n* takeover, acquisition
收回 shōuhuí *v* repossess
收货人 shōuhuòrén *n* consignee
收据 shōujù *n* receipt
收款人 shōukuǎnrén *n* payee
收讫单 shōuqì dān *n* release note
收取 shōuqǔ *v* collect
收入 shōurù *n* income
收受者 shōushòu zhě *n* recipient
收益 shōuyì *n* proceeds
首次公开发行 shǒucì gōngkāi fāxíng initial public offering (IPO)
首席执行官 shǒuxí zhíxíngguān chief executive officer (CEO)
受票人 shòupiàorén *n* drawee
受让人 shòuràngrén *n* assignee
受益人 shòuyìrén *n* beneficiary
售价 shòujià *n* sale price
书面合同 shūmiàn hétong written contract
书面通知 shūmiàn tōngzhī written notice
双边合同 shuāngbiān hétong bilateral contract
税 shuì *n* tax
税法 shuìfǎ *n* tax law
税后回报率 shuìhòu huíbàolǜ after-tax return
税率 shuìlǜ *n* tax rate
税务热线电话 shuìwù rèxiàn diànhuà TeleTax
税务条约 shuìwù tiáoyuē tax treaty
说明书 shuōmíngshū *n* prospectus
损失 sǔnshī *n* loss
所得 suǒdé *n* income

所有权 **suǒyǒuquán** *n* ownership

摊销 **tānxiāo** *n* amortization

贪污 **tānwū** *n* embezzlement

弹性开支账户 **tánxìng kāizhī zhànghù** flexible spending account (FSA)

逃避 **táobì** *n* evasion

讨债 **tǎozhài** *n* debt collection

讨债公司 **tǎozhài gōngsī** debt collection agency

套汇 **tàohuì** *n/v* arbitrage

特许 **tèxǔ** *n* concession

特许财务咨询人 **tèxǔ cáiwùzīxún rén** chartered financial consultant (ChFC)

特许的 **tèxǔ de** *adj* chartered

特许权 **tèxǔquán** *n* concession, franchise

特许商 **tèxǔshāng** *n* franchisor

提供资金 **tígōng zījīn** provide fund

提货单 **tíhuòdān** *n* bill of lading (BL)

提款 **tíkuǎn** *n* withdrawal; *v* draw, withdraw

跳票 **tiàopiào** *n* bounced check

贴现 **tiēxiàn** *n/v* discount

贴现率 **tiēxiànlǜ** *n* discount rate

停止付款 **tíngzhǐ fùkuǎn** stop payment

通知银行 **tōngzhī yínháng** advising bank

统一反欺诈性转移法 **tǒngyī fǎn qīzhàxìng zhuǎnyí fǎ** Uniform Fraudulent Transfers Act (UFTA)

统一费率 **tǒngyī fèilǜ** flat rate

统一商法典 **tǒngyī shāngfǎdiǎn** Uniform Commercial Code (UCC)

投诉 **tóusù** *v* complain, file a complaint

投资 **tóuzī** *n* investment; *v* invest

投资策略 **tóuzī cèluè** investment strategy

投资工具 **tóuzī gōngjù** investment vehicle

投资公司 **tóuzī gōngsī** investment company
投资顾问 **tóuzī gùwèn** investment counselor
投资人 **tóuzīrén** *n* investor
投资委员会 **tóuzī wěiyuánhuì** investment committee
投资账户 **tóuzī zhànghù** investment account
透支 **tòuzhī** *n* overdraft
透支保护支票账户 **tòuzhī bǎohù zhīpiào zhànghù**
    overdraft checking account
退回 支票 **tuìhuí zhīpiào** bounce a check
退货 **tuìhuò** *n* returned goods; *v* return merchandise
退款 **tuìkuǎn** *n/v* refund
退税 **tuìshuì** *n* tax refund, tax rebate
退休 **tuìxiū** *n* retirement; *v* retire
退休计划 **tuìxiū jìhuà** retirement plan
托运 **tuōyùn** *n* consignment, shipment
拖欠 **tuōqiàn** *adj* delinquent; *n* delinquency, arrears;
    n/v default
拖延 **tuōyán** *n/v* delay
外包 **wàibāo** *n* outsourcing
完税后交货 **wánshuì hòu jiāohuò** delivered duty paid
    (DDP)
完税前交货 **wánshuì qián jiāohuò** delivered duty
    unpaid (DDU)
网络钓鱼 **wǎngluò diàoyú** phishing
网络钓语 **wǎngluò diàoyǔ** vishing
网上银行业务 **wǎngshàng yínháng yèwù** online banking
往期财务报表 **wǎngqī cáiwù bàobiǎo** historical
    financial statement
违反保用条款 **wéifǎn bǎoyòng tiáokuǎn** breach of
    warranty
违约 **wéiyuē** *n* breach of contract, default
违约行为 **wéiyuē xíngwéi** non-compliance

Commercial Law

委托人 **wěituōrén** *n* principal

伪造 **wěizào** *n/v* counterfeit

未经许可提取 **wèijīng xǔkě tíqǔ** unauthorized withdrawal

未清余额 **wèiqīng yú'é** outstanding balance

未实现损益 **wèi shíxiàn sǔnyì** unrealized loss or profit

文书 **wénshū** *n* instrument

无线的 **wúxiàn de** *adj* wireless

无效 **wúxiào** *adj* void

无形资产 **wúxíng zīchǎn** intangible assets

洗钱 **xǐqián** *n* money laundering

现货市场 **xiànhuò shìchǎng** cash market

现金 **xiànjīn** *n* cash

现金垫款 **xiànjīn diànkuǎn** cash advance

现金结算 **xiànjīn jiésuàn** cash settlement

现金流动 **xiànjīn liúdòng** cash flow

现金流量 **xiànjīn liúliàng** cash flow

现金支付 **xiànjīn zhīfù** pay in cash

消费品 **xiāofèipǐn** *n* consumer goods

消费税 **xiāofèishuì** *n* excise tax

消费物价指数 **xiāofèi wùjià zhǐshù** consumer price index

消费信用 **xiāofèi xìnyòng** consumer credit

消费信用咨询处 **xiāofèi xìnyòng zīxúnchù** Consumer Credit Counseling Service (CCCS)

消费债务 **xiāofèi zhàiwù** consumer debts

消费者 **xiāofèizhě** *n* consumer

消费者保护法 **xiāofèizhě bǎohùfǎ** Consumer Protection Act

消费者权益 **xiāofèizhě quányì** consumer rights

消费者信用报告公司 **xiāofèizhě xìnyòng bàogào gōngsī** consumer reporting company

消费者租赁法 **xiāofèizhě zūlìnfǎ** Consumer Leasing Act

销货净额 **xiāohuò jìng'é** net sales
销货总额 **xiāohuò zǒng'é** gross sales
销售法 **xiāoshòufǎ** *n* sales law
销售合同 **xiāoshòu hétong** contract of sale
销售税 **xiāoshòushuì** *n* sales tax
小额索赔 **xiǎo'é suǒpéi** small claims
小费 **xiǎofèi** *n* tip
小企业 **xiǎo qǐyè** small business
小企业管理署 **xiǎo qǐyè guǎnlǐshǔ** Small Business
　　Administration (SBA)
协定 **xiédìng** *n* agreement
协议 **xiéyì** *n* agreement
谢尔曼反托拉斯法 **xiè'ěrmàn fǎn tuōlāsī fǎ** Sherman
　　Antitrust Act
信贷额度 **xìndài édù** credit line
信贷员 **xìndàiyuán** *n* loan officer
信件 **xìnjiàn** *n* mail
信件裁决 **xìnjiàn cáijué** letter ruling
信托基金 **xìntuō jījīn** trust fund
信用 **xìnyòng** *n* credit
信用保险 **xìnyòng bǎoxiǎn** credit insurance
信用报告 **xìnyòng bàogào** credit report
信用报告公司 **xìnyòng bàogào gōngsī** credit bureau
信用分数 **xìnyòng fēnshù** credit score
信用卡 **xìnyòngkǎ** *n* credit card
信用卡公司 **xìnyòngkǎ gōngsī** credit card company
信用卡合同 **xìnyòngkǎ hétong** credit card agreement
信用社 **xìnyòngshè** *n* credit union
信用史 **xìnyòngshǐ** credit history
信用限额 **xìnyòng xiàn'é** credit limit
信用修复 **xìnyòng xiūfù** credit repair
信用证 **xìnyòngzhèng** *n* letter of credit

信用状况 **xìnyòng zhuàngkuàng** credit profile
信用咨询人 **xìnyòng zīxúnrén** credit counselor
信用咨询组织 **xìnyòng zīxún zǔzhī** credit counseling
    organization
熊市 **xióngshì** *n* bear market
虚假广告 **xūjiǎ guǎnggào** false advertising
许可证 **xǔkězhèng** *n* permit
续订合同 **xùdìng hétong** renewal of contract
宣传 **xuānchuán** *n* publicity
循环帐户 **xúnhuán zhànghù** revolving account
押金 **yājīn** *n* security deposit
严格产品责任 **yángé chǎnpǐn zérèn** strict products
    liability
衍生证券 **yǎnshēng zhèngquàn** derivative
延迟纳税 **yánchí nàshuì** tax deferred
养老基金 **yǎnglǎo jījīn** pension fund
养老金 **yǎnglǎojīn** *n* pension
要约 **yāoyuē** *n* offer
要约人 **yāoyuērén** *n* offeror
夜间存款 **yèjiān cúnkuǎn** night deposit
一般反避税规则 **yībān fǎn bìshuì guīzé** General
    Anti-Avoidance Rule (GAAR)
一般欺诈侦调计划 **yībān qīzhà zhēndiào jìhuà** General
    Fraud Program
一笔总付 **yībǐ zǒngfù** lump-sum payment
医疗保健税 **yīliáo bǎojiàn shuì** Medicare tax
医药费用 **yīyào fèiyòng** medical expenses
已解除债务的破产人 **yǐ jiěchú zhàiwù de pòchǎnrén**
    discharge in bankruptcy
已实现损益 **yǐ shíxiàn sǔnyì** realized loss or profit
以实物 **yǐ shíwù** in kind
以物代款 **yǐ wù dài kuǎn** in kind

意见一致 **yìjiàn yīzhì** meeting of the minds

银行 **yínháng** *n* bank

银行保密法 **yínháng bǎomìfǎ** Bank Secrecy Act (BSA)

银行账户 **yínháng zhànghù** bank account

隐私政策 **yǐnsī zhèngcè** privacy policy

应付 **yīngfù** *adj* payable

应付帐款 **yīngfù zhàngkuǎn** accounts payable

应计利息 **yīngjì lìxī** accrued interest

应计折旧财产 **yīngjì zhéjiù cáichǎn** depreciable property

应纳税的 **yīng nàshuì de** taxable, liable for tax

应纳税额 **yīng nàshuì'é** tax liability

应收 **yīngshōu** *adj* receivable

应收帐款 **yīngshōu zhàngkuǎn** accounts receivable

营业额 **yíngyè'é** business volume

营业费用 **yíngyè fèiyòng** business expenses

营业日 **yíngyèrì** business days

营业时间 **yíngyè shíjiān** business hours

营业执照 **yíngyè zhízhào** business license

佣金 **yòngjīn** *n* commission

优先的 **yōuxiān de** *adj* preferred

邮购或电话订购规则 **yóugòu huò diànhuà dìnggòu guīzé** Mail or Telephone Order Rule

有偿债能力的 **yǒu chángzhài nénglì de** solvent

有条件背书 **yǒutiáojiàn bèishū** conditional endorsement

有条件转让 **yǒutiáojiàn zhuǎnràng** conditional assignment

有限责任 **yǒuxiàn zérèn** limited liability

有限责任公司 **yǒuxiàn zérèn gōngsī** limited liability company (LLC)

有限责任合伙人 **yǒuxiàn zérèn héhuǒrén** limited partner

有责任的 **yǒu zérèn de** *adj* liable

运费 **yùnfèi** *n* freight

运费付至 **yùnfèi fù zhì** carriage paid to (CPT)

运费加保险费 **yùnfèi jiā bǎoxiǎnfèi** carriage and insurance paid (CIP)

运输 **yùnshū** *n* shipping; *v* ship

逾期费用 **yúqī fèiyòng** late charge

逾期付款 **yúqī fùkuǎn** late payment

语音邮件 **yǔyīn yóujiàn** voicemail

预计的 **yùjì de** *adj* pro forma

预扣所得税 **yùkòu suǒdéshuì** withholding

预提现金 **yùtí xiànjīn** cash advance

预先包装的 **yùxiān bāozhuāng de** *adj* prepackaged

原料 **yuánliào** *n* raw material

员工工资表 **yuángōng gōngzī biǎo** payroll

月结单 **yuèjiédān** monthly bank statement

责任 **zérèn** *n* liability

责任保险 **zérèn bǎoxiǎn** liability insurance

增值税 **zēngzhíshuì** *n* value added tax (VAT)

诈骗 **zhàpiàn** *n/v* scam

债权人 **zhàiquánrén** *n* creditor

债券 **zhàiquàn** *n* bond

债务 **zhàiwù** *n* debt, financial obligation

债务人 **zhàiwùrén** *n* debtor

账单 **zhàngdān** *n* bill

账单错误 **zhàngdān cuòwù** billing error

帐单质疑权 **zhàngdān zhìyíquán** billing rights

账户 **zhànghù** *n* account

账户核查 **zhànghù héchá** account verification

账面价值 **zhàngmiàn jiàzhí** book value

招致 **zhāozhì** *v* incur

召回 **zhàohuí** *n/v* recall

折旧 **zhéjiù** *n* depreciation (*of assets*)

折扣 **zhékòu** *n/v* discount

折扣率 zhékòulǜ *n* discount rate

征税 zhēngshuì *n* taxation; *v* tax

证券 zhèngquàn *n* security

证券化 zhèngquànhuà *n* securitization

证券交易所 zhèngquàn jiāoyìsuǒ stock exchange

证书 zhèngshū *n* certificate

支付 zhīfù *n* payment; *v* pay

支票 zhīpiào *n* check

支票账户 zhīpiào zhànghù checking account

支票支付 zhīpiào zhīfù pay by check

知识产权 zhīshí chǎnquán intellectual property

值 zhí *n* worth

智慧产权 zhìhuì chǎnquán intellectual property

制造商 zhìzàoshāng *n* manufacturer

中央银行 zhōngyāng yínháng central bank

终生人寿保险 zhōngshēng rénshòu bǎoxiǎn whole life
insurance

仲裁 zhòngcái *n* arbitration

州税 zhōushuì *n* state tax

注册 zhùcè *n* registration

注册会计师 zhùcè kuàijìshī certified public accountant
(CPA)

注销 zhùxiāo *v* write off

注销支票 zhùxiāo zhīpiào cancelled check

著作权 zhùzuòquán *n* copyright

专利 zhuānlì *n* patent

转让 zhuǎnràng *n* assignment; *v* assign

转账 zhuǎnzhàng *n* money transfer

装运 zhuāngyùn *n* shipment

装运港船上交货 zhuāngyùn gǎng chuánshàng jiāohuò
free on board (FOB)

追回 zhuīhuí *n* recovery

Commercial Law

准确 **zhǔnquè** *adj* accurate

资本 **zīběn** *n* capital

资本化 **zīběnhuà** *n* capitalization; *v* capitalize

资本损益 **zīběn sǔnyì** capital gain or loss

资本支出 **zīběn zhīchū** capital expenditure

资产 **zīchǎn** *n* asset

资产负债表 **zīchǎn fùzhàibiǎo** balance sheet

资产净值 **zīchǎn jìngzhí** equity

资方 **zīfāng** *n* those representing capital, management

资金 **zījīn** *n* funds

资金短缺 **zījīn duǎnquē** cash crunch

子公司 **zǐgōngsī** *n* subsidiary

自动提款机 **zìdòng tíkuǎnjī** automated teller machine (ATM)

自动销售机 **zìdòng xiāoshòujī** vending machine

自雇税 **zì gù shuì** *n* self-employment tax

自愿遵守 **zìyuàn zūnshǒu** voluntary compliance

总裁 **zǒngcái** *n* president

租金支出 **zūjīn zhīchū** rental expenses

租赁 **zūlìn** *n* lease

租约 **zūyuē** *n* lease

组成公司 **zǔchéng gōngsī** incorporate

最低应付金额 **zuìdī yīngfù jīn'é** minimum payment due

最优惠利率 **zuì yōuhuì lìlǜ** prime rate

遵守 **zūnshǒu** *n* compliance; *v* comply with

作假 **zuòjiǎ** *n* falsification; *v* falsify

商法词汇

刑法词汇
Criminal Law

刑法涉及应予处罚的行为。根据 "法无明文规定不处罚" (nulla poena sine lege) 的罪刑法定主义原则, 一项行为, 法律没有明文规定处罚的, 则不受处罚。根据一罪不二审原则, 一个人被裁定无罪后, 不因同一罪名再受审判。一名被告被起诉后, 根据刑事诉讼法享有为自己辩护的保障。如被判有罪, 则根据罪行的轻重予以处罚。轻罪常判罚金, 重罪则判有期监禁、无期监禁乃至死刑。在美国, 刑法事务由联邦和州政府管辖。

5k信件 **wǔ k xìnjiàn** 5K letter
爱国法 **àiguó fǎ** PATRIOT Act (又称反恐法 *a.k.a.* **fǎnkǒng fǎ**)
安全等级 **ānquán děngjí** security classification
安全阀 **ānquánfá** *n* safety valve
暗杀 **ànshā** *n* assassination; *v* assassinate
帮派 **bāngpài** *n* gang
帮助和教唆 **bāngzhù hé jiàosuō** aiding and abetting
绑架 **bǎngjià** *n* abduction, kidnapping; *v* abduct, kidnap
绑架者 **bǎngjiàzhě** *n* abductor, kidnapper
绑匪 **bǎngfěi** *n* abductor, kidnapper
保释 **bǎoshì** *v* bail, release on bail
保释担保人 **bǎoshì dānbǎorén** bail bondsman
保释担保物 **bǎoshì dānbǎowù** collateral for bail
保释改革法 **bǎoshì gǎigé fǎ** Bail Reform Act

保释金 **bǎoshìjīn** *n* bail

保释听证会 **bǎoshì tīngzhènghuì** bail hearing

暴力 **bàolì** *n* violence, force

暴力罪 **bàolì zuì** *n* crime of violence

暴乱 **bàoluàn** *n* riot

暴徒 **bàotú** *n* rioter, thug

爆炸 **bàozhà** *n* explosion, demolition

被捕 **bèibǔ** *v* be arrested

被告 **bèigào** *n* the accused, the charged, the defendant

被告律师 **bèigàolùshī** defense lawyer, defense counsel

被上诉人 **bèi shàngsùrén** respondent on appeal

辩方 **biànfāng** *n* the defense

辩护 **biànhù** *n* defense; *v* defend

辩护律师 **biànhù lùshī** defense attorney

辩护准备时间 **biànhù zhǔnbèi shíjiān** defense preparation period

辩诉协议 **biàn sù xiéyì** plea agreement, plea bargain, plea-bargaining

便衣警官 **biànyī jǐngguān** undercover police officer

驳回控告 **bóhuí kònggào** dismiss a charge

补救 **bǔjiù** *n* reparation

不当行为 **bùdàng xíngwéi** misconduct

不定期刑 **bùdìngqī xíng** indeterminate sentence

不抗辩 **bùkàngbiàn** no contest

不可采信的证据 **bùkě cǎixìn de zhèngjù** inadmissible evidence

不可抗拒的冲动 **bùkěkàngjù de chōngdòng** irresistible impulse

不可能性 **bùkěnéngxìng** *n* impossibility

不利的 **bùlì de** *adj* prejudicial, harmful

不认罪 **bùrènzuì** plead not guilty; not guilty plea

不完整罪 **bùwánzhěng zuì** inchoate crime

不在犯罪现场的抗辩 **bùzài fànzuì xiànchǎng de kàngbiàn** *n* alibi

不争辩 **bùzhēngbiàn** nolo contendere

裁定无罪 **cáidìng wúzuì** acquit

裁决 **cáijué** *n* verdict

查抄 **cháchāo** *n* confiscation; *v* confiscate

查封 **cháfēng** *n* seizure; *v* seize

拆盗破坏汽车罪 **chāi dào pòhuài qìchē zuì** auto stripping, auto tampering

娼妓 **chāngjì** *n* prostitute

长臂管辖权 **chángbì guǎnxiáquán** long-arm jurisdiction

撤销原判 **chèxiāo yuánpàn** reversal

陈尸所 **chénshīsuǒ** *n* morgue

陈述 **chénshù** *n* statement; *v* make a statement

惩罚性的 **chéngfáxìng de** *adj* punitive

承担责任 **chéngdān zérèn** acceptance of responsibility

持枪歹徒 **chíqiāng dǎitú** gunman

持械职业罪犯 **chíxiè zhíyè zuìfàn** armed career criminal

重婚罪 **chónghūnzuì** *n* bigamy

重新量刑 **chóngxīn liàngxíng** re-sentencing

仇恨犯罪 **chóuhèn fànzuì** hate crime

初犯 **chūfàn** *n* first offense

处罚 **chǔfá** *n* penalty; *v* penalize

处决 **chǔjué** *v* execute, put to death

传唤 **chuánhuàn** *v* subpoena, summon

串通 **chuàntōng** *v* conspire

刺伤 **cìshāng** *v* stab

从犯 **cóngfàn** *n* accessory

篡改 **cuàngǎi** *v* tamper with

大陪审团 **dà péishěntuán** grand jury

大赦 **dàshè** *n* amnesty

逮捕 **dàibǔ** *n/v* arrest

Criminal Law

逮捕记录 **dàibǔ jìlù** arrest history, arrest record, police blotter

逮捕证 **dàibǔzhèng** *n* arrest warrant

单人囚房 **dānrén qiúfáng** cell

道德堕落罪 **dàodé duòluò zuì** crime of moral turpitude

盗窃罪 **dàoqièzuì** *n* theft, larceny

盗用 **dàoyòng** *n* embezzlement; *v* embezzle

盗用身份 **dàoyòng shēnfèn** identity theft

低于量刑指南规定的刑罚 **dīyú liàngxíng zhǐnán guīdìng de xíngfá** sentence below the guideline range

敌对证人 **díduì zhèngrén** adverse witness

地位 **dìwèi** *n* state, status

第五修正案所赋不自证其罪的权利 **dì-wǔ xiūzhèng'àn suǒ fù bù zì zhèng qí zuì de quánlì** Fifth Amendment right against self-incrimination

电子监视 **diànzǐ jiānshì** electronic monitoring, electronic surveillance

调查 **diàochá** *n* investigation; *v* investigate

调查员 **diàocháyuán** *n* investigator

定期刑 **dìngqī xíng** determinate sentence

定罪 **dìngzuì** *n* conviction; *v* convict

斗殴 **dòu'ōu** *n/v* fight, scrap

毒贩 **dúfàn** *n* drug trafficker, drug dealer

独立证据 **dúlì zhèngjù** independent evidence

赌博 **dǔbó** *n/v* gamble

断续监禁判决 **duànxù jiānjìn pànjué** intermittent sentence

对判决提出异议 **duì pànjué tíchū yìyì** challenge a decision

恶意 **èyì** *adj* malicious; *n* malice

恶意破坏他人财产 **èyì pòhuài tārén cáichǎn** malicious mischief

二级谋杀罪 **èrjí móushāzuì** second degree murder

法定强奸罪 **fǎdìng qiángjiānzuì** statutory rape

法定最低刑期 **fǎdìng zuìdī xíngqī** mandatory minimum sentence

法警 **fǎjǐng** *n* bailiff

法网 **fǎwǎng** *n* dragnet

法院拘留所 **fǎyuàn jūliúsuǒ** holding cell

反驳 **fǎnbó** *n* rebuttal

反黑连坐法 **fǎn hēi lián zuò fǎ** Racketeer Influenced and Corrupt Organizations Act (RICO)

反恐法 **fǎnkǒng fǎ** PATRIOT Act (又称爱国法 *a.k.a.* àiguó fǎ)

反诈骗, 操纵和贿赂组织法 **fǎn zhàpiàn cāozòng hé huìlù zǔzhī fǎ** Racketeer Influenced and Corrupt Organizations Act (RICO) (又称反黑连坐法 *a.k.a.* fǎn hēi lián zuò fǎ)

反证 **fǎnzhèng** *n* rebuttal

犯法 **fànfǎ** *v* break the law

犯人 **fànrén** *n* prisoner

犯罪 **fànzuì** *n* crime, offense; *v* commit a crime

犯罪档案 **fànzuì dàng'àn** rap sheet

犯罪记录 **fànzuì jìlù** criminal record, record of convictions

犯罪记录类别 **fànzuì jìlù lèibié** criminal history category

犯罪受害人法 **fànzuì shòuhàirén fǎ** Victims of Crime Act (VOCA)

犯罪嫌疑人 **fànzuì xiányírén** suspect

贩毒者 **fàndúzhě** drug trafficker, drug dealer

贩毒罪 **fàndúzuì** drug trafficking offense

妨碍司法 **fáng'ài sīfǎ** obstruction of justice

放高利贷 **fàng gāolìdài** loan sharking

放弃 **fàngqì** *n* renunciation

非法拘禁 **fēifǎ jūjìn** false imprisonment

非法侵入罪 **fēifǎ qīnrù zuì** criminal trespass

非法侵占他人财产罪 **fēifǎ qīnzhàn tārén cáichǎn zuì**
   larceny

非法影响陪审团 **fēifǎ yǐngxiǎng péishěntuán** tampering
   with jury

非法拥有武器 **fēifǎ yōngyǒu wǔqì** criminal possession
   of a weapon

非监禁刑 **fēi jiānjìn xíng** non-jail sentence, alternative
   sentence

分离诉讼 **fēnlí sùsòng** severance of proceedings

服刑 **fúxíng** *v* serve a sentence

复查 **fùchá** *v* review, reexamine

复核 **fùhé** *v* review, reexamine

复审 **fùshěn** *v* review, rehear

干扰 **gānrǎo** *v* tamper with

高利贷 **gāolìdài** *n* usury

高于量刑指南规定的刑罚 **gāoyú liàngxíng zhǐnán
   guīdìng de xíngfá** sentence above the guideline range

告 **gào** *v* complain, sue, bring a case against

告密 **gàomì** *v* tip off

告密者 **gàomì zhě** *n* informant

攻击 **gōngjī** *n/v* assault

攻击和殴打 **gōngjī hé ōudǎ** assault and battery

公设辩护人 **gōng shè biànhùrén** public defender

公诉人 **gōngsùrén** *n* prosecutor, prosecuting officer

公诉书 **gōngsùshū** *n* information, indictment

共犯 **gòngfàn** *n* accomplice

共谋 **gòngmóu** *n* conspiracy; *v* conspire

共谋者 **gòngmóu zhě** *n* co-conspirator

供认 **gòngrèn** *n* admission, confession; *v* admit, confess

勾引 **gōuyǐn** *n* solicitation

故意 **gùyì** *n* intent

故意的 gùyì de *adj* intentional

故意地 gùyì de *adv* knowingly, intentionally

故意杀人罪 gùyì shārénzuì voluntary manslaughter

拐卖人口 guǎimài rénkǒu human traffic, trafficking in human beings

官诱民犯 guān yòu mín fàn entrapment

惯犯 guànfàn *n* habitual offender

归还 guīhuán *n* restitution

过高保释金 guò gāo bǎoshìjīn excessive bail

过失杀人罪 guòshī shārénzuì involuntary manslaughter

害怕 hàipà *n/v* fear

合并处刑 hébìng chǔxíng concurrent sentence

合并诉讼 hébìng sùsòng consolidation of proceedings

合理根据 hélǐ gēnjù reasonable basis, probable cause, sufficient reason to suspect

合理怀疑 hélǐ huáiyí reasonable doubt

合作协议 hézuò xiéyì cooperation agreement

黑社会 hēishèhuì *n* underworld

还押令 huán yā lìng remanding order

缓刑 huǎnxíng *n* probation

缓刑官 huǎnxíngguān *n* probation officer

缓刑听证会 huǎnxíng tīngzhènghuì probation hearing

恢复原状 huīfù yuánzhuàng *n* restitution

回避 huíbì *n* recusal; *v* recuse

贿赂 huìlù *n* bribery, bribe; *v* bribe

火器 huǒqì *n* firearm

霍布斯法 huòbùsī fǎ Hobbs Act

激情犯罪 jīqíng fànzuì crime of passion

基本罪行级别 jīběn zuìxíng jíbié base offense level

积极抗辩 jījí kàngbiàn affirmative defense

缉拿 jīná *n* apprehension; *v* apprehend

鸡奸 jījiān *n* sodomy

记录在册 **jìlù zàicè** *v* book

纪律诉讼 **jìlǜ sùsòng** disciplinary proceedings

妓女 **jìnǚ** *n* prostitute, hooker

妓院 **jìyuàn** *n* brothel

家庭监禁 **jiātíng jiānjìn** home detention

加重情节 **jiāzhòng qíngjié** aggravating circumstances

假释 **jiǎshì** *n/v* parole

假释官 **jiǎshìguān** *n* parole officer

假释听证会 **jiǎshì tīngzhènghuì** parole hearing

假释委员会 **jiǎshì wěiyuánhuì** parole board

驾车致人死命罪 **jiàchē zhìrén sǐmìng zuì** vehicular manslaughter

监禁 **jiānjìn** *n* imprisonment, confinement, sentence

监禁期 **jiānjìnqī** time in prison

监视 **jiānshì** *n* surveillance

监视录像带 **jiānshì lùxiàngdài** surveillance tape

监狱 **jiānyù** *n* jail, prison

监狱长 **jiānyùzhǎng** *n* warden

监狱看守 **jiānyù kānshǒu** prison guard

监狱囚犯 **jiānyù qiúfàn** inmate

减轻情节 **jiǎnqīng qíngjié** extenuating circumstances

检察官 **jiǎncháguān** *n* prosecutor

检方 **jiǎnfāng** *n* prosecution

检方证人 **jiǎnfāng zhèngrén** prosecution witness

检控 **jiǎnkòng** *v* prosecute

交保 **jiāobǎo** *v* post bail

交通违规 **jiāotōng wéiguī** traffic infraction

教唆 **jiàosuō** *n* instigation; *v* instigate

教养中心 **jiàoyǎng zhōngxīn** *n* penitentiary, correctional center

接受审判的权利 **jiēshòu shěnpàn de quánlì** right to trial

接受脏物 **jiēshòu zāngwù** receiving stolen property

劫持人质 **jiéchí rénzhì** hostage taking; take hostage

诘问证人 **jiéwèn zhèngrén** questioning of witness

介入原因 **jièrù yuányīn** supervening cause

紧急避险辩护 **jǐnjí bìxiǎn biànhùn** necessity defense

近因 **jìnyīn** n proximate cause

禁闭 **jìnbì** n confinement; v confine

禁止 **jìnzhǐ** n prohibition; v prohibit

精神状况 **jīngshén zhuàngkuàng** state of mind

经营淫业 **jīngyíng yínyè** operating a business of
prostitution

警察圈套 **jǐngchá quāntào** entrapment

拘留 **jūliú** n detention; v detain (在中国拘留是一种处
罚，分行政拘留、司法拘留、刑事拘留，拘留期限
一般为15日以下。/ *Under Chinese law a form of
penalty subdivided into administrative, judicial, and
criminal detention. An offender can be detained for
up to 15 days.*)

拘押 **jūyā** n custody

举报人 **jǔbào rén** n informant

举证听证会 **jǔzhèng tīngzhènghuì** evidentiary hearing

举证责任 **jǔzhèng zérèn** burden of proof

具结候审 **jùjié hòushěn** bind over

绝对回避 **juéduì huíbì** peremptory challenge

开枪 **kāiqiāng** v shoot

开枪射杀 **kāiqiāng shèshā** shoot to kill

开审 **kāishěn** v go to trial

开脱证据 **kāituō zhèngjù** exculpatory evidence

可反驳的推定 **kě fǎnbó de tuīdìng** rebuttable presumption

恐怖分子 **kǒngbùfènzǐ** n terrorist

恐怖主义 **kǒngbùzhǔyì** n terrorism

恐惧 **kǒngjù** n fear

恐吓 **kǒnghè** *n/v* menace

控告 **kònggào** *v* charge, sue

控告人 **kònggàorén** *n* accuser

扣押 **kòuyā** *n* seizure; *v* seize

哭诉证人 **kūsù zhèngrén** outcry witness

宽大 **kuāndà** *adj* lenient; *n* leniency, clemency

宽恕 **kuānshù** *n/v* pardon

拉皮条 **lā pítiáo** *n* pimping, procuring

累犯 **lěifàn** *n* recidivist, repeat offender, persistent offender

立即执行 **lìjí zhíxíng** immediate execution

连续判决 **liánxù pànjué** consecutive sentences

联邦监狱局 **liánbāng jiānyù jú** Federal Bureau of Prisons (BOP)

联邦证据规则 **liánbāng zhèngjù guīzé** Federal Rules of Evidence

联邦罪 **liánbāng zuì** federal offense

量刑 **liàngxíng** *n/v* sentence

量刑前调查报告 **liàngxíng qián diàochá bàogào** pre-sentence investigation report

量刑听证会 **liàngxíng tīngzhènghuì** sentencing hearing

量刑指南 **liàngxíng zhǐnán** sentencing guidelines

列队辨认 **lièduì biànrèn** lineup

临时保护身份 **línshí bǎohù shēnfèn** Temporary Protection Status (TPS)

令状 **lìngzhuàng** *n* warrant

乱伦 **luànlún** *n* incest

轮奸 **lúnjiān** *n* gang rape

罗萨里奥规则 **luósàlǐ'ào guīzé** Rosario rule

罗网 **luówǎng** *n* dragnet

卖淫 **màiyín** *n* prostitution

莽撞 **mǎngzhuàng** *adj* reckless; *adv* recklessly; *n* recklessness

莽撞危及他人人身罪 **mǎngzhuàng wēijí tārén rénshēn zuì** reckless endangerment

免责证据 **miǎnzé zhèngjù** exculpatory evidence

美国联邦法典 **měiguó liánbāng fǎdiǎn** United States Code

美国量刑委员会 **měiguó liàngxíng wěiyuánhuì** United States Sentencing Commission

米兰达告诫 **mǐlándá gàojiè** Miranda warnings

秘密行动 **mìmì xíngdòng** undercover operation

面临起诉 **miànlín qǐsù** face charges

民事催收 **mínshì cuī shōu** civil collections

民事自诉状 **mínshì zìsùzhuàng** civil complaint

没收 **mòshōu** *n* forfeiture; *v* forfeit

没收保释金 **mòshōu bǎoshì jīn** forfeit bail

谋杀未遂罪 **móushā wèisuìzuì** attempted murder

谋杀罪 **móushāzuì** *n* murder

目击证人 **mùjī zhèngrén** eyewitness

虐待 **nuèdài** *n/v* abuse

殴打 **ōudǎ** *n* battery

扒窃 **páqiè** *v* pick a pocket

扒手 **páshǒu** *n* pickpocket

排除合理怀疑 **páichú hélǐ huáiyí** beyond a reasonable doubt

排除证据 **páichú zhèngjù** suppression of evidence

排除证据动议 **páichú zhèngjù dòngyì** motion to suppress evidence

排除证据听证会 **páichú zhèngjù tīngzhènghuì** suppression hearing

判决 **pànjué** *n/v* sentence

判决前被告自白 **pànjué qián bèigào zìbái** allocution

判决书摘要 **pànjuéshū zhāiyào** abstract of judgment

判刑 **pànxíng** *n/v* sentence

Criminal Law

判罪 **pànzuì** *n* conviction

赔偿 **péicháng** *n* reparation, restitution

皮条客 **pítiáokè** *n* procurer, procuress, pimp

破案 **pò'àn** *v* solve a case

破坏 **pòhuài** *v* destroy, vandalize, sabotage

破门入室罪 **pòmén rùshì zuì** breaking and entering

欺凌 **qīlíng** *n* hazing; *v* haze

欺诈 **qīzhà** *adj* fraudulent; *n* fraud

起次要作用的参与者 **qǐ cìyào zuòyòng de cānyùzhě** minor participant

起诉 **qǐsù** *v* sue, indict, prosecute

起诉书 **qǐsùshū** *n* bill of complaint, indictment, information

企图 **qǐtú** *n/v* attempt

企图谋杀罪 **qǐtú móushāzuì** attempted murder

前科 **qiánkē** *n* prior conviction

枪支 **qiāngzhī** *n* firearm

强暴 **qiángbào** *n/v* rape, assault

强奸 **qiángjiān** *n/v* rape, assault

强制 **qiángzhì** *n* coercion; *v* coerce

抢劫 **qiǎngjié** *n* robbery; *v* rob, mug

抢劫者 **qiǎngjiézhě** *n* robber, mugger

抢掠 **qiǎnglüè** *n* looting; *v* loot

敲诈勒索 **qiāozhà-lèsuǒ** *n* blackmail, extortion

窃听 **qiètīng** *v* wiretap

窃听录音 **qiètīng lùyīn** wiretap recording

窃听器 **qiètīngqì** *n* bug, wire

侵吞 **qīntūn** *n* embezzlement

清白 **qīngbái** *adj* innocent; *n* innocence

轻判 **qīng pàn** light sentence

轻罪 **qīngzuì** *n* misdemeanor

轻罪法院 **qīngzuì fǎyuàn** misdemeanor court

请求 qǐngqiú *n/v* petition
囚犯 qiúfàn *n* prisoner, convict
驱逐出境 qūzhú chūjìng *n* deportation, removal;
　　v deport, remove
取保 qǔbǎo *v* post bail
取消资格 qǔxiāozīgé disqualification; disqualify
取证 qǔzhèng *n* collection of evidence
缺席 quēxí in absentia
扰乱治安 rǎoluàn zhì'ān disturbing the peace
人身伤害 rénshēn shānghài physical injury
人质 rénzhì *n* hostage
认罪 rènzuì *v* plead guilty, enter a guilty plea
入室盗窃者 rùshì dàoqiè zhě burglar
入室盗窃罪 rùshì dàoqièzuì burglary
入室行盗工具 rùshì xíngdào gōngjù burglar's tools
软禁 ruǎnjìn *n* house arrest
弱势受害人 ruòshì shòuhàirén vulnerable victim
三振出局法 sān zhèn chūjú fǎ three strikes statute
骚扰 sāorǎo *n* harassment; *v* harass
杀人 shārén *n* homicide
杀人罪 shārénzuì *n* manslaughter
删除 shānchú *v* expunge
商店扒手 shāngdiàn páshǒu shoplifter
商店行窃 shāngdiàn xíngqiè shoplifting
上诉案卷 shàngsù ànjuàn record on appeal
少年犯 shàoniánfàn juvenile offender
少年犯管教所 shàoniánfàn guǎnjiàosuǒ reformatory
少年犯罪前科 shàonián fànzuì qiánkē prior juvenile
　　offense
社区服务 shèqū fúwù community service
赦免 shèmiǎn *n* amnesty; *n/v* pardon
身份 shēnfèn *n* identity, status

身体强制 shēntǐ qiángzhì physical restraint
身心障碍 shēnxīn zhàng'ài physical or mental disorder
审后动议 shěn hòu dòngyì motion after trial
审判 shěnpàn n trial; v try
审前陈述 shěn qián chénshù pretrial statements
审前服务部 shěn qián fúwù bù pretrial services
       department
审前羁押 shěn qián jīyā pretrial detention
声明 shēngmíng n statement
实施犯罪 shíshīfànzuì commit a crime
示范刑法典 shìfàn xíngfǎ diǎn Model Penal Code
事后从犯 shìhòu cóngfàn accessory after the fact
释放 shìfàng n/v release
释放条件 shìfàng tiáojiàn conditions of release
释后监督 shì hòu jiāndū post-release supervision
收监令 shōujiān lìng commitment order
手铐 shǒukào n handcuffs
手枪 shǒuqiāng n gun
受害人 shòuhàirén n victim
受害人的权利 shòuhàirén de quánlì victims' rights
受害人和证人援助计划 shòuhàirén hé zhèngrén
       yuánzhù jìhuà victim and witness assistance
       program
受害人影响陈述 shòuhàirén yǐngxiǎng chénshù victim
       impact statement
受贿 shòuhuì v take bribes
受审 shòushěn v go to trial
受损方 shòusǔnfāng injured party
书面详细说明 shūmiàn xiángxì shuōmíng bill of
       particulars
赎金 shújīn n ransom

死缓 **sǐhuǎn** *n* death sentence with a two-year reprieve (*Chinese law*)

死刑 **sǐxíng** *n* capital punishment, death penalty

死刑犯 **sǐxíngfàn** *n* death-row prisoner

死罪 **sǐzuì** *n* capital offense

肆意破坏财产 **sìyì pòhuài cáichǎn** vandalism

搜查 **sōuchá** *n/v* search

搜查证 **sōucházhèng** *n* search warrant

所有物 **suǒyǒuwù** *n* possession

诉讼时效法 **sùsòng shíxiàofǎ** statute of limitations

诉讼转移 **sùsòng zhuǎnyí** transfer of proceedings

诉状 **sùzhuàng** *n* complaint, petition, indictment

他杀 **tāshā** *n* homicide

贪腐 **tānfǔ** *adj* corrupt; *n* corruption

堂讯 **tángxùn** *n* arraignment; *v* arraign

逃犯 **táofàn** *n* escapee, fugitive

逃跑 **táopǎo** *n* flight; *v* flee, escape

逃税 **táoshuì** *n* tax evasion; *v* evade tax

特定故意 **tèdìng gùyì** specific intent

提供证据 **tígōng zhèngjù** proffer

调整后的罪行级别 **tiáozhěng hòu de zuìxíng jíbié** adjusted offense level

投案 **tóu'àn** *v* surrender

徒刑 **túxíng** *n* imprisonment, confinement, sentence

团伙 **tuánhuǒ** *n* gang

团伙攻击罪 **tuánhuǒ gōngjīzuì** gang assault

推定 **tuīdìng** *n* presumption

退出共谋 **tuìchū gòngmóu** withdraw from a conspiracy

违法者 **wéifǎzhě** *n* offender

违规 **wéiguī** *n* infraction

违禁品 **wéijìnpǐn** *n* contraband

伪造品 **wěizàopǐn** *n* counterfeit

伪造者 wěizàozhě *n* counterfeiter, forger

伪造罪 wěizàozuì *n* counterfeiting, forgery

伪证 wěizhèng *n* perjury

猥亵性暴露罪 wěixièxìng bàolùzuì indecent exposure

未经证实的 wèi jīng zhèngshí de *adj* uncorroborated

未受处罚的 wèi shòu chǔfá de *adj* unpunished

无期徒刑 wúqī túxíng life sentence

无证件的 wú zhèngjiàn de *adj* undocumented

无罪 wúzuì *adj* innocent, not guilty

无罪裁定 wúzuì cáidìng acquittal

无罪释放 wúzuì shìfàng acquit

无罪推定 wúzuì tuīdìng presumption of innocence

武力 wǔlì *n* force

武器 wǔqì *n* weapon

洗钱 xǐqián *n* money laundering

先例 xiānlì *n* precedent

县治安官 xiàn zhì'ānguān sheriff

线民 xiànmín *n* informant

限制 xiànzhì *v* confine, limit

限制使用证据动议 xiànzhì shǐyòng zhèngjù dòngyì
      motion to limit the use of evidence

向政府提供重要协助 xiàng zhèngfǔ tígōng zhòngyào
      xiézhù substantial assistance to the government

销毁 xiāohuǐ *v* expunge

携带枪支 xiédài qiāngzhī carrying a firearm

胁迫 xiépò *n* coercion, duress

刑罚 xíngfá *n* penalty

刑事的 xíngshì de *adj* penal

刑事过失罪 xíngshì guòshī zuì criminal negligence

刑事疏忽罪 xíngshì shūhū zuì criminal negligence

刑事诉讼法 xíngshì sùsòngfǎ code of criminal procedure

刑事诉讼规则 **xíngshì sùsòng guīzé** Rules of Criminal
　　Procedure

刑事自诉状 **xíngshì zìsùzhuàng** criminal complaint

行贿 **xínghuì** *v* bribe

性侵犯 **xìng qīnfàn** sexual abuse

性侵犯者 **xìng qīnfànzhě** sexual predator

凶手 **xiōngshǒu** *n* murderer, killer

蓄意 **xùyì** *adj* deliberate, willful

宣誓 **xuānshì** *v* swear, take an oath

悬案 **xuán'àn** *n* unsolved case, pending lawsuit

悬案陪审团 **xuán àn péishěntuán** hung jury

悬赏 **xuánshǎng** *v* post a reward

询问笔录 **xúnwèn bǐlù** record of questioning

迅速审理法 **xùnsù shěnlǐ fǎ** Speedy Trial Act

严格责任 **yángé zérèn** strict liability

严重的 **yánzhòng de** *adj* aggravated

严重人身伤害 **yánzhòng rénshēn shānghài** serious
　　bodily injury

一般故意 **yìbān gùyì** general intent

一级谋杀罪 **yījí móushāzuì** first degree murder

一揽子保释条件 **yīlǎnzi bǎoshì tiáojiàn** bail package

一罪二审 **yī zuì èr shěn** double jeopardy

以貌取人 **yǐmào-qǔrén** profiling

已服刑期 **yǐ fú xíngqī** time served

已决犯 **yǐjuéfàn** *n* convict

已判罪的 **yǐ pànzuì de** *adj* convicted

因表现良好而减刑期 **yīn biǎoxiàn liánghǎo ér jiǎn
　　xíngqī** good behavior time, time off for good behavior

阴谋 **yīnmóu** *n* conspiracy

阴谋者 **yīnmóuzhě** *n* conspirator

应受惩处的 **yīngshòu chéngchǔ de** *adj* culpable

意向 **yìxiàng** *n* intent

有关行为 yǒuguān xíngwéi relevant conduct

有加重情节的重罪 yǒu jiāzhòng qíngjié de zhòngzuì
    aggravated felony

有期徒刑 yǒuqītúxíng fixed-term sentence

有损害的 yǒu sǔnhài de *adj* prejudicial, harmful

有条件豁免 yǒutiáojiàn huòmiǎn qualified immunity

有条件认罪 yǒutiáojiàn rènzuì conditional plea of guilty

有条件释放 yǒutiáojiàn shìfàng conditional release

有预谋的 yǒu yùmóu de *adj* premeditated

有组织犯罪 yǒuzǔzhī fànzuì organized crime

有罪的 yǒuzuì de *adj* guilty

诱拐 yòuguǎi *n* abduction; *v* abduct

诱拐者 yòuguǎizhě *n* abductor

幼年 yòunián *n* infancy

与检方合作 yǔ jiǎnfāng hézuò cooperation with the
    prosecution

约会强奸 yuēhuì qiángjiān date rape

在法庭上的不当行为 zài fǎtíng shàng de bùdàng
    xíngwéi misconduct before the court

暂缓执行判决 zànhuǎn zhíxíng pànjué stay
    enforcement of the judgment

诈骗 zhàpiàn *v* defraud

诈骗罪 zhàpiànzuì *n* fraud, false pretenses

詹克斯法 zhānkèsī fǎ Jencks Act

占有 zhànyǒu *n* possession

侦查 zhēnchá *n* investigation; *v* investigate

侦查员 zhēncháyuán *n* investigator

侦探 zhēntàn *n* detective

证据不足 zhèngjù bùzú insufficient evidence

证据的优势 zhèngjù de yōushì preponderance of the
    evidence

证明无罪 zhèngmíng wúzuì exonerate

证人保护计划 zhèngrén bǎohù jìhuà witness protection
　　plan
正当防卫 zhèngdāng fángwèi self-defense, justifiable
　　defense
执法方式 zhífǎ fāngshì law enforcement methods
执法人员 zhífǎ rényuán law enforcement official (*officer*)
执行逮捕的警员 zhíxíng dàibǔ de jǐngyuán arresting
　　officer
职业杀手 zhíyè shāshǒu gunman, professional killer
指称 zhǐchēng *n* allegation; *v* allege
指控的罪行 zhǐkòng de zuìxíng alleged offense
指纹 zhǐwén *n* fingerprints
致残罪 zhìcánzuì *n* mayhem
致命力 zhìmìng lì deadly force
致命武器 zhìmìng wǔqì deadly weapon
制裁 zhìcái *n/v* sanction
制定法 zhìdìngfǎ *n* statute
终身监禁 zhōngshēn jiānjìn life sentence
终审判决 zhōngshěn pànjué final sentence
种族蔑称 zhǒngzú mièchēng racial slur
重大盗窃罪 zhòngdà dàoqièzuì grand larceny
重大谋杀罪 zhòngdà móushāzuì felony murder
重罪 zhòngzuì *n* felony
重罪犯 zhòngzuìfàn *n* felon
州警 zhōujǐng *n* state trooper
主谋 zhǔmóu *n* mastermind
主张 zhǔzhāng *n* claim, allegation
专门技巧 zhuānmén jìqiǎo specialized skill
状况 zhuàngkuàng *n* state, status
自动投案 zìdòng tóu'àn self-surrender, voluntary surrender
自杀 zìshā *n* suicide; *v* commit suicide
自卫 zìwèi self-defense

自证其罪 **zì zhèng qí zuì** self-incrimination
纵火罪 **zònghuǒzuì** *n* arson
走私 **zǒusī** *n* smuggling; *v* smuggle
走私者 **zǒusīzhě** *n* smuggler
醉酒 **zuìjiǔ** *adj* drunk, intoxicated
罪犯 **zuìfàn** *n* criminal, perpetrator, offender
罪项 **zuì xiàng** *n* count (*of indictment*)
罪行 **zuìxíng** *n* crime, offense
罪行合并 **zuìxíng hébìng** joinder of offenses
罪行级别 **zuìxíng jíbié** offense level
作用最小的参与者 **zuòyòng zuìxiǎo de cānyùzhě**
        minimal participant

家事法词汇
Family Law

家事法是规范家庭关系和家庭事件的法律, 对于结婚年龄、婚姻的效力、婚前协议的执行、分居、离婚、子女权益、抚养和扶养义务、离异双方对子女的监护和探视权利等等, 均有规定。

安全套 ānquántào *n* condom
保护儿童和家庭安全法 bǎohù értóng hé jiātíng ānquán fǎ Keeping Children and Families Safe Act
避孕 bìyùn *n* contraception
避孕药具 bìyùn yàojù contraceptive
表姐妹 biǎojiěmèi *n* female cousins
  表姐 biǎojiě *n* elder female cousin (*father's sister's daughter who is older than you; mother's sibling's daughter who is older than you*)
  表妹 biǎomèi *n* younger female cousin (*father's sister's daughter who is younger than you; mother's sibling's daughter who is younger than you*)
表亲 biǎoqīn *n* cousinship
表兄弟 biǎoxiōngdì *n* male cousins
  表弟 biǎodì *n* younger male cousin (*father's sister's son who is younger than you; mother's sibling's son who is younger than you*)
  表哥 biǎogē *See* 表兄 **biǎoxiōng**
  表兄 biǎoxiōng *n* elder male cousin (*father's sister's son who is older than you; mother's sibling's son who is older than you*)

伯父 **bófù** *n* uncle (*father's elder brother*)

伯母 **bómǔ** *n* aunt (*wife of father's elder brother*)

不付抚养费的父亲 **bùfù fǔyǎngfèi de fùqīn** deadbeat dad

不能和解的分歧 **bùnéng héjiě de fēnqí** irreconcilable differences

不育的 **bùyù de** *adj* infertile

不育症 **bùyùzhèng** *n* infertility

不忠实 (夫妻间) **bùzhōngshí** (*fūqījiān*) *adj* unfaithful; *n* infidelity

产假 **chǎnjià** *n* maternity leave

产科病房 **chǎnkē bìngfáng** maternity ward

重婚罪 **chónghūnzuì** *n* bigamy

出生 **chūshēng** *n* birth; *v* to be born

出生证 **chūshēngzhèng** *n* birth certificate

大伯子 **dàbǎizi** *n* brother-in-law (*husband's elder brother*)

大姑子 **dàgūzi** *n* sister-in-law (*husband's elder sister*)

大姨子 **dàyízi** *n* sister-in-law (*wife's elder sister*)

代孕母亲 **dàiyùn mǔqīn** surrogate mother

单方监护权 **dānfāng jiānhùquán** sole custody

单身 **dānshēn** *adj/n* single

等待期 **děngdàiqī** waiting period

弟弟 **dìdi** *n* younger brother

弟媳 **dìxí** *n* sister-in-law (*younger brother's wife*)

订婚 **dìnghūn** *n* engagement

堕胎 **duòtāi** *n* abortion

儿童 **értóng** *n* child, children

儿媳 **érxí** *n* daughter-in-law

儿子 **érzi** *n* son

法定婚姻障碍 **fǎdìng hūnyīn zhàng'ài** impediment to marriage

法定成年人年龄 **fǎdìng chéngniánrén niánlíng** age of majority

法定结合 **fǎdìng jiéhé** civil union

法定结婚年龄 **fǎdìng jiéhūn niánlíng** marriageable age

法律监护权 **fǎlù jiānhùquán** legal custody

犯重婚罪者 **fàn chónghūnzuì zhě** bigamist

非法的 **fēifǎ de** *adj* illegitimate

非婚生子女 **fēi hūnshēng zǐnǚ** illegitimate children

分居 **fēnjū** *n* separation; *v* live separate and apart

分居协议 **fēnjū xiéyì** separation agreement

分娩 **fēnmiǎn** *n* childbirth

夫妻 **fūqī** *n* couple, husband and wife

夫妻共同财产 **fūqī gòngtóng cáichǎn** community property

扶养 **fúyǎng** *n* spousal support

扶养费 **fúyǎngfèi** *n* alimony, spousal support payment, maintenance

抚养 **fúyǎng** *n* child support

抚养费 **fǔyǎngfèi** *n* child support payment

福祉 **fúzhǐ** *n* well-being

辅导 **fǔdǎo** *n* counseling

辅导员 **fǔdǎoyuán** *n* guidance counselor

父母 **fùmǔ** *n* parents

父母权利 **fùmǔ quánlì** parental rights

父母诱拐 **fùmǔ yòuguǎi** parental abduction, custodial abduction

父亲 **fùqīn** *n* father

哥哥 **gēge** *n* elder brother

个人财产 **gèrén cáichǎn** separate property (与夫妻共同财产相对 / *in contrast to community property*)

工资代扣 **gōngzī dài kòu** wage withholding

公公 **gōnggōng** *n* father-in-law (*husband's father*)

共同监护权 **gòngtóng jiānhùquán** joint custody

姑 **gū** *n* aunt (*father's sister*)

姑父 **gūfu** *n* uncle (*father's sister's husband*)

姑子 **gūzi** *n* sister-in-law (*husband's sister*)

孤儿 **gū'ér** *n* orphan

寡妇 **guǎfù** *n* widow

鳏夫 **guānfū** *n* widower

合法的 **héfǎ de** *adj* legitimate

和解 **héjiě** *n* reconciliation; *v* reconcile

后代 **hòudài** *n* offspring

忽视儿童 **hūshì értóng** neglect of a child

户主 **hùzhǔ** *n* head of household

怀孕 **huáiyùn** *adj* pregnant; *n* pregnancy

婚礼 **hūnlǐ** *n* marriage ceremony, wedding ceremony

婚内强奸 **hūnnèi qiángjiān** marital rape

婚前协议 **hūnqián xiéyì** pre-nuptial agreement

婚生子女 **hūnshēng zǐnǚ** legitimate children, children born in wedlock

婚姻 **hūnyīn** *n* marriage

婚姻财产 **hūnyīn cáichǎn** marital property

婚姻财产协议 **hūnyīn cáichǎn xiéyì** marital settlement agreement

婚姻的 **hūnyīn de** *adj* matrimonial

婚姻关系 **hūnyīn guānxì** matrimony

婚姻债务 **hūnyīn zhàiwù** marital debt

婚姻咨询 **hūnyīn zīxún** marriage counseling

婚姻咨询员 **hūnyīn zīxúnyuán** marriage counselor

婚姻资产 **hūnyīn zīchǎn** marital asset

计划生育 **jìhuà shēngyù** family planning

寄养 **jìyǎng** *n* foster care

寄养家庭 **jìyǎng jiātíng** foster family

继父 **jìfù** *n* stepfather

继母 **jìmǔ** *n* stepmother

家 **jiā** *n* family, home
家事法 **jiāshìfǎ** family law
家事法院 **jiāshì fǎyuàn** family court
家事法院法官 **jiāshì fǎyuàn fǎguān** family court judge
家庭 **jiātíng** *n* family
家庭暴力 **jiātíng bàolì** domestic violence
家庭的 **jiātíng de** *adj* domestic
家庭关系 **jiātíng guānxì** domestic relations
家庭团聚 **jiātíng tuánjù** family reunification
嫁 **jià** *v* marry (*of a woman*)
奸夫 **jiānfū** *n* adulterer
奸妇 **jiānfù** *n* adulteress
监护 **jiānhù** *n* custody, guardianship
监护权 **jiānhùquán** *n* custody, guardianship
监护人 **jiānhùrén** *n* guardian
监护诱拐 **jiānhù yòuguǎi** custodial abduction
健康证明 **jiànkāng zhèngmíng** medical certificate
节制生育 **jiézhì shēngyù** birth control
结婚 **jiéhūn** *n* marriage; *v* marry
结婚证书 **jiéhūn zhèngshū** marriage certificate
姐 **jiě** *n* elder sister
姐夫 **jiěfu** *n* brother-in-law (*husband of elder sister*)
解除婚姻 **jiěchú hūnyīn** dissolution of marriage
解脱 **jiětuō** *v* emancipate
禁止骚扰令 **jìnzhǐ sāorǎo lìng** injunction against
　　molestation
救济 **jiùjì** *n* relief; *v* relieve
舅父 **jiùfù** *n* uncle (*mother's brother*)
舅母 **jiùmǔ** *n* aunt (*wife of mother's brother*)
举行婚礼 **jǔxíng hūnlǐ** solemnize a marriage
绝对离婚 **juéduì líhūn** absolute divorce

Family Law

扣付债务人工资令 kòu fù zhàiwùrén gōngzī lìng *n*
　　garnishment

宽恕 **kuānshù** *n* condonation

离婚 **líhūn** *n/v* divorce

离婚的理由 **líhūn de lǐyóu** grounds for divorce

离婚判决 **líhūn pànjué** divorce decree

离了婚的 **lí le hūn de** *adj* divorced

离了婚的人 **lí le hūn de rén** divorcee

连襟 **liánjīn** *n* brother-in-law (*husband of sister*)

联邦查找父母服务网 **liánbāng cházhǎo fùmǔ fúwù
　　wǎng** Federal Parent Locator Service (FPLS)

联邦子女抚养案登记处 **liánbāng zǐnǚ fǔyǎng àn
　　dēngjìchù** Federal Case Registry (FCR)

临时监护权 **línshí jiānhùquán** temporary custody

临时禁止令 **línshí jìnzhǐ lìng** temporary restraining
　　order (TRO)

临时命令 **línshí mìnglìng** temporary order

妹 **mèi** *n* younger sister

妹夫 **mèifu** *n* brother-in-law (*husband of younger sister*)

母亲 **mǔqīn** *n* mother

奶妈 **nǎimā** *n* wetnurse

男同性恋者 **nán tóngxìngliànzhě** gay male

内兄 **nèixiōng** *n* brother-in-law (*wife's elder brother*)

内弟 **nèidì** *n* brother-in-law (*wife's younger brother*)

能力 **nénglì** *n* competency

能力听证会 **nénglì tīngzhènghuì** competency hearing

女儿 **nǚ'ér** *n* daughter

女同性恋者 **nǚ tóngxìngliànzhě** lesbian

女婿 **nǚxù** *n* son-in-law

虐待 **nuèdài** *n* cruelty; *n/v* abuse

虐待配偶 **nuèdài pèi'ǒu** spousal abuse

判决分居 **pànjué fēnjū** legal separation

赔偿金裁定额 **péichángjīn cáidìng'é** monetary award

配偶 **pèiǒu** *n* spouse

配偶扶养费 **pèi'ǒu fúyǎngfèi** spousal support

贫困家庭临时救济 **pínkùn jiātíng línshí jiùjì** temporary
　　aid for needy families (TANF)

婆母 **pómǔ** *n* mother-in-law (*husband's mother*)

普通法婚姻 **pǔtōngfǎ hūnyīn** common law marriage

妻子 **qīzi** *n* wife

弃家 **qìjiā** *n* abandonment of marital domicile

前夫 **qiánfū** *n* ex-husband

前妻 **qiánqī** *n* ex-wife

强迫堕胎 **qiǎngpò duòtāi** forced abortion

亲属关系 **qīnshǔ guānxì** kinship

青春期 **qīngchūnqī** *n* puberty

青少年 **qīngshàonián** *adj/n* adolescent; *n* teenager

情夫 **qíngfū** *n* male paramour

情妇 **qíngfù** *n* female paramour, mistress

情人 **qíngrén** *n* lover, paramour

娶 **qǔ** *v* marry (*of a man*)

取得独立生活资格的未成年人 **qǔdé dúlì shēnghuó
　　zīgé de wèichéngniánrén** emancipated minor

确认生父的诉讼 **quèrèn shēngfù de sùsòng** paternity
　　proceeding, paternity suit

人工授精 **réngōng shòujīng** artificial insemination

人身监护权 **rénshēn jiānhùquán** physical custody

妊娠 **rènshēn** *adj* pregnant; *n* pregnancy

丧失行为能力的 **sàngshī xíngwéi nénglì de** *adj*
　　incapacitated

嫂子 **sǎozi** *n* sister-in-law (*elder brother's wife*)

赡养 **shànyǎng** *v* support one's parents (*under Chinese law*)

赡养费 **shànyǎngfèi** *n* support payment to one's parents
　　(*under Chinese law*)

赡养义务 **shànyǎng yìwù** duty to support one's parents (*under Chinese law*)

社会服务局 **shèhuì fúwù jú** Department of Social Services

涉外婚姻 **shèwài hūnyīn** foreign marriage

婶母 **shěnmǔ** *n* aunt (*wife of father's younger brother*)

生父 **shēngfù** *n* biological father

生父关系 **shēngfù guānxì** paternity

生母 **shēngmǔ** *n* biological mother

生身父母 **shēngshēn fùmǔ** biological parents

失依子女家庭援助 **shī yī zǐnǚ jiātíng yuánzhù** Aid to Families with Dependent Children (AFDC)

实际分居 **shíjì fēnjū** actual separation

使用与占用 **shǐyòng yǔ zhànyòng** use and possession

试管受精 **shìguǎn shòujīng** in-vitro fertilization (IVF)

试管婴儿 **shìguǎn yīng'ér** in vitro baby, test-tube baby

收入拨付 **shōurù bōfù** earnings assignment

收入代扣 **shōurù dài kòu** income withholding

收入代扣令 **shōurù dàikòu lìng** earnings withholding order

收养 **shōuyǎng** *n* adoption; *v* adopt

收养抵税额 **shōuyǎng dǐshuì'é** adoption tax credit

受养人 **shòuyǎngrén** *n* dependent

受益人 **shòuyìrén** *n* beneficiary

叔父 **shūfù** *n* uncle (*father's younger brother*)

双胞胎 **shuāngbāotāi** *n* twins

双性恋者 **shuāngxìngliànzhě** bisexual

死产 **sǐchǎn** *adj* stillborn

死去的 **sǐqù de** *adj* deceased

死亡 **sǐwáng** *n* death; *v* die

死亡证明书 **sǐwáng zhèngmíngshū** death certificate

死者 **sǐzhě** *n* decedent

诉讼待决期间 sùsòng dàijué qījiān pendente lite

诉讼监护人 sùsòng jiānhùrén guardian ad litem (GAL)

孙女 sūnnǚ *n* granddaughter (*son's daughter*)

孙子 sūnzi *n* grandson (*son's son*)

探视 tànshì *n* visitation

探视权 tànshìquán visitation rights

堂姐妹 tángjiěmèi *n* paternal female cousin

　　堂姐 tángjiě *n* paternal elder female cousins (*father's brother's daughter who is older than you*)

　　堂妹 tángmèi *n* paternal younger female cousin (*father's brother's daughter who is younger than you*)

堂兄弟 tángxiōngdì *n* paternal male cousins

　　堂弟 tángdì *n* paternal younger male cousin (*father's brother's son who is younger than you*)

　　堂兄 tángxiōng *n* paternal elder male cousin (*father's brother's son who is older than you*)

通奸 tōngjiān *n* adultery

通奸男子 tōngjiān nánzǐ adulterer

通奸女子 tōngjiān nǚzǐ adulteress

同居伴侣 tóngjū bànlǚ domestic partner

同性婚姻 tóngxìng hūnyīn same-sex marriage, gay marriage

同性恋者 tóngxìngliànzhě homosexual, gay

同意 tóngyì *n/v* consent

同宗 tóngzōng *n* consanguinity

推定的父亲 tuīdìng de fùqīn putative father

退休 tuìxiū *n* retirement; *v* retire

托儿所 tuō'érsuǒ *n* nursery

托儿中心 tuō'er zhōngxīn *n* child care center

外甥 wàishēng *n* nephew (*sister's son*)

外甥女 wàishēngnǚ *n* niece (*sister's daughter*)

外孙女 wàisūnnǚ *n* granddaughter (*daughter's daughter*)

外孙子 **wàisūnzi** *n* grandson (*daughter's son*)

外孙子女 **wàisūnzǐnǚ** *n* grandchildren (*daughter's children*)

外祖父 **wàizǔfù** *n* maternal grandfather

外祖父母 **wàizǔfùmǔ** *n* maternal grandparents

外祖母 **wàizǔmǔ** *n* maternal grandmother

未成年 **wèichéngnián** *adj* juvenile, minor, underage

未达法定年龄 **wèidá fǎdìng niánlíng** underage

未婚 **wèihūn** *adj* single, unmarried

未婚夫 **wèihūnfū** *n* fiancé

未婚妻 **wèihūnqī** *n* fiancée

未留遗嘱的 **wèi liú yízhǔ de** *adj* intestate

未亡配偶选择权 **wèiwáng pèi'ǒu xuǎnzéquán** right of election by surviving spouse

无过错离婚 **wú guòcuò líhūn** no-fault divorce

无行为能力者 **wú xíngwéi nénglì zhě** incompetent person

无争议离婚 **wú zhēngyì líhūn** uncontested divorce

小产 **xiǎochǎn** *n* miscarriage

小姑子 **xiǎogūzi** *n* sister-in-law (*husband's younger sister*)

小叔子 **xiǎoshūzi** *n* brother-in-law (*husband's younger brother*)

小姨子 **xiǎoyízi** *n* sister-in-law (*wife's younger sister*)

兄弟 **xiōngdi** *n* younger brother

兄弟 **xiōngdì** *n* brothers

兄弟姐妹 **xiōngdì jiěmèi** *n* sibling

宣告婚姻无效 **xuāngào hūnyīn wúxiào** annulment of marriage

血亲 **xuèqīn** *n* consanguinity

阳痿 **yángwěi** *adj* impotent; *n* impotence

养父 **yǎngfù** *n* foster father, adoptive father

养父母 **yǎngfùmǔ** *n* foster parents, adoptive parents

养母 yǎngmǔ *n* foster mother, adoptive mother

遗产 yíchǎn *n* estate

遗产法院程序 yíchǎn fǎyuàn chéngxù surrogate court proceeding

遗产管理人 yíchǎn guǎnlǐrén administrator of an estate

遗产继承人 yíchǎn jìchéngrén *n* distributee

遗产税 yíchǎnshuì *n* estate tax

遗嘱检验 yízhǔ jiǎnyàn probate

遗嘱执行人 yízhǔ zhíxíngrén executor

姨 yí *n* aunt (*mother's sister*)

姨父 yífù *n* uncle (*husband of mother's sister*)

姨子 yízi *n* sister-in-law (*wife's sister*)

已婚的 yǐhūn de *adj* married

异性恋者 yìxìngliànzhě heterosexual

姻亲 yīnqīn *n* in-laws

有监护权的父亲或母亲 yǒu jiānhùquán de fùqīn huò mǔqīn custodial parent

有生育能力的 yǒu shēngyù nénglì de *adj* fertile

远亲 yuǎnqīn *n* distant relative

岳父 yuèfù *n* father-in-law (*wife's father*)

岳母 yuèmǔ *n* mother-in-law (*wife's mother*)

再婚 zàihūn *v* remarry

早产 zǎochǎn *n* premature birth

赠与税 zèngyǔshuì *n* gift tax

丈夫 zhàngfu *n* husband

直系家庭 zhíxì jiātíng immediate family

直系亲属 zhíxì qīnshǔ immediate relative

侄女 zhínü *n* niece (*brother's daughter*)

侄子 zhízi *n* nephew (*brother's son*)

指导方针 zhǐdǎo fāngzhēn guidelines

指导顾问 zhǐdǎo gùwèn guidance counselor

忠实 zhōngshí *n* fidelity

Family Law

终局离婚判决 zhōngjú líhūn pànjué final decree of
　　divorce

妯娌 zhóuli *n* sister-in-law (*wife of your husband's
　　brother*)

助产士 zhùchǎnshì *n* midwife

转让子女抚养费权利 zhuǎnràng zǐnǚ fǔyǎngfèi quánlì
　　assignment of support rights

咨询 zīxún *n* counseling; *v* counsel

子女 zǐnǚ *n* child, children

子女抚养费 zǐnǚ fǔyǎngfèi child support

子女抚养费强制执行机构 zǐnǚ fǔyǎngfèi qiángzhì
　　zhíxíng jīgòu child support enforcement agency or
　　office

子女抚养费指导方针 zǐnǚ fǔyǎngfèi zhǐdǎo fāngzhēn
　　child support guidelines

子女最佳利益 zǐnǚ zuìjiā lìyì best interests of the child

子孙 zǐsūn *n* offspring

自认的配偶 zìrèn de pèi'ǒu putative spouse

祖父 zǔfù *n* paternal grandfather

祖父母 zǔfùmǔ *n* paternal grandparents

祖母 zǔmǔ *n* paternal grandmother

保健法词汇
Health-Care Law

伤病、治疗、医疗保险，为保护公众权益而对行医和
药品销售加以管理, 这些都属于保健法涉及的范围。

癌症 **áizhèng** *n* cancer
艾滋病 (又称爱滋病) **àizībìng** *n* acquired
　　immunodeficiency syndrome (AIDS)
艾滋病毒 (又称爱滋病毒) **àizībìngdú** human
　　immunodeficiency virus (HIV)
白血病 **báixuèbìng** *n* leukemia
保单 **bǎodān** *n* policy
保单持有人 **bǎodān chíyǒurén** policyholder
保单限额 **bǎodān xiàn'é** policy limit
保健 **bǎojiàn** *n* health care
保健管控 **bǎojiàn guǎnkòng** health-care management
保健委托书 **bǎojiàn wěituōshū** health-care proxy
保健组织 **bǎojiàn zǔzhī** health maintenance organization
　　(HMO)
保险 **bǎoxiǎn** *n* insurance
保险单 **bǎoxiǎndān** insurance policy
保险范围 **bǎoxiǎn fànwéi** coverage
保险费 **bǎoxiǎnfèi** *n* premium
保险给付 **bǎoxiǎn jǐfù** policy benefit
保险人 **bǎoxiǎnrén** *n* insurer
报销申请 **bàoxiāo shēnqǐng** claim
抱怨 **bàoyuàn** *n* grievance
被保险人 **bèi bǎoxiǎnrén** *n* insured

扁桃体炎 **biǎntáotǐyán** *n* tonsillitis

标准 **biāozhǔn** *n* standard

补偿 **bǔcháng** *n* compensation; *v* compensate

补偿制度 **bǔcháng zhìdù** compensation system

不达标准的护理 **bùdá biāozhǔn de hùlǐ**
　　substandard care

不需卧床的 **bùxū wòchuáng de** *adj* ambulatory

残疾 **cánjí** *adj* disabled; *n* disability

残疾福利 **cánjí fúlì** disability benefit

残障 **cánzhàng** *adj* handicapped; *n* handicap

产前健康 **chǎnqián jiànkāng** prenatal health

超重 **chāozhòng** *adj* overweight

成人日间护理中心 **chéngrén rìjiān hùlǐ zhōngxīn**
　　adult daycare center

承保人 **chéngbǎorén** *n* insurance carrier

除外 **chúwài** *n* exclusion (*policy*)

除外风险 **chúwài fēngxiǎn** excluded risk

处方 **chǔfāng** *n* prescription

处方药 **chǔfāngyào** *n* prescription drug

处方药给付 **chǔfāngyào jǐfù** prescription drug benefit

传染 **chuánrǎn** *n* infection

传染病 **chuánrǎnbìng** *n* infectious disease

传统医学 **chuántǒng yīxué** traditional medicine

待决索赔 **dàijué suǒpéi** pending claim

毒瘾 **dúyǐn** *n* drug addiction

恶性的 **èxìng de** *adj* malignant

恶性肿瘤 **èxìng zhǒngliú** malignant tumor

法定盲人 **fǎdìng mángrén** legally blind

法定丧失行为能力者 **fǎdìng sàngshī xíngwéi nénglì
　　zhě** legally incapacitated

反式脂肪酸 **fǎnshì zhīfángsuān** trans fats, trans fatty
　　acids

放弃 fàngqì *v* waive

非处方药 fēi chǔfāngyào over-the-counter drug

非传统医学 fēi chuántǒng yīxué non-traditional medicine

非典 fēidiǎn *n* SARS (*severe acute respiratory syndrome /*
严重急性呼吸系统综合征 *yánzhòng jíxìng hūxī*
xìtǒng zōnghézhēng)

肥胖症 féipàngzhèng *n* obesity

肺癌 fèi'ái *n* lung cancer

福利 fúlì *n* benefit

辅助生活 fǔzhù shēnghuó assisted living

辅助生殖中心 fǔzhù shēngzhí zhōngxīn fertility services

附加保险范围 fùjiā bǎoxiǎn fànwéi additional coverage

肝癌 gān'ái *n* liver cancer

感冒 gǎnmào *n* cold

感染 gǎnrǎn *n* infection

高血压 gāoxuèyā *n* hypertension, high blood pressure

工人补偿金 gōngrén bǔchángjīn workman's compensation

共付费 gòngfùfèi *n* co-payment

管控保健组织 guǎnkòng bǎojiàn zǔzhī managed care
organization

过失 guòshī *n* malpractice

过失案件 guòshī ànjiàn malpractice case

过失索赔 guòshī suǒpéi malpractice claim

含铅油漆 hán qiān yóuqī lead paint

合格的 hégé de *adj* eligible

合乎条件的 héhū tiáojiàn de *adj* eligible

忽视 hūshì *n/v* neglect

护理 hùlǐ *n/v* care

护理标准 hùlǐ biāozhǔn standard of care

护理管理 hùlǐ guǎnlǐ care management

护理员 hùlǐyuán *n* caregiver, caretaker

护理之家 hùlǐ zhī jiā nursing home

护士 **hùshi** *n* nurse

化验 **huàyàn** *n/v* test

恢复室 **huīfùshì** *n* recovery room

获得 **huòdé** *n/v* access; *v* acquire

急性病 **jíxìngbìng** *n* acute disease

急性病护理 **jíxìngbìng hùlǐ** acute care

急性的 **jíxìng de** *adj* acute

急诊室 **jízhěnshì** *n* emergency room

疾病 **jíbìng** *n* disease, illness

疾病控制 **jíbìng kòngzhì** disease control

疾病预防 **jíbìng yùfáng** disease prevention

给付 **jǐfù** *n* benefit

给付额 **jǐfù'é** *n* allowance

给付范围内的福利 **jǐfù fànwéi nèi de fúlì** covered benefit

计划 **jìhuà** *n* plan

计划给付额 **jìhuà jǐfù'é** plan allowance

计划外 **jìhuà wài** *adj* out-of-network, out-of-plan

家庭 **jiātíng** *n* family

家庭护理员 **jiātíng hùlǐyuán** home attendant

减肥 **jiǎnféi** *n* weight loss; *v* lose weight

检验 **jiǎnyàn** *v* examine, check, test

健康 **jiànkāng** *n* health, fitness

健康的 **jiànkāng de** *adj* healthy

戒毒 **jièdú** *n* drug rehabilitation

精神病学 **jīngshénbìngxué** *n* psychiatry

精神病医生 **jīngshénbìng yīshēng** *n* psychiatrist

精神的 **jīngshén de** *adj* mental

精神健康 **jīngshén jiànkāng** *n* mental health

救护车 **jiùhùchē** *n* ambulance

居家护理 **jūjiā hùlǐ** at-home nursing care

开业医生 **kāiyè yīshēng** *n* practitioner

康复 **kāngfù** *n* rehabilitation

抗药的 kàngyào de *adj* drug-resistant
可靠性 kěkàoxìng *n* dependability
控制体重 kòngzhì tǐzhòng weight management
扣除额 kòuchú'é *n* deductible
老年保健 lǎonián bǎojiàn elder care
老年的 lǎonián de *adj* elderly
老年法律 lǎonián fǎlǜ elder law
老年人 lǎoniánrén *n* elder, senior citizen
老人服务 lǎorén fúwù senior services
理疗 lǐliáo *n* physical therapy
良性的 liángxìng de *adj* benign
良性肿瘤 liángxìng zhǒngliú benign tumor
疗法 liáofǎ *n* therapy
领取 lǐngqǔ *v* collect
流感 liúgǎn *n* flu, influenza
慢性病 mànxìngbìng *n* chronic disease
门诊病人 ménzhěn bìngrén outpatient
免除 miǎnchú *v* waive
免费的 miǎnfèi de *adj* free, free of charge
免费获得 miǎnfèi huòdé free access
赔偿 péicháng *n* compensation
普通医生 pǔtōng yīshēng general practitioner
器官移植 qìguān yízhí organ transplant
前列腺炎 qiánlièxiànyán *n* prostatitis
禽流感 qín liúgǎn avian influenza, avian flu
龋洞 qǔdòng *n* cavity
全保 quánbǎo *n* comprehensive coverage
全国成人日间护理协会 quánguó chéngrén rìjiān hùlǐ
　　xiéhuì National Adult Day Services Association
　　(NADSA)
全科医生 quánkē yīshēng general practitioner

人禽流感 **rén qín liúgǎn** human avian influenza, human bird flu

丧失 **sàngshī** *n* loss

伤害 **shānghài** *n* injury; *v* injure

申诉 **shēnsù** *n* grievance; *v* file a grievance, appeal

申诉程序 **shēnsù chéngxù** appeal process

身体残障 **shēntǐ cánzhàng** physical handicap

身体伤害 **shēntǐ shānghài** physical injury

生病 **shēngbìng** *adj* ill, sick

生活质量 **shēnghuó zhìliàng** quality of life

生命损失 **shēngmìng sǔnshī** loss of life

失去 **shīqù** *n* loss; *v* lose

失去双手和双脚 **shīqù shuāngshǒu hé shuāngjiǎo** loss of both hands and feet

失去听力 **shīqù tīnglì** loss of hearing

失去同一只手的拇指和食指 **shīqù tóng yīzhīshǒu de mǔzhǐ hé shízhǐ** loss of thumb and index finger of the same hand

失去语言能力 **shīqù yǔyán nénglì** loss of speech

失业 **shīyè** *adj* unemployed; *n* unemployment

失业补偿金 **shīyè bǔchángjīn** unemployment compensation

失业救济金 **shīyè jiùjìjīn** unemployment compensation

石棉 **shímián** *n* asbestos

使用情况审核 **shǐyòng qíngkuàng shěnhé** utilization review

事故 **shìgù** *n* accident

适当护理 **shìdàng hùlǐ** adequate care

手术 **shǒushù** *n* surgery

手术室 **shǒushùshì** *n* operating room

受管制物质 **shòu guǎnzhì wùzhì** controlled substance

受伤 shòushāng *n* injury

受益人 shòuyìrén *n* beneficiary

书面索赔通知 shūmiàn suǒpéi tōngzhī written notice of claim

私人保险 sīrén bǎoxiǎn private insurance

损失 sǔnshī *n* loss

损失证明 sǔnshī zhèngmíng proof of loss

索赔 suǒpéi *n/v* claim

索赔表 suǒpéibiǎo claim form

索赔给付 suǒpéi jǐfù payment of claim

索赔通知 suǒpéi tōngzhī notice of claim

糖尿病 tángniàobìng *n* diabetes

特别护理 tèbié hùlǐ intensive care

体重 tǐzhòng *n* weight

体重减轻 tǐzhòng jiǎnqīng weight loss

替代医学 tìdài yīxué alternative medicine

同意治疗 tóngyì zhìliáo consent to treatment

投保人 tóubǎorén *n* subscriber

退休 tuìxiū *n* retirement; *v* retire

外科医生 wàikē yīshēng surgeon

完全失明 wánquán shīmíng loss of entire sight

危及生命的 wēijí shēngmìng de *adj* life-threatening

维生预嘱 wéishēng yù zhǔ living will

卫生 wèishēng *n* health

胃癌 wèi'ái *n* gastric carcinoma, stomach cancer

无行为能力 wú xíngwéi nénglì incapacity

小儿疾病 xiǎo'ér jíbìng childhood disease

心理的 xīnlǐ de *adj* mental

心血管病 xīnxuèguǎnbìng cardiovascular disease

心脏病护理 xīnzàngbìng hùlǐ cardiac care

行为健康 xíngwéi jiànkāng behavioral health

幸存者 **xìngcúnzhě** *n* survivor

性传疾病 **xìng chuán jíbìng** sexually transmitted disease

牙科的 **yákē de** *adj* dental

牙医 **yáyī** *n* dentist

眼镜 **yǎnjìng** *n* eyeglasses

验光师 **yànguāngshī** *n* optometrist

阳痿 **yángwěi** *adj* impotent; *n* impotence

药品 **yàopǐn** *n* drug, medicine

医患关系 **yīhuàn guānxì** provider-patient relationship

医疗保健计划 **yīliáo bǎojiàn jìhuà** Medicare

医疗补助计划 **yīliáo bǔzhù jìhuà** Medicaid

医疗的 **yīliáo de** *adj* medical

医疗服务提供者 **yīliáo fúwù tígōngzhě** medical service
    provider

医疗事故 **yīliáo shìgù** medical accident

医生 **yīshēng** *n* doctor, physician

医学 **yīxué** *n* medicine

医学的 **yīxué de** *adj* medical

医学上必要的治疗 **yīxué shàng bìyào de zhìliáo**
    medically necessary treatment

医院 **yīyuàn** *n* hospital

遗嘱 **yízhǔ** *n* will

疫苗 **yìmiáo** *n* vaccine

意外死亡和伤残 **yìwài sǐwán hé shāngcán** accidental
    death and dismemberment

瘾 **yǐn** *n* addiction

隐形镜片 **yǐnxíng jìngpiàn** contact lenses

应享的 **yīngxiǎng de** *adj* entitled

永久残疾 **yǒngjiǔ cánjí** permanent disability

永久局部残疾 **yǒngjiǔ júbù cánjí** permanent partial
    disability

永久完全残疾 **yǒngjiǔ wánquán cánjí** permanent total
　　disability

有毒的 **yǒudú de** *adj* toxic

有管控的保健 **yǒu guǎnkòng de bǎojiàn** managed care

预防 **yùfáng** *n* prevention; *v* prevent

预防的 **yùfáng de** *adj* preventive

预防性筛查 **yùfángxìng shāichá** preventive screening

预防医学 **yùfáng yīxué** preventive medicine

预约 **yùyuē** *n* appointment; *v* make an appointment

暂时残疾 **zànshí cánjí** temporary disability

遭遇天灾与失踪给付 **zāoyù tiānzāi yǔ shīzōng jǐfù**
　　exposure and disappearance benefit

针灸 **zhēnjiǔ** *n* acupuncture

诊所 **zhěnsuǒ** *n* clinic

知情的同意 **zhīqíng de tóngyì** informed consent

职业健康 **zhíyè jiànkāng** occupational health

指定受益人 **zhǐdìng shòuyìrén** beneficiary designation

治疗 **zhìliáo** *n* treatment, therapy; *v* cure, treat

治愈 **zhìyù** *v* cure

致癌物 **zhì'áiwù** *n* carcinogen

智力迟钝 **zhìlì chídùn** mental retardation

智障 **zhìzhàng** *n* mental handicap

终止 **zhōngzhǐ** *v* terminate

终止和拒绝 **zhōngzhǐ hé jùjué** terminations and denials

住院 **zhùyuàn** *n* hospitalization; *v* hospitalize

住院病人 **zhùyuàn bìngrén** inpatient

住院前核准 **zhùyuàn qián hézhǔn** pre-admission
　　certification

住院前审核 **zhùyuàn qián shěnhé** pre-admission review

专门技能 **zhuānmén jìnéng** expertise

专业的 **zhuānyè de** *adj* professional

转诊 **zhuǎnzhěn** *n* referral
转诊电话 **zhuǎnzhěn diànhuà** referral line
转诊服务 **zhuǎnzhěn fúwù** referral service
自付限额 **zìfù xiàn'é** out-of-pocket maximum
最低标准 **zuìdī biāozhǔn** minimum standard

住房法词汇
Housing Law

住房法涉及不动产规则、公寓等居住单位的使用和维护规定、租赁契约、房东和房客的权利与义务、房屋抵押贷款等等。在美国, 住房法事务归州和地方政府管理。

安宁享受 ānníng xiǎngshòu quiet enjoyment
安宁享受专约 ānníng xiǎngshòu zhuānyuē covenant of quiet enjoyment
按揭 ànjiē *n* mortgage (又称房屋抵押贷款 *a.k.a.* fángwū dǐyā dàikuǎn)
按揭权人 ànjiēquánrén *n* mortgagee
按揭人 ànjiērén *n* mortgagor
白蚁检查 báiyǐ jiǎnchá termite inspection
搬出 bānchū *v* vacate
搬迁通知 bānqiān tōngzhī notice to quit
包裹按揭 bāoguǒ ànjiē wraparound mortgage
保险价值 bǎoxiǎn jiàzhí insured value
边界线 biānjièxiàn *n* metes and bounds
补贴住房 bǔtiē zhùfáng subsidized housing
不动产 bùdòngchǎn *n* real estate
不封口按揭 bùfēngkǒu ànjiē open-end mortgage
不适宜居住的 bùshìyí jūzhù de *adj* uninhabitable
财产 cáichǎn *n* property
财产权 cáichǎnquán *n* property right
财产权益 cáichǎn quányì property interest
财产税 cáichǎnshuì *n* property tax

Housing Law

餐厅 **cāntīng** *n* dining room

层 **céng** *n* story, level

产权 **chǎnquán** *n* title

产权保险 **chǎnquán bǎoxiǎn** title insurance

产权调查 **chǎnquán diàochá** title search

产权归属诉讼 **chǎnquán guīshǔ sùsòng** quiet title

产权租赁 **chǎnquán zūlìn** proprietary lease

偿清 **chángqīng** *n* redemption; *v* redeem, pay off

车库 **chēkù** *n* garage

撤销 **chèxiāo** *n* revocation; *v* revoke, cancel

成本法 **chéngběn fǎ** cost approach

承租人 **chéngzūrén** *n* lessee, tenant

持有期间 **chíyǒu qījiān** holding period

重新贷款 **chóngxīn dàikuǎn** refinancing

重新占有 **chóngxīn zhànyǒu** repossession

出租 **chūzū** *n/v* lease

出租人 **chūzūrén** *n* lessor

厨房 **chúfáng** *n* kitchen

储存室 **chǔcúnshì** *n* storage room

次级按揭 **cìjí ànjiē** subprime mortgage

贷款 **dàikuǎn** *n* loan, financing

贷款价值比 **dàikuǎn jiàzhí bǐ** loan-to-value ratio

担保契据 **dānbǎo qìjù** warranty deed

低收入者住房 **dīshōurùzhě zhùfáng** low-income housing

抵押贷款 **dǐyā dàikuǎn** *n* mortgage

地籍图 **dìjítú** *n* plat

地库 **dìkù** *n* basement

地块 **dìkuài** *n* lot

地下室 **dìxiàshì** *n* basement

地役权 **dìyìquán** *n* easement

点数 **diǎnshù** *n* points

氡检查 **dōng jiǎnchá** radon inspection

独家代理契约 dújiā dàilǐ qìyuē exclusive agency listing

独家销售权契约 dújiā xiāoshòuquán qìyuē exclusive
right-to-sell listing

多家庭住房 duō jiātíng zhùfáng multi-family housing

二房客 èrfángkè *n* sublessee, subtenant

二级按揭 èrjí ànjiē secondary mortgage

二级按揭市场 èrjí ànjiē shìchǎng secondary mortgage
market

二家庭住房 èr jiātíng zhùfáng two-family home

法拍 fǎpāi *n* foreclosure; *v* foreclose

法院契据 fǎyuàn qìjù judicial deed

法院下令逐客 fǎyuàn xiàlìng zhúkè court-ordered
eviction

反向占有 fǎnxiàng zhànyǒu adverse possession

房地产 fángdìchǎn *n* real estate

房地产经纪人 fángdìchǎn jīngjìrén real estate broker

房地产转让契据 fángdìchǎn zhuǎnràng qìjù bargain
and sale deed

房地进入权 fángdì jìnrùquán access to premises

房东 fángdōng *n* landlord

房客 fángkè *n* tenant

房屋 fángwū *n* house

房屋抵押贷款 fángwū dǐyā dàikuǎn *n* mortgage
(又称按揭 *a.k.a.* ànjiē)

房屋法院 fángwū fǎyuàn housing court

房屋净值贷款 fángwū jìngzhí dàikuǎn home equity loan

房屋净值信贷额度 fángwū jìngzhí xìndài édù home
equity line of credit

房屋销售合同 fángwū xiāoshòu hétong listing contract

放弃权利证书 fàngqì quánlì zhèngshū quitclaim deed

非法占用者 fēifǎ zhànyòngzhě squatter

非自愿留置权 fēizìyuàn liúzhìquán involuntary lien

废物 fèiwù *n* waste

分割 fēngē *n/v* partition

分权共有 fènquán gòngyǒu tenancy in common

分租 fēnzū *v* sublease, sublet

浮动租金租约 fúdòng zūjīn zūyuē graduated lease

附加条款 fùjiā tiáokuǎn rider

附件 fùjiàn *n* rider

附属单元 fùshǔ dānyuán accessory apartment

附属的 fùshǔ de *adj* accessory

附属用途 fùshǔ yòngtú accessory uses

复归 fùguī *n* reversion

复归权益 fùguī quányì reversionary interest

改正契据 gǎizhèng qìjù deed of correction

隔间 géjiān *n* partition

公开销售契约 gōngkāi xiāoshòu qìyuē open-listing agreement

公开展示 gōngkāi zhǎnshì open house

公平住房 gōngpíng zhùfáng fair housing

公用区 gōngyòngqū common elements

公用事业 gōngyòng shìyè utilities

公寓 gōngyù *n* apartment

公寓楼 gōngyù lóu apartment building

供暖 gōngnuǎn *n* heating

共用墙 gòngyòng qiáng party wall

共有公寓 gòngyǒu gōngyù condominium, condo

估价 gūjià *n* appraisal, valuation

估价员 gūjiàyuán *n* appraiser, assessor

固定附着物 gùdìng fùzhuówù fixture

过户会 guòhùhuì *n* closing

海滨产权 hǎibīn chǎnquán littoral rights

海滨住宅 hǎibīn zhùzhái beach home, beach house

豪华住宅 háohuá zhùzhái luxury home

河岸权 hé'ànquán riparian rights

合作公寓 hézuò gōngyù co-operative, co-op

会员经纪人 huìyuán jīngjìrén realtor

活动房 huódòng fáng mobile home

活跃成人社区 huóyuè chéngrén shèqū active adult community

基本租金 jīběn zūjīn base rent

积极专约 jījí zhuānyuē positive covenant

计税估价 jìshuì gūjià assessed value

寄宿舍 jìsùshè rooming house

技工留置权 jìgōng liúzhìquán mechanic's lien

加速条款 jiāsù tiáokuǎn acceleration clause

家庭厅 jiātíng tīng *n* family room

检查 jiǎnchá *n* inspection; *v* inspect

建材供应商留置权 jiàncái gōngyìngshāng liúzhìquán materialman's lien

建筑商 jiànzhùshāng *n* builder

建筑物 jiànzhùwù *n* building

经纪人 jīngjìrén *n* broker

净值 jìngzhí *n* equity

交割会 jiāogēhuì *n* closing

居民 jūmín *n* resident

居民的 jūmín de *adj* residential

居所 jūsuǒ *n* residence

居住 jūzhù *n* occupancy

居住的 jūzhù de *adj* residential

拒绝发放按揭 jùjué fāfàng ànjiē redlining; redline

开发商 kāifāshāng *n* developer

康斗 kāngdǒu *n* condo, condominium

可调利率按揭 kětiáo lìlǜ ànjiē adjustable rate mortgage (ARM)

客厅 kètīng *n* living room, front room

联邦住房抵押贷款公司 liánbāng zhùfáng dǐyā dàikuǎn gōngsī Federal Home Loan Mortgage Corporation (*Freddie Mac*)

联邦住房管理局 liánbāng zhùfáng guǎnlǐ jú Federal Housing Administration (FHA)

联邦住房和城市发展部 liánbāng zhùfáng hé chéngshì fāzhǎn bù Department of Housing and Urban Development (HUD)

联名房产权 liánmíng fángchǎnquán joint tenancy

联权共有 liánquán gòngyǒu joint tenancy

留置权 liúzhìquán *n* lien

楼房 lóufáng *n* building

买低 mǎidī *n* buydown

模块房 mókuài fáng modular home

磨损 mósǔn *n* wear and tear

农村住房服务局 nóngcūn zhùfáng fúwù jú Rural Housing Service (RHS)

平房 píngfáng *n* bungalow

气球式按揭 qìqiúshì ànjiē balloon mortgage

弃产 qì chǎn abandonment of premises

弃权契据 qìquán qìjù quitclaim deed

弃屋 qì wū abandonment of premises

契据 qìjù *n* deed

墙 qiáng *n* wall

区划 qūhuà *n* zoning

驱逐房客 qūzhú fángkè *n* tenant eviction; *v* evict a tenant

取消赎回权 qǔxiāo shúhuíquán *n* foreclosure; *v* foreclose

全权契据 quánquán qìjù general warranty deed

认可 rènkě *n* ratification; *v* ratify

擅自进入 shànzì jìnrù *n/v* trespass

商用不动产 shāngyòng bùdòngchǎn commercial property

商用租赁 shāngyòng zūlìn commercial lease

上市房地产 shàngshì fángdìchǎn listed property

生存者取得权 shēngcúnzhě qǔdé quán right of survivorship

时效占有 shíxiào zhànyǒu adverse possession

市场价值 shìchǎng jiàzhí market value

适于居住 shìyú jūzhù habitable

收回 shōuhuí *n* repossession

受让人 shòuràngrén *n* grantee

售方按揭 shòufāng ànjiē purchase money mortgage

赎回 shúhuí *n* redemption; *v* redeem

税契 shuìqì *n* tax deed

税收留置权 shuìshōu liúzhìquán tax lien

随意租约 suíyì zūyuē estate at will

所有人 suǒyǒurén *n* owner

特别担保契据 tèbié dānbǎo qìjù special warranty deed

特别用途许可证 tèbié yòngtú xǔkězhèng special use permit

提前清偿条款 tíqián qīngcháng tiáokuǎn prepayment clause

土地租约 tǔdì zūyuē ground lease

推定逐客 tuīdìng zhúkè constructive eviction

退休房 tuìxiū fáng retirement home

退休社区 tuìxiū shèqū retirement community

完全担保契据 wánquán dānbǎo qìjù full covenant and warranty deed

完全共有 wánquán gòngyǒu tenancy by the entirety

维护 wéihù *n* maintenance; *v* maintain

卫生间 wèishēngjiān *n* bathroom

文书 wénshū *n* deed

卧室 wòshì *n* bedroom

屋主自售 **wūzhǔ zìshòu** sale by owner

无负担专约 **wú fùdān zhuānyuē** covenant against
　　encumbrances

无条件产权 **wútiáojiàn chǎnquán** fee simple absolute

物业 **wùyè** *n* real estate, property

洗衣室 **xǐyīshì** *n* laundry room

先购权 **xiāngòuquán** right of first refusal

限期租约 **xiànqī zūyuē** estate for years

限制性专约 **xiànzhìxìng zhuānyuē** restrictive covenant

消极专约 **xiāojí zhuānyuē** negative covenant

销售代理 **xiāoshòu dàilǐ** sales agent

信托契据 **xìntuō qìjù** deed of trust

许可证 **xǔkězhèng** *n* permit

续签选择 **xùqiān xuǎnzé** option to renew

学区 **xuéqū** *n* school district

押金 **yājīn** *n* security deposit

业主 **yèzhǔ** *n* owner

一级按揭 **yījí ànjiē** primary mortgage

一家庭住房 **yī jiātíng zhùfáng** single-family home

一室公寓房 **yīshì gōngyù fáng** studio apartment

遗产管理人契据 **yíchǎn guǎnlǐrén qìjù** administrator's
　　deed

遗产执行人契据 **yíchǎn zhíxíngrén qìjù** executor's deed

遗弃 **yíqì** *n* abandonment; *v* abandon

佣金 **yòngjīn** *n* commission

有条件产权 **yǒutiáojiàn chǎnquán** fee simple defeasible

逾期房客 **yúqī fángkè** holdover tenant

预制房 **yùzhì fáng** manufactured home

赠与契据 **zèngyǔ qìjù** deed of gift

栅栏 **zhàlan** *n* fence

占有 **zhànyǒu** *n* possession

执法官契据 zhífǎguān qìjù sheriff's deed
直接费用 zhíjiē fèiyòng direct costs
制造街区恐慌 zhìzào jiēqū kǒnghuāng blockbusting
终身地产权 zhōngshēn dìchǎnquán life estate
主要居所 zhǔyào jūsuǒ principal residence
主要用途 zhǔyào yòngtú principal uses
住房 zhùfáng *n* housing, house, home, shelter
住房工程 zhùfáng gōngchéng housing project
住宅市场 zhùzhái shìchǎng residential market
住宅市场分析 zhùzhái shìchǎng fēnxī residential
　　market analysis
住宅用不动产 zhùzhái yòng bùdòngchǎn residential
　　property
专约 zhuānyuē *n* covenant
转让 zhuǎnràng *n* conveyance; *v* convey, grant
转让契据 zhuǎnràng qìjù cession deed
转让人 zhuǎnràngrén *n* grantor
转租 zhuǎnzū *v* sublease, sublet
转租承租人 zhuǎnzū chéngzūrén sublessee, subtenant
转租房客 zhuǎnzū fángkè sublessee, subtenant
自主持有地产权 zìzhǔ chíyǒu dìchǎnquán free-hold
　　estate
租得 zūdé *v* lease
租金 zūjīn *n* rent
租金管制 zūjīn guǎnzhì rent regulation
租金控制 zūjīn kòngzhì rent control
租金稳定 zūjīn wěndìng rent stabilization
租赁 zūlìn *v* lease
租赁持有地产权 zūlìn chíyǒu dìchǎnquán lease-hold
　　estate
租赁条件 zūlìn tiáojiàn lease term

租约 **zūyuē** *n* lease agreement
租约期满 **zūyuē qīmǎn** expiration of lease term, lease
　　expiration
租约转让 **zūyuē zhuǎnràng** assignment of lease
组合地块 **zǔhé dìkuài** plottage

移民法词汇
Immigration Law

外国人入境美国, 探亲, 经商, 留学, 申请永久居留, 归化入籍, 这些都属移民法的范围。移民法事务现由国土安全部管辖。

A-1 签证 a-yī qiānzhèng A-1 Visa (外交签证 / *for diplomats*)

A-2 签证 a-èr qiānzhèng A-2 Visa (公务签证 / *for official business*)

A-3 签证 a-sān qiānzhèng A-3 Visa (*A-1、A-2 签证持有者的私人随行人员签证 / for attendants, servants, and personal employees of A-1 and A-2 visa holders*)

B-1 签证 b-yī qiānzhèng B-1 Visa (商务签证 / *for business-related activities*)

B-2 签证 b-èr qiānzhèng B-2 Visa (旅游签证 / *for tourists*)

F-1 签证 f-yī qiānzhèng F-1 Visa (学生签证 / *for foreign students*)

K-1 签证 k-yī qiānzhèng K-1 Visa (未婚夫、未婚妻签证 / *nonimmigrant visa for fiancé(e) to travel to the United States for marriage*)

M-1 签证 m-yī qiānzhèng M-1 Visa (职业培训签证 / *for vocational students*)

安全第三国 ānquán dì-sān guó safe third country

澳门特别行政区 àomén tèbié xíngzhèngqū Macao Special Administrative Region, Macao SAR

办事处 **bànshìchù** *n* suboffice (移民支局下设机构 / *of a district office, USCIS*)

保持身份和离境担保金 **bǎochí shēnfèn hé líjìng dānbǎojīn** maintenance of status and departure bond

被动庇护程序 **bèidòng bìhù chéngxù** defensive asylum process

被殴儿童 **bèi ōu értóng** battered child

被殴配偶 **bèi ōu pèi'ǒu** battered spouse

被殴配偶豁免 **bèi ōu pèi'ǒu huòmiǎn** battered spouse waiver

庇护 **bìhù** *n* asylum

庇护官 **bìhùguān** *n* asylum officer

庇护申请 **bìhù shēnqǐng** asylee application

庇护所 **bìhùsuǒ** *n* safe haven

边境巡逻 **biānjìng xúnluó** border patrol

边境巡逻区 **biānjìng xúnluóqū** Border Patrol Sector

补充庇护申请 **bǔchōng bìhù shēnqǐng** supplemental asylum application

不出庭 **bùchūtíng** failure to appear

不合格 **bùhégé** *adj* ineligible

不离境 **bùlíjìng** failure to depart

不披露 **bùpīlù** nondisclosure

不投案 **bùtóu'àn** failure to surrender

材料合格的 **cáiliào hégé de** documentarily qualified

撤销 **chèxiāo** *n* withdrawal, rescission; *v* withdraw, cancel, rescind

撤销驱逐出境 **chèxiāo qūzhú chūjìng** cancellation of removal

撤销身份的程序 **chèxiāo shēnfèn de chéngxù** rescission process

撤销身份的意向 chèxiāo shēnfèn de yìxiàng intention
　　to rescind

重新安置 chóngxīn ānzhì resettlement

重新设定担保金额听证会 chóngxīn shèdìng dānbǎojīn'é
　　tīngzhènghuì custody redetermination hearing

抽签 chōuqiān *n* lottery

初看合格 chūkàn hégé prima facie eligibility

出生国 chūshēng guó country of birth

出庭通知 chūtíng tōngzhī notice to appear (NTA)

从属关系 cóngshǔ guānxì affiliation

打指印 dǎ zhǐyìn *v* fingerprint

大使馆 dàshǐguǎn *n* embassy

担保人 dānbǎorén *n* sponsor

当前身份 dāngqián shēnfèn current status

道德堕落 dàodé duòluò moral turpitude

登记日期 dēngjì rìqī registry date

递解出境 dìjiè chūjìng *n* deportation; *v* deport

递解出境听证会 dìjiè chūjìng tīngzhènghuì deportation
　　hearing

地方办事处 dìfāng bànshìchù field office (移民支局下
　　设机构 / *of a district office, USCIS*)

第一 (第二、第三、第四、第五) 优先 dì-yī (dì-èr,
　　dì-sān, dì-sì, dì-wǔ) yōuxiān first (second, third,
　　fourth, fifth) preference

定居的 dìngjū de *adj* domiciled

对迫害的真切恐惧 duì pòhài de zhēnqiè kǒngjù
　　genuine fear of persecution

对社区的威胁 duì shèqū de wēixié danger to the
　　community

多元化国家 duōyuánhuà guójiā diversity country

多元化签证抽签 duōyuánhuà qiānzhèng chōuqiān
　　Diversity Visa Lottery

Immigration Law

多元化移民 **duōyuánhuà yímín** diversity immigrant (DV)

多元化移民签证计划 **duōyuánhuà yímín qiānzhèng jìhuà** Diversity Immigrant Visa Program

反恐和有效死刑法 **fǎnkǒng hé yǒuxiào sǐxíng fǎ** Antiterrorism and Effective Death Penalty Act (AEDPA)

犯罪的外国人 **fànzuì de wàiguórén** criminal alien

防止 **fángzhǐ** *n* preclusion, prevention; *v* preclude, prevent

非法逗留 **fēifǎ dòuliú** unlawful stay

非法居留 **fēifǎ jūliú** unlawfully present

非法移民 **fēifǎ yímín** illegal immigrant, undocumented alien

非法移民改革和移民责任法 **fēifǎ yímín gǎigé hé yímín zérèn fǎ** Illegal Immigration Reform and Immigrant Responsibility Act

非居民外国人 **fēi jūmín wàiguórén** nonresident alien

非全日学生 **fēi quánrì xuéshēng** part-time student

非学位学生 **fēi xuéwèi xuéshēng** nonacademic student

非移民 **fēi yímín** *adj* nonimmigrant

非移民签证 **fēi yímín qiānzhèng** nonimmigrant visa

费用 **fèiyòng** *n* fee

分局 **fēnjú** *n* regional office (移民局所属机构 / *of USCIS*)

服务中心 **fúwù zhōngxīn** service center (移民局所属机构 / *of USCIS*)

复核申请 **fùhé shēnqǐng** petition for review

负面因素 **fùmiàn yīnsù** negative factor

改变身份 **gǎibiàn shēnfèn** change of status

告知权利 **gàozhī quánlì** advisal of rights

个案编号 **gè'àn biānhào** case number

个人简历 **gèrén jiǎnlì** biographical (biographic) information

各国签证限额 **gèguó qiānzhèng xiàn'é** per-country limit

工卡 **gōngkǎ** *n* employment authorization

工作 **gōngzuò** *n* work, employment

工作许可 **gōngzuò xǔkě** employment authorization

公共负担 **gōnggòng fùdān** public charge

公民 **gōngmín** *n* citizen

公民身份 **gōngmín shēnfèn** citizenship

公民证书 **gōngmín zhèngshū** certificate of citizenship

公民资格 **gōngmín zīgé** citizenship

共同担保人 **gòngtóng dānbǎorén** joint sponsor

共同申请人 **gòngtóng shēnqǐngrén** co-applicant

孤身未成年人 **gūshēn wèichéngniánrén** unaccompanied minor

规定离境 **guīdìng líjìng** required departure

归化 **guīhuà** *n* naturalization; *v* naturalize

归化法院 **guīhuà fǎyuàn** naturalization court

归化公民 **guīhuà gōngmín** naturalized citizen

归化申请 **guīhuà shēnqǐng** naturalization application

归化文件 **guīhuà wénjiàn** naturalization papers

归化仪式 **guīhuà yíshì** naturalization ceremony

归化证书 **guīhuà zhèngshū** certificate of naturalization

国籍 **guójí** *n* nationality

国家利益 **guójiā lìyì** national interest

国家利益豁免 **guójiā lìyì huòmiǎn** national interest waiver (NIV)

国务院的批复 **guówùyuàn de pīfù** State Department response

过渡期扣押规则 **guòdùqī kòuyā guīzé** Transition Period Custody Rules

过境外国人 **guòjìng wàiguórén** transit alien

过期 **guòqī** *n* expiration; *v* expire

过期日 **guòqīrì** expiration date

海员 **hǎiyuán** *n* crewman

合法化的 **héfǎhuà de** *adj* legitimated

合法入境 **héfǎ rùjìng** lawfully admitted

合法移民家庭公平法 **héfǎ yímín jiātíng gōngpíng fǎ**
   Legal Immigration Family Equity Act

合法永久居民 **héfǎ yǒngjiǔ jūmín** lawful permanent
   resident (LPR)

合格 **hégé** *adj* eligible; *n* eligibility

合乎规定的家庭关系 **héhū guīdìng de jiātíng guānxì**
   qualifying family relationship

核准难民入境人数 **hézhǔn nànmín rùjìng rénshù**
   refugee authorized admissions

很高的可能性 **hěn gāo de kěnéngxìng** significant
   possibility

后果 **hòuguǒ** *n* consequence

护照 **hùzhào** *n* passport

华侨 **huáqiáo** *n* overseas Chinese

华人 **huárén** *n* Chinese, foreign citizens of Chinese origin

华裔美国人 **huáyì měiguórén** Chinese American

回美的居民外国人 **huíměi de jūmín wàiguórén**
   returning resident alien

回美证 **huíměizhèng** *n* advance parole

婚姻欺诈 **hūnyīn qīzhà** marriage fraud

婚姻状况 **hūnyīn zhuàngkuàng** marital status

机器可读护照 **jīqì kědú hùzhào** machine-readable
   passport (MRP)

机器可读签证 **jīqì kědú qiānzhèng** machine-readable
   visa (MRV)

机组人员 **jīzǔ rényuán** *n* crewman

极端残酷 **jíduān cánkù** extreme cruelty

极端困难 **jíduān kùnnan** extreme hardship

记入 **jìrù** *v* charge

记入国 jìrù guó country of chargeability

加速驱逐程序 jiāsù qūzhú chéngxù expedited removal
proceeding

家属 jiāshǔ *n* dependents

家庭第一 (第二、第三、第四) 优先 jiātíng dì-yī
(dì-èr, dì-sān, dì-sì) yōuxiān family-sponsored first
(second, third, fourth) preference

家庭收入 jiātíng shōurù household income

家庭团聚计划 jiātíng tuánjù jìhuà Family Unity
Program

假结婚 jiǎ jiéhūn false marriage

监督离境 jiāndū líjìng departure under safeguards

检查记录 jiǎnchá jìlù records check

见证 jiànzhèng *n* attestation

健康豁免 jiànkāng huòmiǎn medical waiver

交换学者 jiāohuàn xuézhě exchange visitor, exchange
alien

教育水平 jiàoyù shuǐpíng level of education

杰出教授 jiéchū jiàoshòu Outstanding Professor
(EB-1(b))

杰出人才 jiéchū réncái alien of extraordinary ability
(EB-1(a))

杰出研究员 jiéchū yánjiūyuán Outstanding Researcher
(EB-1(b))

结婚证书 jiéhūn zhèngshū marriage certificate

截止日期 jiézhǐ rìqī cut-off date

禁止庇护 jìnzhǐ bìhù bar to asylum

禁止入境 jìnzhǐ rùjìng *n* exclusion, inadmissibility

禁止入境的外国人 jìnzhǐ rùjìng de wàiguórén
excludable alien, inadmissible alien

禁止再入境 jìnzhǐ zài rùjìng bar to readmission

经济担保书 **jīngjì dānbǎoshū** Affidavit of Support
(*I-864 表 / Form I-864*)

就业 **jiùyè** *n* employment, work

居民外国人 **jūmín wàiguórén** resident alien

可记入 **kě jìrù** *adj* chargeable

恐怖主义活动 **kǒngbùzhǔyì huódòng** terrorist activity

跨国公司调派人员 **kuàguógōngsī diàopài rényuán**
     intracompany transferee

跨国公司经理 **kuàguógōngsī jīnglǐ** Managers and
     Executive Transferees (EB-1(c))

跨界往来者 **kuàjiè wǎnglái zhě** border crosser

劳工部 **láogōngbù** Department of Labor (DOL)

劳工情况申请表 **láogōng qíngkuàng shēnqǐngbiǎo**
     Labor Condition Application (LCA)

劳工证 **láogōngzhèng** labor certification (又称劳工纸
     a.k.a. **láogōng zhǐ**)

离境移民 **líjìng yímín** *n* emigrant

例外情况 **lìwài qíngkuàng** exceptional circumstances

连续居住 **liánxù jūzhù** continuous residence

连续实际住在 **liánxù shíjì zhùzài** continuous physical
     presence

联邦贫穷线指导方针 **liánbāng pínqióngxiàn zhǐdǎo
     fāngzhēn** Federal Poverty Guidelines

两年规则 **liǎngnián guīzé** two-year rule

临时保护身份 **línshí bǎohù shēnfèn** Temporary
     Protection Status (TPS)

临时工人 **línshí gōngrén** temporary worker

临时居民 **línshí jūmín** temporary resident

领事 **lǐngshì** *n* consul

领事官 **lǐngshìguān** *n* consular officer

领事馆 **lǐngshìguǎn** *n* consulate

流动农工 liúdòng nónggōng migrant farm (agricultural) worker

留学 liúxué *v* study abroad

留学生 liúxuéshēng *n* student studying abroad, foreign student

轮到 lúndào *adj* current (又称有名额 *a.k.a.* yǒu míng'é)

绿卡 lǜkǎ green card

美国公民与移民服务局 měiguó gōngmín yǔ yímín fúwù jú U.S. Citizenship and Immigration Services (USCIS) (简称移民局 *a.k.a.* yímínjú, *formerly known as the Immigration and Naturalization Service [INS]*)

美籍华人 měijí huárén Chinese American

面试 miànshì *n/v* interview

面谈需携带资料 miàntán xū xiédài zīliào appointment package

难民 nànmín *n* refugee

难民批准人数 nànmín pīzhǔn rénshù refugee approvals

难民入境人数 nànmín rùjìng rénshù refugee arrivals

难民身份 nànmín shēnfèn refugee status

年度限额 niándù xiàn'é annual limit

农工 nónggōng *n* agricultural worker

排期表 páiqī biǎo Visa Bulletin (又称签证公报 *a.k.a.* qiānzhèng gōngbào)

派生公民身份 pàishēng gōngmín shēnfèn derivative citizenship

派生身份 pàishēng shēnfèn derivative status

派生受益人 pàishēng shòuyìrén derivative beneficiary

陪伴签证 péibàn qiānzhèng accompanying visa

配额 pèi'é *n* quota

批准通知 pīzhǔn tōngzhī approval notice

平信徒杂役 píngxìntú záyì lay worker

签证 **qiānzhèng** *n* visa

签证公报 **qiānzhèng gōngbào** Visa Bulletin
(又称移民排期表 *a.k.a.* yímín páiqī biǎo)

签证豁免计划 **qiānzhèng huòmiǎn jìhuà** Visa Waiver
Program (VWP)

签证延期 **qiānzhèng yánqī** visa extension

强制羁押 **qiángzhì jīyā** mandatory detention

遣返 **qiǎnfǎn** *n* repatriation; *v* repatriate

清楚、可信、无疑的证据 **qīngchǔ kěxìn wúyí de
zhèngjù** clear, convincing, and unequivocal evidence

清楚无疑 **qīngchǔ wúyí** clearly and beyond a doubt

情事变更 **qíngshì biàngēng** changed circumstances

驱逐程序 **qūzhú chéngxù** removal process, removal
proceeding

驱逐出境 **qūzhú chūjìng** *n* removal, expulsion

驱逐出境听证会 **qūzhú chūjìng tīngzhènghuì** removal
hearing

驱逐令下达后扣押审查 **qūzhúlìng xiàdá hòu kòuyā
shěnchá** post order custody review (POCR)

取得合法居留身份的外国人 **qǔdé héfǎ jūliú shēnfèn
de wàiguórén** legalized alien

全国服务中心 **quánguó fúwù zhōngxīn** National Benefit
Center (NBC) (移民局所属机构 / *of USCIS*)

全国自动化移民审查系统 **quánguó zìdònghuà yímín
shěnchá xìtǒng** Automated Nationwide System for
Immigration Review (ANSIR)

全日学生 **quánrì xuéshēng** full-time student

权宜入境许可 **quányí rùjìng xǔkě** parole

权宜入境者 **quányí rùjìng zhě** parolee

权宜入境的外国人 **quányí rùjìng de wàiguórén**
paroled aliens

权宜许可入境美国 **quányí xǔkě rùjìng měiguó** parole
  someone into the U.S.
确定难民资格 **quèdìng nànmín zīgé** establish eligibility
  as a refugee
确认 **quèrèn** *n* affirmation
人口走私 **rénkǒu zǒusī** people smuggling
人蛇 **rénshé** *n* stowaway (*lit.* human snake)
入籍 **rùjí** *n* naturalization; *v* naturalize
入籍宣誓 **rùjí xuānshì** swear in citizens
入境 **rùjìng** *n* admission, entry
入境-出境卡 **rùjìng-chūjìng kǎ** Arrival-Departure Card
  (*I-94 表 / Form I-94*)
入境口岸 **rùjìng kǒu'àn** port of entry
入境类别 **rùjìng lèibié** arrival category
入境日期 **rùjìng rìqī** arrival date
入境申请人 **rùjìng shēnqǐngrén** applicant for admission
入境外国人 **rùjìng wàiguórén** arriving alien
入境移民 **rùjìng yímín** *n* immigrant, immigration
丧失合法身份 **sàngshī héfǎ shēnfèn** out of status
商务非移民 **shāngwù fēi yímín** business non-immigrant
上一个住所 **shàng yīgè zhùsuǒ** last residence
蛇头 **shétóu** *n* leader of a human smuggling ring (*lit.*
  snakehead)
社区 **shèqū** *n* community
申请 **shēnqǐng** *n* application, petition; *v* apply, petition
申请撤销驱逐出境 **shēnqǐng chèxiāo qūzhú chūjìng**
  application for cancellation of removal
申请费 **shēnqǐngfèi** *n* filing fee
申请书 **shēnqǐngshū** *n* application, petition
申请调整身份 **shēnqǐng tiáozhěng shēnfèn** application
  for adjustment of status

申请签证 **shēnqǐng qiānzhèng** apply for a visa, make a request for a visa

申请人 **shēnqǐngrén** *n* applicant, petitioner

申请入境 **shēnqǐng rùjìng** application for admission

申请协助中心 **shēnqǐng xiézhù zhōngxīn** application support center (ASC)

身份 **shēnfèn** *n* status

身份不符通知 **shēnfèn bùfú tōngzhī** no-match letter

身份审查 **shēnfèn shěnchá** status review

身份有效期 **shēnfèn yǒuxiàoqī** duration of status

身份证 **shēnfènzhèng** *n* identification card

事先检查 **shìxiān jiǎnchá** pre-inspection

受庇护者 **shòu bìhù zhě** asylee

受庇护者身份 **shòu bìhù zhě shēnfèn** asylee status

受到殴打的 **shòudào ōudǎ de** *adj* battered

受虐外国人 **shòu nuè wàiguórén** abused alien

受虐移民配偶 **shòu nuè yímín pèi'ǒu** abused immigrant spouse

数量限制 **shùliàng xiànzhì** numerical limit

诉讼程序结束后自动离境 **sùsòng chéngxù jiéshù hòu zìdòng líjìng** voluntary departure at the conclusion of proceedings

诉讼程序结束前自动离境 **sùsòng chéngxù jiéshù qián zìdòng líjìng** voluntary departure prior to completion of proceedings

速办听证会 **sùbàn tīngzhènghuì** expedited hearing

随后团聚 **suíhòu tuánjù** following to join

琐屑性申请 **suǒxièxìng shēnqǐng** frivolous application

探亲 **tànqīn** *v* visit relatives

特别归化规定 **tèbié guīhuà guīdìng** special naturalization provisions

特别农工 **tèbié nónggōng** special agricultural worker (SAW)

特别严重的罪行 **tèbié yánzhòng de zuìxíng** particularly serious crime

特别移民 **tèbié yímín** special immigrant

特殊专业 **tèshū zhuānyè** specialty occupation

替代记入 **tìdài jìrù** alternate chargeability

替代驱逐出境令 **tìdài qūzhú chūjìng lìng** alternate order of removal

条约国商人 **tiáoyuē guó shāngrén** treaty trader

条约国投资人 **tiáoyuē guó tóuzīrén** treaty investor

调整 **tiáozhěng** *n* adjustment; *v* adjust

调整身份 **tiáozhěng shēnfèn** adjustment of status

听证记录 **tīngzhèng jìlù** record of proceeding (ROP)

通信地址总录 **tōngxìn dìzhǐ zǒnglù** central address file

偷渡 **tōudù** *n* stowaway, illegal entry

偷渡集团 **tōudù jítuán** people-smuggling syndicate

偷渡者 **tōudùzhě** *n* stowaway

外国人 **wàiguórén** *n* alien

外国人登记号码 **wàiguórén dēngjì hàomǎ** alien registration number

外国人登记收据卡 **wàiguórén dēngjì shōujù kǎ** alien registration receipt card

外国人劳工证 **wàiguórén láogōngzhèng** alien labor certification

未婚子女 **wèihūn zǐnǚ** unmarried sons and daughters

未轮到 **wèi lúndào** *adj* noncurrent (又称无名额 *a.k.a.* **wú míng'é**)

无国籍的 **wú guójí de** *adj* stateless

无害注销 **wúhài zhùxiāo** cancelled without prejudice

无家的 **wújiā de** *adj* homeless

无名额 **wú míng'é** *adj* noncurrent

无签证过境 **wú qiānzhèng guòjìng** Transit Without Visa (TWOV)

无证外国人 **wú zhèng wàiguórén** undocumented aliens

无资格的 **wú zīgé de** *adj* ineligible

香港特别行政区 **xiānggǎng tèbié xíngzhèngqū** Hong Kong Special Administrative Region, Hong Kong SAR

偕行亲属 **xiéxíng qīnshǔ** accompanying relative

行政上诉办公室 **xíngzhèng shàngsù bàngōngshì** Administrative Appeals Office (AAO)

性别迫害 **xìngbié pòhài** gender-related persecution

宣誓 **xuānshì** *v* swear, take an oath

宣誓仪式 **xuānshì yíshì** swearing-in ceremony, swearing-in session

学生 **xuéshēng** *n* student

寻求庇护者 **xúnqiú bìhù zhě** asylum seeker

亚裔美国人 **yàyì měiguórén** Asian American

延后决定 **yánhòu juédìng** reserved decision

延期停留 **yánqī tíngliú** extension of stay

一年规则 **yīnián guīzé** one-year rule

依血统取得的公民身份 **yī xuètǒng qǔdé de gōngmín shēnfèn** acquired citizenship

移交移民法官的通知 **yíjiāo yímín fǎguān de tōngzhī** notice of referral to immigration judge

移民 **yímín** *n* immigrant, immigration

移民法官 **yímín fǎguān** immigration judge

移民官 **yímínguān** immigration officer

移民记录 **yímín jìlù** immigration record

移民局 **yímínjú** USCIS (全称美国公民与移民服务局, 其前身是移民与归化局 / *United States Citizenship and Immigration Services, formerly known as the Immigration and Naturalization Service [INS]*)

移民扣留令 **yímín kòuliú lìng** immigration hold

移民律师 **yímín lùshī** immigration lawyer, immigration attorney

移民签证 **yímín qiānzhèng** immigrant visa

移民上诉委员会 **yímín shàngsù wěiyuánhuì** Board of Immigration Appeals (BIS)

移民申请 **yímín shēnqǐng** immigrant petition

移民诉讼局 **yímín sùsòng jú** Office of Immigration Litigation (OIL)

移民与国籍法 **yímín yǔ guójí fǎ** Immigration and Nationality Act (INA)

移民与海关执行局 **yímín yǔ hǎiguān zhíxíng jú** Immigration and Customs Enforcement (ICE)

已婚子女 **yǐhūn zǐnǚ** married sons and daughters

已永久安置 (难民) **yǐ yǒngjiǔ ānzhì** firmly resettled (*refugees*)

因刑事犯罪驱逐出境 **yīn xíngshì fànzuì qūzhú chūjìng** criminal removal

应递解出境的外国人 **yīng dìjiè chūjìng de wàiguórén** deportable alien

应驱逐出境的外国人 **yīng qūzhú chūjìng de wàiguórén** removable alien

应予入境的 **yīng yǔ rùjìng de** entitled to be admitted

英语水平 **yīngyǔ shuǐpíng** English proficiency

永久居民 **yǒngjiǔ jūmín** permanent resident

永久居民卡 **yǒngjiǔ jūmín kǎ** permanent resident card (PRC) (俗称绿卡 *a.k.a.* **lǜkǎ**)

优先 **yōuxiān** *n* preference, priority

优先类别 **yōuxiān lèibié** preference category

优先日期 **yōuxiān rìqī** priority date

优先移民 **yōuxiān yímín** preference immigrant

优先制度 **yōuxiān zhìdù** preference system

Immigration Law

有名额 **yǒu míng'é** current

有条件居留签证 **yǒutiáojiàn jūliú qiānzhèng** conditional residence visa

有条件居民 **yǒutiáojiàn jūmín** conditional resident

有条件准予 **yǒutiáojiàn zhǔnyǔ** conditional grant

有效的 **yǒuxiào de** *adj* valid

逾期逗留 **yúqī dòuliú** *v* overstay

预先入境许可 **yùxiān rùjìng xǔkě** advance parole

再入境许可 **zài rùjìng xǔkě** re-entry permission

暂缓递解出境 **zànhuǎn dìjiè chūjìng** withholding of deportation

暂缓驱逐出境 **zànhuǎn qūzhú chūjìng** withholding of removal

暂缓执行的判决 **zànhuǎn zhíxíng de pànjué** deferred sentence

展期申请 **zhǎnqī shēnqǐng** renewal application

证明文件 **zhèngmíng wénjiàn** supporting document

政治庇护 **zhèngzhì bìhù** political asylum

政治庇护申请人 **zhèngzhì bìhù shēnqǐngrén** applicant for political asylum

支持性文件 **zhīchíxìng wénjiàn** supporting document

支局 **zhījú** district office (移民局下设机构 / *of USCIS*)

直系家庭 **zhíxì jiātíng** immediate family

直系亲属 **zhíxì qīnshǔ** immediate relative

职业 **zhíyè** *n* occupation

职业第一 (第二、第三、第四、第五) 优先 **zhíyè dì-yī (dì-èr, dì-sān, dì-sì, dì-wǔ) yōuxiān** employment-based first (second, third, fourth, fifth) preference

职业培训学生 **zhíyè péixùn xuéshēng** vocational student (*M-1 Visa*)

只关庇护听证会 **zhǐ guān bìhù tīngzhènghuì** asylum-only hearing

指定移民医生 zhǐdìng yímín yīshēng panel physician
指南材料袋 zhǐnán cáiliào dài instruction package
指印 zhǐyìn *n* fingerprint, fingerprinting
中国大陆 zhōngguó dàlù China's mainland
终止动议 zhōngzhǐ dòngyì motion for termination
主动庇护程序 zhǔdòng bìhù chéngxù affirmative
　　asylum process
主要受益人 zhǔyào shòuyìrén primary beneficiary
主要外国人 zhǔyào wàiguórén principal alien
住所 zhùsuǒ *n* domicile, residence
酌情裁量权 zhuóqíng cáiliàngquán discretion
酌情救济 zhuóqíng jiùjì discretionary relief
自动离境 zìdòng líjìng voluntary departure, voluntary
　　removal
自动离境担保金 zìdòng líjìng dānbǎojīn voluntary
　　departure bond
自动离境令 zìdòng líjìng lìng voluntary departure order
总领事馆 zǒnglǐngshìguǎn *n* consulate general
阻止 zǔzhǐ *v* preclude, prevent
最后一次入境地点 zuìhòu yīcì rùjìng dìdiǎn place of
　　last entry
最终驱逐令 zuìzhōng qūzhú lìng final order of removal

Immigration Law

交通法词汇
Traffic Law

交通法规范机动车辆在公路上的行驶规则。交通法要求驾驶人必须考取驾照，购买保险，开车要系安全带，不得酒后驾驶。交通法还规定对交通违规行为进行处罚。在美国，交通法事务归州政府管辖。

安全带法 ānquándài fǎ seat belt law
安全责任法 ānquán zérèn fǎ Safety Responsibility Law
安全责任听证会 ānquán zérèn tīngzhènghuì safety
　　responsibility hearing
案件编号 ànjiàn biānhào case number
保持车距 bǎochí chējù don't tailgate
保险费 bǎoxiǎnfèi *n* insurance premium
保险卡 bǎoxiǎnkǎ *n* insurance identification card
保险理赔 bǎoxiǎn lǐpéi insurance settlement
保险违规 bǎoxiǎn wéiguī insurance violation
保险证明 bǎoxiǎn zhèngmíng proof of insurance
爆胎 bàotāi *n* tire blowout
被扣押车辆 bèi kòuyā chēliàng impounded vehicle
被没收驾照 bèi mòshōu jiàzhào confiscated license
鞭打式损伤 biāndǎshì sǔnshāng whiplash
标志限速 biāozhì xiànsù posted speed limit
泊车 bóchē *n* parking; *v* park
泊车罚单 bóchē fádān parking ticket
泊车违规 bóchē wéiguī parking violations
不当超车 bùdàng chāochē improper passing
不当的 bùdàng de *adj* improper

不当换车道 **bùdàng huàn chēdào** making unsafe lane changes

不付罚款 **bùfù fákuǎn** failure to pay fine (FTP)

不给人行横道上的行人让路 **bùgěi rénxíng héngdào shàng de xíngrén rànglù** failure to yield to pedestrian in crosswalk

不顾他人权利或安全 **bùgù tārén quánlì huò ānquán** disregard of the rights or safety of others

不抗辩 **bùkàngbiàn** no contest plea

不让路 **bùrànglù** failure to yield right of way

不受理 **bùshòulǐ** dismiss

不遵守交通控制装置 **bùzūnshǒu jiāotōng kòngzhì zhuāngzhì** failure to obey traffic control device

财产损失 **cáichǎn sǔnshī** property damage

财务责任 **cáiwù zérèn** financial responsibility

侧面碰撞 **cèmiàn pèngzhuàng** side collision

查看 **chákàn** *n* probation

超车 **chāochē** *n* overtaking and passing; *v* overtake and pass

超出 **chāochū** in excess of

超过最高限速 **chāoguò zuìgāo xiànsù** exceeding maximum speed limit

超速 **chāosù** *n* speeding

超速罚单 **chāosù fádān** speeding ticket

超速行驶 **chāosù xíngshǐ** traveling in excess of the speed limit

超停着的校车 **chāo tíngzhe de xiàochē** passing a stopped school bus

车窗贴膜 **chēchuāng tiēmó** window tint

车道违规 **chēdào wéiguī** lane violation

车祸致人死命罪 **chēhuò zhìrén sǐmìng zuì** vehicular homicide

车检 **chējiǎn** *n* inspection
车检标签 **chējiǎn biāoqiān** inspection sticker
车辆伤害罪 **chēliàng shānghài zuì** vehicular assault
车牌 **chēpái** *n* license plate
车速太慢阻碍交通 **chēsù tàimàn zǔ'ài jiāotōng** slow
　speed blocking traffic
撤销 **chèxiāo** *n* cancellation; *v* cancel
闯红灯 **chuǎng hóngdēng** run a red light
闯交通灯 **chuǎng jiāotōngdēng** failure to stop for
　traffic light
闯停车标志 **chuǎng tíngchē biāozhì** run a stop sign
惩罚 **chéngfá** *n/v* sanction
出庭日 **chūtíng rì** court appearance date
处罚 **chǔfá** *n* penalty
穿行安全岛 **chuānxíng ānquándǎo** driving through
　safety zone
传票 **chuánpiào** *n* citation
粗心驾驶 **cūxīn jiàshǐ** careless driving
窜改 **cuàngǎi** *n* falsification; *v* falsify
答复罚单 **dáfù fádān** answer a ticket
担保 **dānbǎo** *n* collateral
道路 **dàolù** *n* road
道路标志 **dàolù biāozhì** traffic sign
道路交叉口 **dàolù jiāochākǒu** *n* intersection
登记 **dēngjì** *n* registration
抵押 **dǐyā** *n* collateral
第二次违规 **dì-èrcì wéiguī** second offense
第三次违规 **dì-sāncì wéiguī** third offense
第一次违规 **dì-yīcì wéiguī** first offense
吊销驾照 **diàoxiāo jiàzhào** revocation of driver's license
吊销驾照通知 **diàoxiāo jiàzhào tōngzhī** notice of
　revocation of driver's license

Traffic Law

斗气 **dòuqì** *n* road rage

对交通罚单提出抗辩 **duì jiāotōng fádān tíchū kàngbiàn** fight a traffic ticket

儿童保护措施法 **értóng bǎohù cuòshī fǎ** child restraint law

发还扣留驾照手续费 **fāhuán kòuliú jiàzhào shǒuxùfèi** suspension termination fee

罚单 **fádān** *n* ticket

罚款 **fákuǎn** *n/v* fine

法定 **fǎdìng** *adj* mandatory

法定出庭的交通违规行为 **fǎdìng chūtíng de jiāotōng wéiguī xíngwéi** mandatory appearance violations

法定限速 **fǎdìng xiànsù** statutory speed limit

翻车 **fānchē** *n* roll-over; *v* overturn

反应距离 **fǎnyìng jùlí** reaction distance

反应时间 **fǎnyìng shíjiān** reaction time

防御性驾驶 **fángyùxìng jiàshǐ** defensive driving

非法定出庭的违规行为 **fēi fǎdìng chūtíngde wéiguī xíngwéi** non-mandatory appearance violations

非法使用隔离带 **fēifǎ shǐyòng gélídài** unlawful use of median strip

非居民违规公约 **fēi jūmín wéiguī gōngyuē** Nonresident Violator Compact (NRVC)

非行车违规 **fēi xíngchē wéiguī** non-moving violation

附加费 **fùjiāfèi** *n* surcharge

改善驾驶辅导班 **gǎishàn jiàshǐ fǔdǎobān** driver improvement program

高速公路 **gāosù gōnglù** *n* highway

高速公路巡警 **gāosù gōnglù xúnjǐng** highway patrol

高速公路赛车 **gāosù gōnglù sàichē** racing on the highway

跟车过近 **gēnchē guò jìn** tailgate, follow too closely

跟车距离 gēnchē jùlí following distance

公园路 gōngyuán lù *n* parkway

攻击性驾驶 gōngjīxìng jiàshǐ aggressive driving

攻击性驾驶辅导班 gōngjīxìng jiàshǐ fǔdǎobān
　　aggressive driver program

国家高速公路交通安全局 guójiā gāosù gōnglù
　　jiāotōng ānquán jú National Highway Traffic
　　Safety Administration (NHTSA)

过路护卫 guòlù hùwèi crossing guard

过失 guòshī *n* fault

红灯 hóngdēng *n* red light

呼吸测试 hūxī cèshì breath test

缓刑 huǎnxíng *n* probation

换边泊车 huànbiān bóchē alternate side parking

黄灯 huángdēng *n* yellow light

恢复驾驶特权 huīfù jiàshǐ tèquán reinstatement of
　　driving privileges

回应 huíyìng *n* response; *v* respond

基本速度规则 jīběn sùdù guīzé basic speed rule

机动车 jīdòngchē *n* motor vehicle

机动车驾驶人 jīdòngchē jiàshǐrén motorist

机动车辆管理局 jīdòng chēliàng guǎnlǐ jú motor
　　vehicle authority

即决违规行为 jíjué wéiguī xíngwéi summary offense

记分 jìfēn *n* point

记分制度 jìfēn zhìdù point system

系安全带 jì ānquándài wear seat belts, buckle up

驾驶记录 jiàshǐ jìlù driver record

驾驶能力受损后开车 jiàshǐ nénglì shòusǔn hòu kāichē
　　driving while ability impaired (DWAI)

驾驶人 jiàshǐrén *n* driver, operator

驾驶人不在场的机动车辆 jiàshǐrén bùzàichǎng de jīdòng chēliàng unattended motor vehicle

驾驶特权 jiàshǐ tèquán driving privilege

驾照 jiàzhào *n* driver's license

驾照被扣留期间开车 jiàzhào bèi kòuliú qījiān kāichē driving while license suspended

驾照公约 jiàzhào gōngyuē Driver's License Compact (DLC)

驾照过期开车 jiàzhào guòqī kāichē driving with an expired license

肩带 jiāndài *n* shoulder harness

监禁 jiānjìn *n* imprisonment

减分 jiǎnfēn *n* reduction in points

减速 jiǎnsù *v* slow down

见习驾驶人辅导班 jiànxí jiàshǐrén fǔdǎobān probationary driver program

见习驾照 jiànxí jiàzhào provisional driver's license

交叉口 jiāochākǒu *n* junction

交通标志 jiāotōng biāozhì traffic sign

交通部 jiāotōngbù Department of Transportation (DOT)

交通罚单 jiāotōng fádān traffic tickets

交通法规 jiāotōng fǎguī vehicle code

交通法庭 jiāotōng fǎtíng traffic court

交通路口不当转弯 jiāotōng lùkǒu bùdàng zhuǎnwān improper turn at traffic light

交通违规 jiāotōng wéiguī traffic offenses

交通违规的对等处理 jiāotōng wéiguī de duìděng chǔlǐ traffic violations reciprocity

交通违规事务处 jiāotōng wéiguī shìwù chù traffic violations bureau

交通违规学校 jiāotōng wéiguī xuéxiào traffic school

紧急车辆 jǐnjí chēliàng emergency vehicles

紧急停车 jǐnjí tíngchē emergency stop
禁止泊车 jìnzhǐ bóchē no parking
禁止停车 jìnzhǐ tíngchē no stopping
禁止停留 jìnzhǐ tíngliú no standing
警报器 jǐngbàoqì *n* siren
警察报告 jǐngchá bàogào police report
酒后开车 jiǔ hòu kāichē driving under the influence
　　(DUI), driving while intoxicated (DWI), drunk driving
酒后开车辅导班 jiǔhòu kāichē fǔdǎobān drinking
　　driver program (DDP)
酒精饮料 jiǔjīng yǐnliào alcoholic beverage
救护车 jiùhùchē *n* ambulance
拒付罚款的交通违规者 jùfù fákuǎn de jiāotōng
　　wéiguīzhě scofflaw
拒绝接受呼吸测试 jùjué jiēshòu hūxī cèshì refuse to
　　submit to a breath test
拒绝接受化学测试 jùjué jiēshòu huàxué cèshì refuse to
　　submit to a chemical test
开车特权 kāichē tèquán driving privilege
开罚单的警官 kāi fádānde jǐngguān issuing officer
开封法 kāifēngfǎ open container law
抗辩 kàngbiàn *v* contest
靠边停车 kàobiān tíngchē pull over
扣车场 kòuchē chǎng *n* impound lot
扣留驾照 kòuliú jiàzhào suspension of driver's license
扣留驾照通知 kòuliú jiàzhào tōngzhī notice of
　　suspension of driver's license
扣押车辆 kòuyā chēliàng impound a vehicle
快速公路 kuàisù gōnglù *n* expressway
雷达探测器 léidá tàncèqì radar detector
累积记分 lěijī jìfēn accumulation of points
零容忍法 língróngrěn fǎ zero tolerance law

鲁莽驾驶 **lǔmǎng jiàshǐ** reckless driving

路肩超车 **lùjiān chāochē** passing on the shoulder

路权 **lùquán** *n* right of way

绿灯 **lùdēng** *n* green light

鸣喇叭 **míng lǎba** honk

默示同意 **mòshì tóngyì** implied consent

逆行 **nìxíng** *v* move against traffic

判决前查看 **pànjué qián chákàn** probation before judgment (PBJ)

判罪 **pànzuì** *n* conviction

碰撞 **pèngzhuàng** *n* collision, impact; *v* collide, crash

前排乘客 **qiánpái chéngkè** front-seat occupants

强制性的 **qiángzhìxìng de** *adj* mandatory

抢道超车 **qiǎngdào chāochē** cutting

桥 **qiáo** *n* bridge

轻微违规 **qīngwēi wéiguī** infraction

请求庭审 **qǐngqiú tíngshěn** claim trial

求助示意 **qiúzhù shìyì** signal for help

缺席判罪 **quēxí pànzuì** default conviction

让路 **rànglù** *v* yield

人身伤害保护险 **rénshēn shānghài bǎohù xiǎn** personal injury protection (PIP)

赛车 **sàichē** *n* speed contest, race

擅离事故现场 **shànlí shìgù xiànchǎng** leaving the scene of an accident

伤害 **shānghài** *n* injury; *v* injure

上交驾照 **shàngjiāo jiàzhào** turn in a license

身份 **shēnfèn** *n* identity

身份证 **shēnfènzhèng** *n* identity card, ID card

身份证明 **shēnfèn zhèngmíng** proof of identity

设备违规 **shèbèi wéiguī** mechanical violation

失去驾驶特权 shīqù jiàshǐ tèquán loss of driving
privileges

时速 shísù *n* miles per hour (mph)

实行过失制的州 shíxíng guòshīzhì de zhōu at-fault state

实行无过失制的州 shíxíng wú guòshīzhì de zhōu
no-fault state

事故 shìgù *n* accident

事故报告 shìgù bàogào accident report

事故现场 shìgù xiànchǎng scene of an accident

收费 shōufèi *adj/n/v* toll

收费路/桥/隧道 shōufèi lù/qiáo/suìdào/ toll road/bridge/
tunnel

收费站 shōufèi zhàn toll booth

手机法 shǒujī fǎ cell phone law

数码驾照 shùmǎ jiàzhào digital driver's license (DDL)

双重泊车 shuāngchóng bóchē double parking

司机 sījī *n* driver, operator

死亡 sǐwáng *n* death; *v* die

速度限制 sùdù xiànzhì speed limit

隧道 suìdào *n* tunnel

特权 tèquán *n* privilege

庭审 tíngshěn *n* court trial

停车 tíngchē *v* stop

停车标志 tíngchē biāozhì stop sign

停车违规 tíngchē wéiguī stopping violations

停留违规 tíngliú wéiguī standing violation

停止 tíngzhǐ *v* stop

危险 wēixiǎn *n* hazard

违规 wéiguī *n* non-compliance, offense, violation

违规过马路 wéiguī guò mǎlù jaywalk

违规驾驶人学校 wéiguī jiàshǐrén xuéxiào traffic
violator school

违规者 **wéiguīzhě** *n* violator

伪造 **wěizào** *n* falsification; *v* falsify

未保险车辆 **wèi bǎoxiǎn chēliàng** uninsured vehicle

无不良驾驶记录 **wú bùliáng jiàshǐ jìlù** clean driving record

先行权 **xiānxíngquán** right of way

限制 **xiànzhì** *n* restriction

校车 **xiàochē** *n* school bus

校区 **xiàoqū** *n* school zone

行车违规 **xíngchē wéiguī** moving violation

修车罚单 **xiūchē fádān** fix-it-ticket

需出庭的违规行为 **xū chūtíng de wéiguī xíngwéi** court appearance violations

血液酒精浓度 **xuèyè jiǔjīng nóngdù** blood alcohol concentration (BAC)

严重人身伤害 **yánzhòng rénshēn shānghài** serious physical injury

严重无照驾驶 **yánzhòng wúzhào jiàshǐ** aggravated unlicensed operation (AUO)

野蛮驾驶 **yěmán jiàshǐ** reckless driving

迎面相撞 **yíngmiàn xiāngzhuàng** head-on collision

邮寄支付 **yóujì zhīfù** pay by mail

有条件驾照 **yǒutiáojiàn jiàzhào** conditional license

右边超车 **yòubian chāochē** passing on the right

迂回穿行 **yūhuí chuānxíng** weaving

预付费停车证 **yùfùfèi tíngchēzhèng** paid parking permit

原告过失 **yuángào guòshī** contributory negligence

匝道 **zādào** *n* ramp

责任保险 **zérèn bǎoxiǎn** liability insurance

肇事逃逸 **zhàoshì táoyì** hit and run

正面碰撞 **zhèngmiàn pèngzhuàng** frontal impact

执法 **zhífǎ** *n* law enforcement

执法部门 **zhífǎ bùmén** law enforcement
致命事故 **zhìmìng shìgù** fatal accident
致命性 **zhìmìngxìng** *n* fatality
中毒 **zhòngdú** *n* intoxication
州际高速公路 **zhōujì gāosù gōnglù** interstate highway
转弯不打灯 **zhuǎnwān bùdǎdēng** failure to use turn
    signals
撞车 **zhuàngchē** *v* crash, collide
追尾 **zhuīwěi** rear-end collision
阻碍交通 **zǔ'ài jiāotōng** impeding traffic
醉酒 **zuìjiǔ** *adj* drunk, intoxicated
最低速度规则 **zuìdī sùdù guīzé** minimum speed rule
遵守 **zūnshǒu** *v* obey

English-Chinese

（英汉）

General and Procedural Terms
一般和程序性词汇

This section covers procedural terms and terms that are of a more general character. Some terms listed here may appear in other sections.

abandon *v* 放弃 fàngqì, 遗弃 yíqì
abandonment *n* 放弃 fàngqì, 遗弃 yíqì
abrogate *v* 废除 fèichú, 取消 qǔxiāo
abstract *n* 摘要 zhāiyào
abstract of judgment 判决摘要 pànjué zhāiyào
abuse *n/v* 虐待 nuèdài, 滥用 lànyòng, 侵犯 qīnfàn
abuse of power 滥用权力 lànyòng quánlì
abuse of trust 滥用信任 lànyòng xìnrèn
acknowledgment of satisfaction of judgment
    履行判决收据 lǚxíng pànjué shōujù
act *n* 作为 zuòwéi
act of God 天灾 tiānzāi, 不可抗力 bùkěkànglì
action *n* 诉讼 sùsòng
ad litem *adj* 为诉讼目的 wèi sùsòng mùdì
addict *n* 上瘾的人 shàngyǐn de rén
addiction *n* 瘾 yǐn
addiction to alcohol 酒瘾 jiǔyǐn
addiction to drugs 毒瘾 dúyǐn
adjourn *v* 休庭 xiūtíng
adjourned *adj* 休庭的 xiūtíng de
adjournment *n* 休庭 xiūtíng
adjudicate *v* 判决 pànjué, 裁定 cáidìng

adjudication *n* 判决 pànjué, 裁定 cáidìng

adjuster (*insurance*) *n* (保险) 理算人 (bǎoxiǎn) lǐsuànrén

administer *v* 执行 zhíxíng

administration *n* 管理 guǎnlǐ

administrative *adj* 管理的 guǎnlǐ de, 行政的 xíngzhèng de

administrator *n* 管理人 guǎnlǐrén

admissible evidence 可采信的证据 kě cǎixìn de zhèngjù

admission *n* 供述 gòngshù, 入境 rùjìng

admonish *v* 警告 jǐnggào

admonition *n* 警告 jǐnggào

adult *adj* 成年的 chéngnián de; *n* 成年人 chéngniánrén

adversarial system 抗辩制 kàngbiànzhì, 对抗制 duìkàngzhì

adverse witness 敌对证人 díduì zhèngrén

affair *n* 事务 shìwù, 事件 shìjiàn, 私通 sītōng

affidavit *n* 宣誓书 xuānshìshū, 证明书 zhèngmíngshū, 保证书 bǎozhèngshū

affidavit of support (AOS) 经济担保书 jīngjì dānbǎoshū

affirm *v* 维持原判 wéichí yuánpàn, 确认 quèrèn

affirmance (*of a decision*) *n* 维持原判 wéichí yuánpàn

affirmative action 平权措施 píngquán cuòshī

affix signature 签名 qiānmíng

age *n* 年龄 niánlíng

aggrieved party 受损害方 shòu sǔnhài fāng

agreement *n* 协议 xiéyì, 协定 xiédìng, 合同 hétong

alcohol *n* 酒精 jiǔjīng, 酒 jiǔ

alcoholic *adj* 酒精的 jiǔjīng de, 酗酒的 xùjiǔ de; *n* 酗酒者 xùjiǔzhě

alcoholism *n* 酗酒 xùjiǔ

alien *adj* 外国的 wàiguó de; *n* 外国人 wàiguórén

allegation *n* 指控 zhǐkòng, 主张 zhǔzhāng

allege *v* 指控 zhǐkòng, 主张 zhǔzhāng

alter *v* 更改 gēnggǎi, 改动 gǎidòng

alternate *adj* 替补的 tìbǔ de, 替换的 tìhuàn de

Amber Alert 安珀警报 ānpò jǐngbào

amend *v* 修改 xiūgǎi, 修正 xiūzhèng

amendment *n* 修正 xiūzhèng, 修正案 xiūzhèng'àn

amount *n* 数额 shù'é

amphetamine *n* 苯丙胺 běnbǐng'àn, 安非他明 ānfēitāmíng

annul *v* 废除 fèichú, 取消 qǔxiāo

AOS 见 affidavit of support

appeal *n/v* 上诉 shàngsù

appear in court 出庭 chūtíng

appearance *n* 出庭 chūtíng

appellant *n* 上诉人 shàngsùrén

appellee *n* 被上诉人 bèi shàngsùrén

application *n* 申请 shēnqǐng

argue *v* 争辩 zhēngbiàn

argument *n* 辩论 biànlùn, 论证 lùnzhèng

arrears *n* 拖欠 tuōqiàn

article *n* 条 tiáo, 物品 wùpǐn

assign *v* 转让 zhuǎnràng

assignee *n* 受让人 shòuràngrén

assignment *n* 转让 zhuǎnràng

assignor *n* 出让人 chūràngrén

assist *v* 协助 xiézhù

at your own risk 后果自负 hòuguǒ zìfù

attendance *n* 照料 zhàoliào, 出席 chūxí

attorney *n* 律师 lǜshī, 法律代理人 fǎlǜ dàilǐrén, 检察官 jiǎncháguān

attorney of record 备案律师 bèi'àn lǜshī

attorney's fee 律师费 lǜshī fèi

authentic *adj* 作准的 zuòzhǔn de

award *n* 判决 pànjué; *v* 判给 pàngěi

bad faith 失信 shīxìn, 不诚信 bùchéngxìn

bail *n* 保释 bǎoshì, 保释金 bǎoshìjīn; *v* 保释 bǎoshì

bailiff *n* 法警 fǎjǐng, 执达官 zhídáguān

bar *n* 律师业 lǜshīyè, 律师界 lǜshījiè; *v* 阻止zǔzhǐ

bearer *n* 持有人 chíyǒurén

bench trial 法官审理 fǎguān shěnlǐ

bodily injury or harm 身体伤害 shēntǐ shānghài

bodily search; body search 搜身 sōushēn

bond *n* 担保金 dānbǎojīn, 债券 zhàiquàn

brain contusion 脑挫伤 nǎo cuòshāng

brain damage 脑损伤 nǎo sǔnshāng

breach *n/v* 违反 wéifǎn, 不遵守 bùzūnshǒu

breach of duty 失职 shīzhí, 不履行义务 bùlǚxíng yìwù

brief *n* 辩护要点 biànhù yàodiǎn, 诉讼要点 sùsòng yàodiǎn

burden of proof 举证责任 jǔzhèng zérèn

bylaws *n* 条例 tiáolì, 地方法规 dìfāng fǎguī, 公司章程 gōngsī zhāngchéng

CAFA 见 Class Action Fairness Act

cannabis *n* 大麻 dàmá

case *n* 案件 ànjiàn, 案例 ànlì

case file 案卷 ànjuàn

case law 判例法 pànlìfǎ

case worker 办案员 bàn'ànyuán

caseflow management 案件流程管理 ànjiàn liúchéng guǎnlǐ

Central Intelligence Agency (CIA) 中央情报局 zhōngyāng qíngbàojú

certificate *n* 证书 zhèngshū

certified mail 保证信 bǎozhèngxìn, 保证邮件 bǎozhèng yóujiàn

challenge *n/v* 质疑 zhìyí, 要求回避 yāoqiú huíbì

charge to the jury 对陪审团的指示 duì péishěntuán de zhǐshì

chattel *n* 动产 dòngchǎn

child molester 猥亵儿童者 wěixiè értóng zhě

CIA 见 Central Intelligence Agency

circumstantial evidence 情节证据 qíngjié zhèngjù, 间接证据 jiànjiē zhèngjù

circumvent *v* 规避 guībì

claim *v* 权利主张 quánlì zhǔzhāng, 要求 yāoqiú, 索赔 suǒpéi, 诉讼 sùsòng

claimant *n* 要求人 yāoqiúrén, 索赔人 suǒpéirén, 原告 yuángào

class action 集体诉讼 jítǐ sùsòng

Class Action Fairness Act (CAFA) 集体诉讼公平法 jítǐ sùsòng gōngpíng fǎ

clause *n* 条款 tiáokuǎn

clinical examination 临床检查 línchuáng jiǎnchá

closing argument 最后辩论 zuìhòu biànlùn

coca *n* 古柯 gǔkē

cocaine *n* 可卡因 kěkǎyīn

collect evidence 收集证据 shōují zhèngjù

collection agency 代收公司 dàishōu gōngsī

commission *n* 委托 wěituō, 佣金 yòngjīn, 实施 (犯罪) shíshī (*fànzuì*)

commit (*confine*) *v* 监禁 jiānjìn, 押交 yājiāo

commit (*crime*) *v* 实施犯罪 shíshī fànzuì

compensation *n* 补偿 bǔcháng

compensatory damages 补偿性损害赔偿金 bǔchángxìng sǔnhài péichángjīn

competent to stand trial 有能力承受审判 yǒunénglì chéngshòu shěnpàn

competent to testify 有能力作证 yǒunénglì zuòzhèng

complain *v* 控告 kònggào
complainant *n* 控告人 kònggàorén, 原告 yuángào
complaint (*civil*) *n* 民事控诉 mínshì kòngsù
comply with *v* 遵守 zūnshǒu
conceal *v* 隐藏 yǐncáng
conciliation *n* 调解 tiáojiě, 和解 héjiě
condemnation *n* 定罪 dìngzuì, 判刑 pànxíng, 征用 zhēngyòng
conditional *adj* 有条件的 yǒutiáojiàn de
confidential *adj* 机密的 jīmì de
consent *n* 同意 tóngyì
conservatee *n* 受监护人 shòu jiānhùrén
conservator *n* 监护人 jiānhùré
conservatorship *n* 监护权 jiānhùquán
consolidation of actions 合并诉讼 hébìng sùsòng
constitution *n* 宪法 xiànfǎ
constitutional *adj* 宪法的 xiànfǎ de, 符合宪法的 fúhé xiànfǎ de
consumer *n* 消费者 xiāofèizhě
contempt of court 藐视法庭罪 miǎoshì fǎtíng zuì
continuance *n* 推迟审理 tuīchí shěnlǐ
contract *n* 合同 hétong
contractual *adj* 合同的 hétong de, 约定的 yuēdìng de
convention *n* 公约 gōngyuē
coroner *n* 验尸官 yànshīguān
corroborate *v* 确证 quèzhèng, 确认 quèrèn
corroborated *adj* 经过确证的 jīngguò quèzhèng de
corrupt *adj* 贪腐的 tānfǔ de; *v* 贪腐 tānfǔ
corruption *n* 贪腐 tānfǔ
cosignor *n* 连署人 liánshǔrén
cost *n* 诉讼费 sùsòngfèi, 费用 fèiyòng; *v* 花费 huāfèi
counsel *n* 律师 lùshī, 法律顾问 fǎlùgùwèn

counterclaim *n/v* 反诉 fǎnsù

course of conduct 系列行为 xìliè xíngwéi

court *n* 法院 fǎyuàn, 法庭 fǎtíng

court clerk 法院书记员 fǎyuàn shūjìyuán

court clerk's office 法院书记员办公室 fǎyuàn shūjìyuán
   bàngōngshì

court costs 法庭费用 fǎtíng fèiyòng

court of appeals *n* 上诉法院 shàngsù fǎyuàn

court reporter 法院速记员 fǎyuàn sùjìyuán

court trial 见 bench trial

courtroom *n* 审判室 shěnpànshì

credibility *n* 可靠性 kěkàoxìng, 可信性 kěxìnxìng

credible *adj* 可靠的 kěkào de, 可信的 kěxìn de

crime *n* 犯罪 fànzuì, 罪行 zuìxíng

cross-complaint *n* 交叉诉讼状 jiāochā sùsòngzhuàng

cross-examination *n* 交叉诘问 jiāochā jiéwèn

cross-examine *v* 交叉诘问 jiāochā jiéwèn

culpability *n* 有罪 yǒuzuì, 应受惩罚 yīngshòu chéngfá

custody *n* 扣押 kòuyā, 拘禁 jūjìn, 保管 bǎoguǎn,
   监护 jiānhù

custody of evidence 证据保管 zhèngjù bǎoguǎn

customs *n* 海关 hǎiguān, 关税 guānshuì

damages *n* 损害赔偿金 sǔnhài péichángjīn

date *n* 日期 rìqī

dead man's statute 死者证言不可采信规则 sǐzhě
   zhèngyán bùkě cǎixìn guīzé

death certificate 死亡证明书 sǐwáng zhèngmíngshū

decedent *n* 死者 sǐzhě

deceive *v* 欺骗 qīpiàn

declarant *n* 陈述人 chénshùrén, 申诉人 shēnsùrén

declaration *n* 宣告 xuāngào, 陈述 chénshù, 起诉状
   qǐsùzhuàng

declare *v* 宣告 xuāngào, 陈述 chénshù

decree *n* 法令 fǎlìng, 判决 pànjué

deed *n* 行为 xíngwéi, 契据 qìjù, 文书 wénshū

defamation *n* 诋毁名誉 dǐhuǐ míngyù

default *n/v* 缺席 quēxí, 未到庭 wèi dàotíng, 违约 wéiyuē, 拖欠 tuōqiàn

default judgment 缺席判决 quēxí pànjué

defend *v* 辩护 biànhù

defendant *n* 被告 bèigào

defense *n* 辩护 biànhù, 抗辩 kàngbiàn, 被告方 bèigàofāng

delay *n/v* 延期 yánqī, 推迟 tuīchí

deliberate *adj* 蓄意的 xùyì de; *v* 讨论 tǎolùn

delinquency *n* 未成年人犯罪 wèichéngniánrén fànzuì, 不履行义务或债务 bùlǚxíng yìwù huò zhàiwù

delinquent *n* 未成年罪犯 wèichéngnián zuìfàn, 拖欠债务者 tuōqiàn zhàiwù zhě

denial *n* 否认 fǒurèn, 拒绝 jùjué, 剥夺 bōduó

deny *v* 否认 fǒurèn, 拒绝 jùjué

deny a motion 拒绝一项动议 jùjué yī xiàng dòngyì

Department of Homeland Security (DHS) 国土安全部 guótǔ ānquán bù

deponent *n* 宣誓证人 xuānshì zhèngrén

depose *v* 宣誓证明 xuānshì zhèngmíng

deposition *n* 庭外取证 tíngwài qǔzhèng, 庭外证词笔录 tíngwài zhèngcí bǐlù

detective *n* 侦探 zhēntàn

DHS 见 Department of Homeland Security

direct examination 直接诘问 zhíjiē jiéwèn

direct income withholding 直接代扣收入 zhíjiē dài kòu shōurù

disbursement *n* 付款 fùkuǎn, 支出 zhīchū

disclose *v* 揭露 jiēlù, 披露 pīlù

disclosure *n* 揭露 jiēlù, 披露 pīlù

discontinuance *n* 终止 zhōngzhǐ, 撤诉 chèsù

discovery *n* 证据开示 zhèngjù kāishì

dismiss *v* 驳回 bóhuí

dismiss with prejudice 驳回起诉, 不可再诉 bóhuí qǐsù, bùkě zàisù

dismiss without prejudice 驳回起诉, 但可再诉 bóhuí qǐsù, dàn kě zàisù

dismissal *n* 驳回 bóhuí

disposable income 可支配收入 kě zhīpèi shōurù

dispute *n* 争执 zhēngzhí, 争议 zhēngyì, 纠纷 jiūfēn

disqualification *n* 取消资格 qǔxiāo zīgé

disqualified *adj* 被取消资格的 bèi qǔxiāo zīgé de

disqualify *v* 取消资格 qǔxiāo zīgé

distinguish between right and wrong 分辨是非 fēnbiàn shìfēi

district *n* 区 qū, 地方 dìfāng

district attorney (DA) 地方检察官 dìfāng jiǎncháguān

district court 联邦地方法院 liánbāng dìfāng fǎyuàn, 州地方法院 zhōu dìfāng fǎyuàn

DNA 脱氧核糖核酸 tuōyǎng hétáng hésuān

DNA test DNA 鉴定 DNA jiàndìng

docket *n* 待审案件目录 dài shěn ànjiàn mùlù, 诉讼摘录 sùsòng zhāilù

documentary evidence 书证 shūzhèng

domicile *n* 住所 zhùsuǒ

drug *n* 毒品 dúpǐn

drunk *adj* 醉酒的 zuìjiǔ de; *n* 酗酒者 xùjiǔzhě

drunkenness *n* 醉酒 zuìjiǔ

due process 适当法律程序 shìdàng fǎlù chéngxù

duty of care 注意义务 zhùyì yìwù

eavesdropping *n* 窃听 qiètīng

一般和程序性词汇

eligibility *n* 合格 hégé, 资格 zīgé, 适当 shìdàng

eligible *adj* 合格的 hégé de, 适当的 shìdàng de

eminent domain 政府征用权 zhèngfǔ zhēngyòngquán

enforcement (*of judgment*) *n* 强制执行 qiángzhì zhíxíng

enjoyment (*of rights*) *n* 享有 (权利) xiǎngyǒu (quánlì)

equality under the law 法律面前人人平等 fǎlǜ
   miànqián rénrén píngděng

euthanasia *n* 安乐死 ānlèsǐ

evidence *n* 证据 zhèngjù

evidence ruling 证据裁定 zhèngjù cáidìng

evidentiary *adj* 提供证据的 tígōng zhèngjù de

examination of witness 诘问证人 jiéwèn zhèngrén

examine *v* 诘问 jiéwèn, 询问 xúnwèn

examine the facts 审查事实 shěnchá shìshí

excited utterance 激情表述 jīqíng biǎoshù

execute *v* 执行 zhíxíng

execution *n* 执行 zhíxíng

executor *n* 执行人 zhíxíngrén

exhaustion of remedies 竭尽救济原则 jiéjìn jiùjì yuánzé

exhibit *n* 呈庭证据 chéngtíng zhèngjù

expert *n* 专家 zhuānjiā

expert examination 诘问专家 jiéwèn zhuānjiā

expert opinion *n* 专家意见 zhuānjiā yìjiàn

expert witness *n* 专家证人 zhuānjiā zhèngrén

expertise *n* 专门知识 zhuānmén zhīshi, 专门技能
   zhuānmén jìnéng

expiration *n* 期满 qīmǎn

expire *v* 到期 dàoqī

extension of period of stay 延长延缓期 yáncháng
   yánhuǎnqī

extenuating *adj* 减轻的 jiǎnqīng de

facilitate *v* 协助 xiézhù

fact finding 事实调查 shìshí diàochá

failure to appear (FTA) 不出庭 bùchūtíng, 逃庭 táotíng

fax; facsimile *n/v* 传真 chuánzhēn

FBI 见 Federal Bureau of Investigation

Federal Bureau of Investigation (FBI) 联邦调查局 liánbāng diàochájú

Federal Emergency Management Agency (FEMA) 联邦紧急情况管理局 liánbāng jǐnjí qíngkuàng guǎnlǐ jú

FEMA 见 Federal Emergency Management Agency

fiduciary *adj* 托付的 tuōfù de; *n* 受托人 shòutuōrén

finding *n* 调查结果 diàochá jiéguǒ, 认定 rèndìng

fine *n* 罚金 fájīn; *v* 处以罚金 chǔyǐ fájīn

foreman of jury 陪审团团长 péishěntuán tuánzhǎng

forensic *adj* 法庭的 fǎtíng de, 法医的 fǎyī de

foreseeable *adj* 可预见的 kě yùjiàn de

forfeit *v* 没收 mòshōu

fraudulent intent 欺诈意图 qīzhà yìtú

FTA 见 failure to appear

fundamental right 基本权利 jīběn quánlì

gang *n* 团伙 tuánhuǒ, 帮派 bāngpài

garnishment *n* 扣押工资令 kòuyā gōngzī lìng, 扣押财产令 kòuyā cáichǎn lìng

give evidence 作证 zuòzhèng, 提供证据 tígōng zhèngjù

give notice 通知 tōngzhī

grace period 宽限期 kuānxiànqī

grand juror 大陪审团陪审员 dà péishěntuán péishěnyuán

grand jury 大陪审团 dà péishěntuán

grant a motion 同意一项动议 tóngyì yīxiàng dòngyì

grievance *n* 冤情 yuānqíng

gross negligence 重大过失 zhòngdà guòshī

ground *n* 根据 gēnjù, 理由 lǐyóu

grounds for re-trial 重审理由 chóngshěn lǐyóu

habeas corpus 人身保护令 rénshēn bǎohù lìng

handwriting *n* 笔迹 bǐjì, 手书 shǒushū

harassment *n* 骚扰 sāorǎo

hardship *n* 困窘 kùnjiǒng

harm *n/v* 伤害 shānghài, 损害 sǔnhài

harmful *adj* 有害的 yǒuhài de

hashish *n* 印度大麻 yìndù dàmá

hearing *n* 听证 tīngzhèng, 听证会 tīngzhènghuì

hearsay *n* 传闻 chuánwén

heir *n* 继承人 jìchéngrén

hemp *n* 大麻 dàmá

illegal *adj* 非法的 fēifǎ de

illegal entry 非法进入 fēifǎ jìnrù, 非法入境 fēifǎ rùjìng

imminent danger 紧迫危险 jǐnpò wēixiǎn

impeach *v* 弹劾 tánhé, 控告 kònggào

implicated *adj* 牵连在内的 qiānlián zàinèi de

in session (*court*) 开庭 kāitíng

inadmissible evidence 不可采信的证据 bùkě cǎixìn de zhèngjù

incident report 事件报告 shìjiàn bàogào

incite *v* 煽动 shāndòng, 鼓动 gǔdòng

income *n* 收入 shōurù, 所得 suǒdé

induce *v* 引诱 yǐnyòu

informed consent 知情的同意 zhīqíng de tóngyì

inherit *v* 继承 jìchéng

inheritance *n* 继承 jìchéng

injunction *n* 禁制令 jìnzhì lìng

injured party 受害方 shòuhàifāng

injury *n* 损害 sǔnhài, 伤害 shānghài

inquest *n* 死因审理 sǐyīn shěnlǐ

inquest jury 死因调查陪审团 sǐyīn diàochá péishěntuán

inquire *v* 询问 xúnwèn, 调查 diàochá
inquiry *n* 询问 xúnwèn, 调查 diàochá
insane *adj* 精神错乱的 jīngshén cuòluàn de
insanity *n* 精神错乱 jīngshén cuòluàn
intend *v* 意图 yìtú
intention *n* 意图 yìtú, 故意 gùyì
international judicial assistance 国际司法协助 guójì
    sīfǎ xiézhù
interpret *v* 口译 kǒuyì, 解释 jiěshì
interpretation *n* 口译 kǒuyì, 解释 jiěshì
interpreter *n* 口译员 kǒuyìyuán
interrogate *v* 讯问 xùnwèn
intestate *adj* 未留遗嘱的 wèi liú yízhǔ de
intimidate *v* 恐吓 kǒnghè
intoxication *n* 中毒
    alcohol intoxication 酒精中毒 jiǔjīng zhòngdú
    narcotic intoxication 毒品中毒 dúpǐn zhòngdú
investigate *v* 调查 diàochá, 侦查 zhēnchá
investigation *n* 调查 diàochá, 侦查 zhēnchá
involuntary *adj* 非自愿的 fēi zìyuàn de, 非故意的 fēi
    gùyì de
irrebuttable presumption 不可反驳的推定 bùkě fǎnbó
    de tuīdìng
issue *v* 发行 fāxíng, 发出 fāchū
judge *n* 法官 fǎguān; *v* 判决 pànjué
judgment *n* 判决 pànjué
judicial review 司法复核 sīfǎ fùhé
jurisdiction *n* 管辖权 guǎnxiáquán
jurisdictional limit 管辖范围 guǎnxiá fànwéi
juror *n* 陪审员 péishěnyuán
jury *n* 陪审团 péishěntuán
jury challenge 要求陪审员回避 yāoqiú péishěnyuán huíbì

一般和程序性词汇

jury charge 法官对陪审员的指示 fǎguān duì péishěnyuán de zhǐshì

jury duty 担任陪审员 dānrèn péishěnyuán, 担任陪审员的义务 dānrèn péishěnyuán de yìwù

justice 正义 zhèngyì, 法官 fǎguān

justice court 治安法院 zhì'ān fǎyuàn

juvenile *adj* 未成年的 wèichéngnián de; *n* 未成年人 wèichéngniánrén, 少年 shàonián

knowingly *adv* 故意地 gùyì de

lack of jurisdiction 无管辖权 wú guǎnxiáquán

law *n* 法律 fǎlǜ

lawsuit *n* 诉讼 sùsòng

lawyer *n* 律师 lǜshī

leading question 诱导性提问 yòudǎoxìng tíwèn

leave to appeal 上诉许可 shàngsù xǔkě

legal *adj* 法律上的 fǎlǜ shàng de, 合法的 héfǎ de

legal representative 法律代理人 fǎlǜ dàilǐrén, 诉讼代理人 sùsòng dàilǐrén, 遗嘱执行人 yízhǔ zhíxíngrén

legalization *n* 合法化 héfǎhuà

LEP 见 limited English proficiency

lewd conduct 猥亵行为 wěixiè xíngwéi

liability *n* 责任 zérèn, 义务 yìwù

liable *adj* 有责任的 yǒu zérèn de, 有义务的 yǒu yìwù de

libel *n* 诽谤罪 fěibàngzuì

lie detector *n* 测谎器 cèhuǎngqì

limited English proficiency (LEP) 英语水平有限 yīngyǔ shuǐpíng yǒuxiàn

liquidated damages 事先协定的赔偿金 shìxiān xiédìng de péichángjīn

lis pendens 未决诉讼 wèijué sùsòng

litigant *n* 诉讼当事人 sùsòng dāngshìrén

litigate *v* 诉讼 sùsòng

litigation *n* 诉讼 sùsòng

litigation cost 诉讼费用 sùsòng fèiyòng

losing party 败诉方 bàisùfāng

magistrate judge 辅助法官 fǔzhù fǎguān, 治安法官 zhì'ān fǎguān

malfeasance *n* 违法行为 wéifǎ xíngwéi, 渎职 dúzhí

mandatory *adj* 强制的 qiángzhì de, 法定的 fǎdìng de

manslaughter *n* 杀人罪 shārénzuì

marijuana *n* 大麻 dàmá

mediate *v* 调解 tiáojiě

mediation *n* 调解 tiáojiě

mediator *n* 调解人 tiáojiěrén

medical report 医疗报告 yīliáo bàogào

mental deficiency 精神缺陷 jīngshén quēxiàn

mental depression 精神抑郁症 jīngshén yìyùzhèng

mental disorder 精神失常 jīngshén shīcháng

methamphetamine *n* 甲基苯丙胺 jiǎjī běnbǐng'àn (俗称冰毒 *a.k.a* bīngdú)

minor *adj* 未成年的 wèichéngnián de; *n* 未成年人 wèichéngniánrén

misconduct *n* 不当行为 bùdàng xíngwéi

mistake *n* 错误 cuòwù

mistrial *n* 流审 liúshěn, 失审 shīshěn, 无效审理 wúxiào shěnlǐ

mitigating *adj* 减轻的 jiǎnqīng de

mob *n* 团伙 tuánhuǒ, 帮派 bāngpài

modify *v* 更改 gēnggǎi, 改动 gǎidòng

money laundering 洗钱 xǐqián

motion *n* 动议 dòngyì, 提议 tíyì

motive *n* 动机 dòngjī

narcotics *n* 麻醉品 mázuìpǐn, 毒品 dúpǐn

nationality *n* 国籍 guójí

neglect *v* 疏忽 shūhū

negligence *n* 疏忽 shūhū, 过失 guòshī

negligent *adj* 疏忽的 shūhū de, 过失的 guòshī de

net worth 净值 jìngzhí

new trial of a case 案件重审 ànjiàn chóngshěn

notarial *adj* 公证的 gōngzhèng de

notary *n* 公证人 gōngzhèngrén

notice *n/v* 通知 tōngzhī

notice of appeal 上诉通知 shàngsù tōngzhī

notify *v* 通知 tōngzhī

null and void *adj* 无效的 wúxiào de

oath *n* 誓言 shìyán, 宣誓 xuānshì

obey *v* 服从 fúcóng

objection *n* 异议 yìyì, 反对 fǎnduì

obscenity *n* 猥亵 wěixiè, 淫秽 yínhuì

offense *n* 违法行为 wéifǎ xíngwéi, 违规行为 wéiguī xíngwéi, 犯罪 fànzuì

offset *n* 抵销 dǐxiāo, 补偿 bǔcháng

opening statement 开场陈述 kāichǎng chénshù

operation of law (by) 依据法律 yījù fǎlù

oral argument 口头辩论 kǒutóu biànlùn

oral proceedings 口头程序 kǒutóu chéngxù

order *n/v* 命令 mìnglìng

ordinance *n* 条例 tiáolì, 地方法规 dìfāng fǎguī

overrule an objection 驳回异议 bóhuí yìyì

panel of judges 合议庭 héyìtíng

parole *n/v* 假释 jiǎshì

party *n* 当事人 dāngshìrén

passport *n* 护照 hùzhào

penalty *n* 刑罚 xíngfá, 处罚 chǔfá, 罚金 fájīn

pendente lite 诉讼待决期间 sùsòng dàijué qījiān

period *n* 期间 qījiān, 期限 qīxiàn

perjury *n* 伪证 wěizhèng

permit *n* 执照 zhízhào, 许可证 xǔkězhèng

person *n* 人 rén

personal jurisdiction 属人管辖权 shǔrén guǎnxiáquán

personalty *n* 动产 dòngchǎn

petit juror 小陪审团陪审员 xiǎo péishěntuán péishěnyuán

petit jury 小陪审团 xiǎo péishěntuán

petition *n/v* 申诉 shēnsù, 申请 shēnqǐng; *n* 起诉状 qǐsùzhuàng

physical evidence 物证 wùzhèng

physical injury or harm 身体伤害 shēntǐ shānghài

plaintiff *n* 原告 yuángào

plea *n* 抗辩 kàngbiàn, 答辩 dábiàn

plead guilty 认罪 rènzuì

plead not guilty 不认罪 bùrènzuì

pleading *n* 诉状 sùzhuàng, 辩状 biànzhuàng

police *n* 警察 jǐngchá, 警方 jǐngfāng

policeman; police officer *n* 警察 jǐngchá, 警员 jǐngyuán

polygraph *n* 测谎器 cèhuǎngqì

postpone *v* 延期 yánqī, 推迟 tuīchí

power of attorney 授权书 shòuquánshū, 委托书 wěituōshū

prejudicial *adj* 有害的 yǒuhài de, 不利的 bùlì de

preside over *v* 主持 zhǔchí, 主审 zhǔshěn

presiding judge 法院院长 fǎyuàn yuànzhǎng, 主审法官 zhǔshěn fǎguān

presume *v* 推定 tuīdìng

presumption *n* 推定 tuīdìng

prevailing party 胜诉方 shèngsùfāng

prima facie *adj* 初步印象的 chūbù yìnxiàng de, 表面的 biǎomiàn de

一般和程序性词汇

probate *n* 遗嘱检验 yízhǔ jiǎnyàn

probative value 证明价值 zhèngmíng jiàzhí

procedure *n* 程序 chéngxù, 手续 shǒuxù

proceed *v* 起诉 qǐsù

proceedings *n* 诉讼程序 sùsòng chéngxù

proof *n* 证明 zhèngmíng, 证据 zhèngjù

property *n* 财产 cáichǎn

proprietary *adj* 所有权的 suǒyǒuquán de, 专有的 zhuānyǒu de, 专利的 zhuānlì de

protective order 保护令 bǎohùlìng

prove *v* 证明 zhèngmíng, 检验 jiǎnyàn

psychiatric evaluation 精神病医学鉴定 jīngshénbìng yīxué jiàndìng

public prosecutor 公诉人 gōngsùrén

puncture wound 刺伤 cì shāng

punitive damages 惩罚性赔偿金 chéngfáxìng péichángjīn

put on notice 通知 tōngzhī, 警告 jǐnggào

qualified immunity 有条件豁免 yǒu tiáojiàn huòmiǎn

quash *v* 撤销 chèxiāo, 使无效 shǐ wúxiào

question *v* 诘问 jiéwèn, 询问 xúnwèn

racial profiling 种族貌相 zhǒngzú màoxiàng

reasonable basis; reasonable ground 合理根据 hélǐ gēnjù, 合理理由 hélǐ lǐyóu

rebuttable *adj* 可反驳的 kě fǎnbó de

rebuttal *n* 反驳 fǎnbó

record of investigation 调查记录 diàochá jìlù

re-cross examination 再交叉诘问 zài jiāochā jiéwèn

recusal *n* 回避 huíbì

recuse *v* 回避 huíbì, 要求回避 yāoqiú huíbì

rehabilitate *v* 恢复 huīfù

rehabilitation *n* 恢复 huīfù

remand *v* 案件发回重审 ànjiàn fāhuí chóngshěn, 被告还押候审 bèigào huán yā hòushěn

removal to federal court 移送联邦法院 yísòng liánbāng fǎyuàn

repeal *n/v* 撤销 chèxiāo, 废除 fèichú

represent *v* 代表 dàibiǎo, 代理 dàilǐ

representative *n* 代表 dàibiǎo, 代理人 dàilǐrén

res judicata 已决案件 yǐ jué ànjiàn, 一案不二诉原则 yī àn bù èr sù yuánzé

rescind *v* 撤销 chèxiāo, 解除 jiěchú

rescission *n* 撤销 chèxiāo, 解除 jiěchú

respondent on appeal 被上诉人 bèi shàngsùrén

responsibility *n* 责任 zérèn

responsible *adj* 应负责任的 yīng fùzérèn de

resume *v* 恢复 huīfù

re-trial *n* 重审 chóngshěn

reverse *v* 撤销 chèxiāo

revocation *n* 撤销 chèxiāo

revoke *v* 撤销 chèxiāo

rider *n* 附件 fùjiàn, 附加条款 fùjiā tiáokuǎn

ruling *n* 裁决 cáijué, 决定 juédìng

schizophrenia *n* 精神分裂症 jīngshén fēnlièzhèng

search *n/v* 搜查 sōuchá

self dealing 自利交易 zì lì jiāoyì

serve (*a writ, an indictment, a subpoena*) *v* 送达 sòngdá (令状 lìngzhuàng, 诉状 sùzhuàng, 传票 chuánpiào)

service (*of a writ, an indictment, a subpoena*) *n* 送达 sòngdá (令状 lìngzhuàng, 诉状 sùzhuàng, 传票 chuánpiào)

settlement *n* 解决 jiějué, 清偿 qīngcháng

severance of proceedings 分离诉讼 fēnlí sùsòng

sex *n* 性别 xìngbié

sexual harassment 性骚扰 xìngsāorǎo

sexual intercourse 性交 xìngjiāo

sign *v* 签名 qiānmíng, 署名 shǔmíng

signature *n* 签名 qiānmíng, 署名 shǔmíng

Social Security Administration (SSA) 社会保障署 shèhuì bǎozhàng shǔ (又称社会安全局 *a.k.a.* shèhuì ānquán jú)

Social Security number (SSN) 社会保障号码 shèhuì bǎozhàng hàomǎ (又称社会安全号码 *a.k.a.* shèhuì ānquán hàomǎ)

social worker 社会工作者 shèhuì gōngzuòzhě

spokesman *n* 代言人 dàiyánrén

SSA 见 Social Security Administration

SSN 见 Social Security number

stab wound 刺伤 cì shāng

stalking *n* 跟踪罪 gēnzōngzuì

state trooper 州警 zhōujǐng

statement *n* 陈述 chénshù

status *n* 法律地位 fǎlǜ dìwèi, 法律身份 fǎlǜ shēnfèn

statute *n* 制定法 zhìdìngfǎ

statute of limitations 诉讼时效法 sùsòng shíxiàofǎ

statutory *adj* 制定法的 zhìdìngfǎ de

subject-matter jurisdiction 事项管辖权 shìxiàng guǎnxiáquán, 诉讼标的管辖权 sùsòng biāodì guǎnxiáquán

suborn *v* 教唆 jiàosuō

subornation *n* 教唆罪 jiàosuōzuì

substantial error 实质性错误 shízhìxìng cuòwù

sue *v* 控告 kònggào, 起诉 qǐsù

suicide *n* 自杀 zìshā

suit *n* 诉讼 sùsòng

summary judgment 简易判决 jiǎnyì pànjué

summary proceeding 简易程序 jiǎnyì chéngxù
summation *n* 总结性陈述 zǒngjiéxìng chénshù
summon *v* 传唤 chuánhuàn
summons *n* 传唤 chuánhuàn, 传票 chuánpiào
surprise *n* 意外 yìwài, 惊奇 jīngqí
surrender *n/v* 投案 tóu'àn, 到案 dào'àn, 交回 jiāohuí
surrogate court 遗产法院 yíchǎn fǎyuàn
survivor *n* 生存者 shēngcúnzhě
swear *v* 宣誓 xuānshì
tamper with *v* 篡改 cuàngǎi
tangible *adj* 有形的 yǒuxíng de
term *n* 期间 qījiān, 期限 qīxiàn
territorial jurisdiction 属地管辖权 shǔdì guǎnxiáquán,
    区域管辖权 qūyù guǎnxiáquán
testify *v* 作证 zuòzhèng
testimony *n* 证言 zhèngyán, 证词 zhèngcí
threat *n* 威胁 wēixié
threaten *v* 威胁 wēixié
tort *n* 侵权行为 qīnquán xíngwéi
tortfeasor *n* 侵权行为人 qīnquán xíngwéirén
tortious *adj* 侵权的 qīnquán de
transcript *n* 庭审纪录 tíngshěn jìlù
traumatic *adj* 创伤的 chuāngshāng de
treaty *n* 条约 tiáoyuē
trial *n* 庭审 tíngshěn, 审理 shěnlǐ, 审判 shěnpàn
trial court 初审法院 chūshěn fǎyuàn
trial date 审理日 shěnlǐrì
trial judge 庭审法官 tíngshěn fǎguān
trial lawyer 庭审律师 tíngshěn lùshī
trial procedure 审理程序 shěnlǐ chéngxù
trial record 庭审纪录 tíngshěn jìlù
truancy *n* 旷课 kuàngkè, 逃学 táoxué

trust *n* 信托 xìntuō, 委托 wěituō

trustee *n* 受托人 shòutuōrén

unconstitutional *adj* 违宪的 wéixiàn de

United States Attorney 联邦检察官 liánbāng jiǎncháguān

United States Department of Justice (USDOJ) 美国司法部 měiguó sīfǎbù

unless otherwise agreed 除非另有约定 chúfēi lìngyǒu yuēdìng

USDOJ 见 United States Department of Justice

user *n* 享用 xiǎngyòng, 用户 yònghù

usher *n* 传达员 chuándáyuán

valid *adj* 有效的 yǒuxiào de

value *n* 价值 jiàzhí

verbatim records 逐字纪录 zhúzì jìlù

verdict *n* 裁决 cáijué

victim *n* 受害人 shòuhàirén

voluntarily *adv* 自愿地 zìyuàn de

voluntary *adj* 自愿的 zìyuàn de, 故意的 gùyì de

waive (*a right*) 放弃 (权利) fàngqì (*quánlì*)

waiver *n* 放弃 fàngqì

weapon *n* 武器 wǔqì

will *n* 遗嘱 yízhǔ

willful commission 蓄意作为 xùyì zuòwéi

willfulness *n* 蓄意 xùyì

willingly *adv* 自愿地 zìyuàn de

with prejudice *adv* 影响当事人权利 yǐngxiǎng dāngshìrén quánlì (*a final decision by a judge about a legal matter that prevents further pursuit of the same matter in any court* / 指当事人不可再诉)

withdraw *v* 撤回 chèhuí

without prejudice *adv* 不影响当事人权利 bùyǐngxiǎng
   dāngshìrén quánlì (*a claim, lawsuit, or proceeding
   has been brought to a temporary end but no legal
   rights have been determined, waived, or lost by the
   result* / 指当事人可以再诉)
witness *n* 证人 zhèngrén; *v* 目击 mùjī, 见证 jiànzhèng
work-related injury 工伤 gōngshāng
wound *n* 伤口 shāngkǒu
written answer 书面回答 shūmiàn huídá
written statement 书面陈述 shūmiàn chénshù
wrongful death 过失致死 guòshī zhìsǐ

General and Procedural Terms

Commercial Law
商法词汇

Commercial law deals with contractual and business relationships, finance, banking, investments, insurance, and rules governing the sale of goods and services to consumers.

401(k) Plan 401(k) 退休计划 sì ling yī (k) tuìxiū jìhuà
above par 超面值 chāo miànzhí
accelerated depreciation 加速折旧法 jiāsù zhéjiùfǎ
acceptance *n* 承兑 chéngduì, 接受 jiēshòu
account *n* 账户 zhànghù
account verification 账户核查 zhànghù héchá
accountant *n* 会计师 kuàijìshī
accounting *n* 会计 kuàijì
accounts payable 应付帐款 yīngfù zhàngkuǎn
accounts receivable 应收帐款 yīngshōu zhàngkuǎn
accrual basis 权责发生制 quánzé fāshēngzhì, 应计制 yīngjìzhì
accrue *v* 产生 chǎnshēng, 积累 jīlěi
accrued interest 应计利息 yīngjì lìxī
accurate *adj* 准确的 zhǔnquè de
acquisition *n* 取得 qǔdé, 收购 shōugòu
ad valorem 从价 cóngjià
ad valorem duty 从价税 cóngjiàshuì
advertising; advertisement; ads *n* 广告 guǎnggào
advising bank 通知银行 tōngzhī yínháng
affiliate *n* 附属公司 fùshǔ gōngsī
after-tax return 税后回报率 shuìhòu huíbàolù

agency *n* 代理 dàilǐ

agent *n* 代理人 dàilǐrén

aggressive growth fund 进取型增长基金 jìnqǔxíng zēngzhǎng jījīn

agreement *n* 合同 hétong, 协定 xiédìng, 协议 xiéyì

agreement for sale and purchase 买卖合同 mǎimài hétong

agreement to discharge a contract 解约协议 jiěyuē xiéyì

amortization *n* 摊销 tānxiāo

analyst report 分析报告 fēnxī bàogào

annual fee 年费 niánfèi

annual percentage rate (APR) 年利率 niánlìlǜ

annual percentage yield (APY) 年收益率 niánshōuyìlǜ

antitrust law 反托拉斯法 fǎn tuōlāsī fǎ

appreciation in value 升值 shēngzhí

APR 见 annual percentage rate

APY 见 annual percentage yield

arbitrage *n* 套汇 tàohuì

arbitration *n* 仲裁 zhòngcái

arrears *n* 欠款 qiànkuǎn, 拖欠 tuōqiàn

articles of association 公司章程 gōngsī zhāngchéng

assess *v* 评估 pínggū

assessment *n* 估价 gūjià, 估定税额 gūdìng shuì'é

assessor *n* 评估员 pínggūyuán

asset *n* 资产 zīchǎn

assign *v* 转让 zhuǎnràng

assignee *n* 受让人 shòuràngrén

assignment *n* 转让 zhuǎnràng

assignor *n* 出让人 chūràngrén

at sight 见票即付 jiàn piào jí fù

ATM 见 automated teller machine

attempt to evade tax 企图逃税 qǐtú táoshuì

auction *n/v* 拍卖 pāimài

audit *n/v* 审计 shěnjì, 查账 cházhàng

audit opinion 审计意见 shěnjì yìjiàn

auditor *n* 审计员 shěnjìyuán, 查账员 cházhàngyuán

automated teller machine (ATM) 自动提款机 zìdòng tíkuǎnjī

average daily balance 日平均余额 rì píngjūn yú'é

backup withholding 后备性预扣税 hòubèixìng yù kòushuì

bad debt 坏账 huàizhàng

balance *n* 结存 jiécún, 结余 jiéyú

balance sheet 资产负债表 zīchǎn fùzhàibiǎo

balloon payment 气球式偿还 qìqiúshì chánghuán

bank *n* 银行 yínháng

bank account 银行账户 yínháng zhànghù

bank check 本票 běnpiào

Bank Secrecy Act (BSA) 银行保密法 yínháng bǎomìfǎ

bank statement 银行报表 yínháng bàobiǎo, 月结单 yuèjiédān

bankrupt *adj* 破产的 pòchǎn de; *n* 破产人 pòchǎnrén; *v* 破产 pòchǎn

bankruptcy *n* 破产 pòchǎn

Bankruptcy Code 破产法 pòchǎnfǎ

bankruptcy court 破产法院 pòchǎn fǎyuàn

bear market 熊市 xióngshì

bearer *adj* 不记名 bùjìmíng; *n* 来人 láirén, 持票人 chípiàorén

bearer check 来人支票 láirén zhīpiào

beneficiary *n* 受益人 shòuyìrén

benefit *n* 福利 fúlì

benefits manager 福利经理 fúlì jīnglǐ

bilateral contract 双边合同 shuāngbiān hétong

bill *n* 账单 zhàngdān; *v* 开账单 kāi zhàngdān

Commercial Law

bill of exchange 汇票 huìpiào
bill of lading (B/L) 提货单 tíhuòdān
billing cycle 结账周期 jiézhàng zhōuqī
billing error 账单错误 zhàngdān cuòwù
billing rights 帐单质疑权 zhàngdān zhìyíquán
black market 黑市 hēishì
blue law 蓝法 lánfǎ
board of directors 董事会 dǒngshìhuì
bona fide 善意的 shànyì de
bond *n* 债券 zhàiquàn
bonus *n* 奖金 jiǎngjīn, 红利 hónglì
book value 账面价值 zhàngmiàn jiàzhí
borrow *v* 借入 jièrù
borrower *n* 借款人 jièkuǎnrén, 借方 jièfāng
bounce a check *v* 退回 (支票) tuìhuí zhīpiào
bounced check 跳票 tiàopiào, 退票 tuìpiào
brand name 商标名称 shāngbiāo míngchēng, 名牌
      míngpái
breach of contract 违约 wéiyuē
breach of warranty 违反保用条款 wéifǎn bǎoyòng
      tiáokuǎn
bribery *n* 贿赂 huìlù
broke *adj* 破产的 pòchǎn de
broker *n* 经纪人 jīngjìrén
BSA 见 Bank Secrecy Act
bubble company 泡沫公司 pàomò gōngsī
business *n* 商业 shāngyè, 企业 qǐyè, 生意 shēngyì
business contract 商业合同 shāngyè hétong
business days 营业日 yíngyèrì
business expenses 营业费用 yíngyè fèiyòng
business hours 营业时间 yíngyè shíjiān
business license 营业执照 yíngyè zhízhào

business registration 企业注册 qǐyè zhùcè

business secret 商业秘密 shāngyè mìmì

business torts 商业侵权行为 shāngyè qīnquán xíngwéi

business volume 营业额 yíngyè'é

businessman *n* 商人 shāngrén

buyer *n* 买方 mǎifāng

buy-sell agreement 买卖协议 mǎimài xiéyì

bylaws *n* 公司章程 gōngsī zhāngchéng

calendar quarter 日历季度 rìlì jìdù

calendar year 日历年度 rìlì niándù

cancellation clause 撤销条款 chèxiāo tiáokuǎn

cancellation of debt 取消债务 qǔxiāo zhàiwù

cancelled check 注销支票 zhùxiāo zhīpiào

capital *n* 资本 zīběn

capital assets 固定资产 gùdìng zīchǎn

capital expenditure 资本支出 zīběn zhīchū

capital gain or loss 资本损益 zīběn sǔnyì

capitalize *v* 资本化 zīběnhuà

capitalized interest 化作本金的利息 huàzuò běnjīn
de lìxī

cargo *n* 货物 huòwù

carrier *n* 承运人 chéngyùnrén

carry over 结转 jiézhuǎn

cash *n* 现金 xiànjīn; *v* 兑现 duìxiàn

cash advance 预提现金 yùtí xiànjīn, 现金垫款 xiànjīn
diànkuǎn

cash cow 金牛 jīnniú

cash crunch 资金短缺 zījīn duǎnquē

cash flow 现金流动 xiànjīn liúdòng, 现金流量 xiànjīn
liúliàng

cash market 现货市场 xiànhuò shìchǎng

cash settlement 现金结算 xiànjīn jiésuàn

Commercial Law

cashier's check 本票 běnpiào

caveat emptor 购者当心 gòuzhě dāngxīn

CCCS 见 Consumer Credit Counseling Service

CD 见 certificate of deposit

central bank 中央银行 zhōngyāng yínháng

CEO 见 chief executive officer

certificate *n* 证书 zhèngshū

certificate of deposit (CD) 定期存单 dìngqī cúndān

certified check 保付支票 bǎofù zhīpiào

certified public accountant (CPA) 注册会计师 zhùcè kuàijìshī

CFR/CF (cost and freight) 成本加运费 chéngběn jiā yùnfèi

chairman *n* 董事会主席 dǒngshìhuì zhǔxí, 董事长 dǒngshìzhǎng

chamber of commerce 商会 shānghuì

Chapter 7 bankruptcy 第七章破产 dì-qī zhāng pòchǎn

Chapter 13 bankruptcy 第十三章破产 dì-shísān zhāng pòchǎn

charge *n* 费用 fèiyòng; *v* 收费 shōufèi, 记账 jìzhàng

chartered *adj* 特许的 tèxǔ de

chartered financial consultant (ChFC) 特许财务咨询人 tèxǔ cáiwù zīxúnrén

check *n* 支票 zhīpiào

checking account 支票账户 zhīpiào zhànghù

chief executive officer (CEO) 首席执行官 shǒuxí zhíxíngguān

CIF (cost, insurance and freight) 成本、保险费加运费 chéngběn bǎoxiǎnfèi jiā yùnfèi

CIP (carriage and insurance paid) 运费加保险费 yùnfèi jiā bǎoxiǎnfèi

client *n* 客户 kèhù

collateral *n* 担保品 dānbǎopǐn

collect *adj* 对方付费 (电话) duìfāng fùfèi (*diànhuà*);
 v 收取 shōuqǔ, 领取 lǐngqǔ

collecting bank 代收行 dàishōuháng

collection agency 催收公司 cuīshōu gōngsī, 讨债公司
 tǎozhài gōngsī

commerce *n* 商业 shāngyè

commercial bank 商业银行 shāngyè yínháng

commercial dispute 商业纠纷 shāngyè jiūfēn

commercial law 商业法 shāngyèfǎ, 商法 shāngfǎ

commercial litigation 商业诉讼 shāngyè sùsòng

commission *n* 佣金 yòngjīn

commodity *n* 初级商品 chūjí shāngpǐn

commodity exchange 商品交易所 shāngpǐn jiāoyìsuǒ

company *n* 公司 gōngsī

company law 公司法 gōngsīfǎ

company report 公司报告 gōngsī bàogào

compensation *n* 赔偿 péicháng

competition *n* 竞争 jìngzhēng

competitor *n* 竞争者 jìngzhēngzhě

compliance *n* 遵守 zūnshǒu

compound interest 复利 fùlì, 利滚利 lì gǔn lì

concession *n* 特许 tèxǔ, 特许权 tèxǔquán

conclusion of contract 订立合同 dìnglì hétong

conditional assignment 有条件转让 yǒutiáojiàn
 zhuǎnràng

conditional endorsement 有条件背书 yǒutiáojiàn bèishū

confirming bank 保兑银行 bǎoduì yínháng

consideration *n* 对价 tèxǔ, 代价 dàijià

consignee *n* 收货人 shōuhuòrén, 承销人 chéngxiāorén

consignment *n* 托运 tuōyùn

consolidated financial statement 合并财务报表 hébìng cáiwù bàobiǎo

consumer *n* 消费者 xiāofèizhě

consumer credit 消费信用 xiāofèi xìnyòng

Consumer Credit Counseling Service (CCCS) 消费信用咨询处 xiāofèi xìnyòng zīxúnchù

consumer debts 消费债务 xiāofèi zhàiwù

consumer goods 消费品 xiāofèipǐn

Consumer Leasing Act 消费者租赁法 xiāofèizhě zūlìnfǎ

consumer price index 消费物价指数 xiāofèi wùjià zhǐshù

Consumer Protection Act 消费者保护法 xiāofèizhě bǎohùfǎ

consumer reporting company 消费者信用报告公司 xiāofèizhě xìnyòng bàogào gōngsī

consumer rights 消费者权益 xiāofèizhě quányì

contract *n* 合同 hétong

contract law 合同法 hétongfǎ

contract of adhesion 格式合同 géshì hétong, 附意合同 fùyì hétong

contract of guarantee 担保合同 dānbǎo hétong

contract of indemnity 赔偿合同 péicháng hétong

contract of sale 销售合同 xiāoshòu hétong

contracting party 订约方 dìngyuēfāng

contractor *n* 承包人 chéngbāorén, 定约人 dìngyuērén

copyright *n* 版权 bǎnquán, 著作权 zhùzuòquán

corner the market 垄断市场 lǒngduàn shìchǎng

corporation *n* 公司 gōngsī

cosigner *n* 共同签字人 gòngtóng qiānzìrén

counterclaim *n* 反诉 fǎnsù, 反索赔 fǎn suǒpéi

counterfeit *adj* 假造的 jiǎzào de; *n* 伪造 wěizào

counteroffer *n* 反要约 fǎn yāoyuē

CPA 见 certified public accountant

CPT (carriage paid to) 运费付至 yùnfèi fù zhì

credit *n* 信用 xìnyòng, 赊欠 shēqiàn, 贷记 dàijì, 贷方 dàifāng, 抵税 dǐshuì, 抵扣额 dǐkòu'é

credit bureau 信用报告公司 xìnyòng bàogào gōngsī

credit card 信用卡 xìnyòngkǎ

credit card agreement 信用卡合同 xìnyòngkǎ hétong

credit card company 信用卡公司 xìnyòngkǎ gōngsī

credit counseling organization 信用咨询组织 xìnyòng zīxún zǔzhī

credit counselor 信用咨询人 xìnyòng zīxúnrén

credit history 信用史 xìnyòngshǐ

credit insurance 信用保险 xìnyòng bǎoxiǎn

credit limit 信用限额 xìnyòng xiàn'é

credit line 信贷额度 xìndài édù

credit profile 信用状况 xìnyòng zhuàngkuàng

credit repair 信用修复 xìnyòng xiūfù

credit report 信用报告 xìnyòng bàogào

credit reporting agency 见 credit bureau

credit score 信用分数 xìnyòng fēnshù

credit union 信用社 xìnyòngshè

creditor *n* 债权人 zhàiquánrén

customer service 客户服务 kèhù fúwù, 客服 kèfú

DAF (delivered at frontier) 边境交货 biānjìng jiāohuò

daily balance 日余额 rìyú'é

daily periodic rate 日利率 rìlìlǜ

DDP (delivered duty paid) 完税后交货 wánshuì hòu jiāohuò

DDU (delivered duty unpaid) 完税前交货 wánshuì qián jiāohuò

dealer *n* 交易人 jiāoyìrén

debit *n* 借记 jièjì

debit card 借记卡 jièjìkǎ

debt *n* 债务 zhàiwù
debt collection 讨债 tǎozhài
debt collection agency 讨债公司 tǎozhài gōngsī
debtor *n* 债务人 zhàiwùrén
deceptive *adj* 欺骗 qīpiàn
deduction 见 tax deduction
default *n/v* 违约 wéiyuē, 拖欠 tuōqiàn
defraud *v* 欺诈 qīzhà
delayed *adj* 拖延的 tuōyán de
delinquency *n* 拖欠 tuōqiàn
delinquent *adj* 拖欠 tuōqiàn
delivery *n* 交付 jiāofù, 交货 jiāohuò
deposit *n* 押金 yājīn, 定金 dìngjīn; *n/v* 存款 cúnkuǎn
depreciable property 应计折旧财产 yīngjì zhéjiù cáichǎn
depreciation *n* 折旧 zhéjiù
DEQ (delivered ex quay) 目的港码头交货 mùdì gǎng mǎtóu jiāohuò
derivative *n* 衍生证券 yǎnshēng zhèngquàn
DES (delivered ex ship) 目的港船上交货 mùdì gǎng chuánshàng jiāohuò
director *n* 董事 dǒngshì
discharge *n/v* 解除 jiěchú
discharge in bankruptcy 已解除债务的破产人 yǐ jiěchú zhàiwù de pòchǎnrén
discharge of contract 解除合同 jiěchú hétong
discharge of debt 解除债务 jiěchú zhàiwù
disclosure *n* 公布 gōngbù, 披露 pīlù
discount *n/v* 折扣 zhékòu, 贴现 tiēxiàn
discount rate 折扣率 zhékòulǜ, 贴现率 tiēxiànlǜ
distressed debt 廉价债务 liánjià zhàiwù
distressed price 廉价 liánjià, 贱卖 jiànmài
distributorship *n* 经销权 jīngxiāoquán

diversify *v* 多样化 duōyànghuà
dividend *n* 股利 gǔlì, 股息 gǔxī, 红利 hónglì
dot-com company 达康公司 dákāng gōngsī
double billing 重复计费 chóngfù jìfèi
double counting 重复计算 chóngfù jìsuàn
draft *n* 汇票 huìpiào
draw *v* 提款 tíkuǎn
drawee *n* 受票人 shòupiàorén
drawer *n* 出票人 chūpiàorén
due date 到期日 dàoqīrì
due diligence 尽职 jìnzhí, 尽责 jìnzé
duties *n* 关税 guānshuì
early withdrawal penalty 到期前支取罚金 dàoqī qián zhīqǔ fájīn
e-banking *n* 电子银行 diànzǐ yínháng
e-business *n* 电子商务 diànzǐ shāngwù
e-commerce *n* 电子商业 diànzǐ shāngyè
EFT 见 electronic fund transfer
electronic fund transfer (EFT) 电子资金转账 diànzǐ zījīn zhuǎnzhàng
Electronic Funds Transfer Act 电子资金转帐法 diànzǐ zījīn zhuǎnzhàng fǎ
e-mail *n* 电子邮件 diànzǐ yóujiàn
embezzlement *n* 侵吞 qīntūn, 贪污 tānwū
employment tax 雇用税 gùyòngshuì
endorse *v* 背书 bèishū
endorsee *n* 被背书人 bèi bèishūrén
endorsement *n* 背书 bèishū
endorser *n* 背书人 bèishūrén
enterprise *n* 企业 qǐyè
Equal Credit Opportunity Act (ECOA) 平等信用机会法 píngděng xìnyòng jīhuì fǎ

equity *n* 权益 quányì, 股本 gǔběn, 资产净值 zīchǎn
  jìngzhí
estimated tax 估计税额 gūjì shuì'é
evasion *n* 逃避 táobì
exchange rate 汇率 huìlǜ
excise tax 消费税 xiāofèishuì
exempt assets 豁免资产 huòmiǎn zīchǎn
expense account 开支账户 kāizhī zhànghù
export *n/v* 出口 chūkǒu
exporter *n* 出口商 chūkǒushāng
EXW (ex works) 工厂交货 gōngchǎng jiāohuò
Fair Credit Billing Act (FCBA) 公平信用结账法
  gōngpíng xìnyòng jiézhàng fǎ
Fair Credit Reporting Act (FCRA) 公平信用报告法
  gōngpíng xìnyòng bàogào fǎ
Fair Debt Collection Practices Act (FDCPA)
  公平债务催收作业法 gōngpíng zhàiwù cuīshōu
  zuòyè fǎ
fair market value (FMV) 公平市价 gōngpíng shìjià
false advertising 虚假广告 xūjiǎ guǎnggào
falsification *n* 弄虚作假 nòngxūzuòjiǎ
FAS (free alongside ship) 船边交货 chuánbiān jiāohuò
FCA (free carrier) 货交承运人 huò jiāo chéngyùnrén
FDIC 见 Federal Deposit Insurance Corporation
Federal Deposit Insurance Corporation (FDIC)
  联邦储蓄保险公司 liánbāng chǔxù bǎoxiǎn gōngsī
Federal Reserve Bank (FRB) 联邦储备银行 liánbāng
  chǔbèi yínháng
federal tax 联邦税 liánbāngshuì
Federal Trade Commission (FTC) 联邦贸易委员会
  liánbāng màoyì wěiyuánhuì
fee *n* 费用 fèiyòng, 收费 shōufèi

finance *n* 金融 jīnróng, 财务 cáiwù; *v* 筹资 chóuzī, 理财 lǐcái

finance charge 金融费用 jīnróng fèiyòng

financial advisor 理财顾问 lǐcái gùwèn

financial institution 金融机构 jīnróng jīgòu

financial investigator 财务调查员 cáiwù diàocháyuán

financial obligation 财务义务 cáiwù yìwù, 债务 zhàiwù

financial statement 财务报表 cáiwù bàobiǎo

financial transaction 财务交易 cáiwù jiāoyì

fine *n/v* 罚金 fájīn

firm *n* 公司 gōngsī

fiscal year 财政年度 cáizhèng niándù, 会计年度 kuàijì niándù

flat rate 统一费率 tǒngyī fèilù

flexible spending account (FSA) 弹性开支账户 tánxìng kāizhī zhànghù

float (*loan, bond, etc.*) *v* 发行 (公债) fāxíng (*gōngzhài*), 筹募 (贷款) chóumù (*dàikuǎn*)

FOB (free on board) 装运港船上交货 zhuāngyùn gǎng chuánshàng jiāohuò

form 表 biǎo

Form W-2 W-2表 (工资和扣税表) w-èr biǎo (*gōngzī hé kòushuì biǎo*)

Form W-4 W-4表 (预扣税减免表) w-sì biǎo (*yù kòushuì jiǎnmiǎn biǎo*)

Fortune 500 财富500强 cáifù wǔbǎi qiáng

franchise *n* 特许权 tèxǔquán, 专卖权 zhuānmàiquán, 经销权 jīngxiāoquán

franchisee *n* 加盟商 jiāméngshāng

franchisor *n* 特许商 tèxǔshāng

fraud *n* 欺诈 qīzhà

fraudulent *adj* 欺诈的 qīzhà de

fraudulent claim 欺诈性索赔 qīzhàxìng suǒpéi

fraudulent conveyance 欺诈性财产转让 qīzhàxìng cáichǎn zhuǎnràng

free of charge 免费 miǎnfèi

freeze *v* 冻结 dòngjié

freight *n* 运费 yùnfèi

fringe benefit 附加福利 fùjiā fúlì

FTC 见 Federal Trade Commission

fund *v* 提供资金 tígōng zījīn

funding *n* 提供资金 tígōng zījīn

funds *n* 资金 zījīn

General Anti-Avoidance Rule (GAAR)
一般反避税规则 yībān fǎn bìshuì guīzé

General Fraud Program 一般欺诈侦调计划 yībān qīzhà zhēndiào jìhuà

general partner 普通合伙人 pǔtōng héhuǒrén

golden parachute 金降落伞 jīn jiàngluòsǎn

good faith 诚信 chéngxìn, 善意 shànyì, 诚意 chéngyì

goods *n* 货物 huòwù

grace period 宽限期 kuānxiànqī, 免息期 miǎnxīqī

grievance *n* 投诉 tóusù

gross dividends 股利总额 gǔlì zǒng'é

gross income 毛所得 máo suǒdé

gross sales 销货总额 xiāohuò zǒng'é

half-year report 半年报告 bànnián bàogào

hedge fund 对冲基金 duìchōng jījīn

high-risk investment 高风险投资 gāo fēngxiǎn tóuzī

historical financial statement 往期财务报表 wǎngqī cáiwù bàobiǎo

home office 家庭办公室 jiātíng bàngōngshì

home-based business 家庭公司 jiātíng gōngsī

hostile takeover 恶意收购 èyì shōugòu

house mark 公司标记 gōngsī biāojì
identity theft 盗用身份 dàoyòng shēnfèn
illegal business operations 非法经营 fēifǎ jīngyíng
import *n/v* 进口 jìnkǒu
importer *n* 进口商 jìnkǒushāng
in kind 以实物 yǐ shíwù, 以物代款 yǐ wù dài kuǎn
income *n* 所得 suǒdé, 收入 shōurù
incorporate *v* 组成公司 zǔchéng gōngsī
incur *v* 招致 zhāozhì, 发生 fāshēng
indemnification *n* 赔偿 péicháng
indemnify *v* 赔偿 péicháng
independent contractor 独立承包商 dúlì
        chéngbāoshāng
individual retirement account (IRA) 个人退休金账户
        gèrén tuìxiūjīn zhànghù
initial public offering (IPO) 首次公开发行 shǒucì
        gōngkāi fāxíng
insider trading 内线交易 nèixiàn jiāoyì, 局内人交易
        júnèirén jiāoyì
insolvency *n* 破产 pòchǎn
installment *n* 分期付款 fēnqī fùkuǎn
instrument *n* 文书 wénshū
insurance *n* 保险 bǎoxiǎn
insurance premium 保险费 bǎoxiǎnfèi
insured *n* 被保险人 bèi bǎoxiǎnrén
intangible assets 无形资产 wúxíng zīchǎn
intellectual property 知识产权 zhīshí chǎnquán,
        智慧产权 zhìhuì chǎnquán
interest *n* 利息 lìxī
interest expense 利息费用 lìxī fèiyòng
interest rate 利率 lìlǜ

Internal Revenue Code (IRC) 国内税收法 guónèi shuìshōu fǎ

Internal Revenue Service (IRS) 国内税收署 guónèi shuìshōu shǔ (又译国税局 *a.k.a.* guóshuìjú)

international money order 国际汇票 guójì huìpiào

inventory *n* 库存 kùcún

investment *n* 投资 tóuzī

investment account 投资账户 tóuzī zhànghù

investment committee 投资委员会 tóuzī wěiyuánhuì

investment company 投资公司 tóuzī gōngsī

investment counselor 投资顾问 tóuzī gùwèn

investment strategy 投资策略 tóuzī cèluè

investment vehicle 投资工具 tóuzī gōngjù

investor *n* 投资人 tóuzīrén

invoice *n* 发票 fāpiào

IPO 见 initial public offering

IRA 见 individual retirement account

issuing bank 开证行 kāizhènghángú, 发卡行 fākǎháng

joint account 联名账户 liánmíng zhànghù

joint venture 合资企业 hézī qǐyè, 合营企业 héyíng qǐyè

kickback *n* 回扣 huíkòu

know your client (KYC) 了解客户 liǎojiě kèhù

KYC 见 know your client

late charge 逾期费用 yúqī fèiyòng

late payment 逾期付款 yúqī fùkuǎn

lease *n* 租赁 zūlìn, 租约 zūyuē; *v* 出租 chūzū, 租得 zūdé

ledger *n* 分类账 fēnlèizhàng

legal person 法人 fǎrén

legal tender 法定货币 fǎdìng huòbì

lend *v* 借出 jièchū

lender *n* 贷方 dàifāng, 贷款人 dàikuǎnrén

let the buyer beware 购者当心 gòuzhě dāngxīn

letter of credit 信用证 xìnyòngzhèng
letter ruling 信件裁决 xìnjiàn cáijué
liability *n* 负债 fùzhài, 责任 zérèn
liability insurance 责任保险 zérèn bǎoxiǎn
liable *adj* 有责任的 yǒu zérèn de, 应纳税的 yīng nàshuì de
LIBOR 见 London Interbank Offered Rate
license *n* 牌照 páizhào, 许可证 xǔkězhèng
lien *n* 留置权 liúzhìquán
lien holder 留置权持有人 liúzhìquán chíyǒurén
life insurance 人寿保险 rénshòu bǎoxiǎn
limited liability 有限责任 yǒuxiàn zérèn
limited liability company (LLC) 有限责任公司
     yǒuxiàn zérèn gōngsī
limited partner 有限责任合伙人 yǒuxiàn zérèn héhuǒrén
liquid asset 流动资产 liúdòng zīchǎn
liquidation *n* 清算 qīngsuàn, 清偿 qīngcháng, 变现
     biànxiàn
liquidity *n* 流动性 liúdòngxìng
listed company 上市公司 shàngshì gōngsī
LLC 见 limited liability company
loan *n* 贷款 dàikuǎn
loan consolidation 贷款合并 dàikuǎn hébìng
loan officer 信贷员 xìndàiyuán
local tax 地方税 dìfāngshuì
London Interbank Offered Rate (LIBOR)
     伦敦银行同业拆放利率 lúndūn yínháng tóngyè
     chāifàng lìlǜ
loss *n* 损失 sǔnshī
lump-sum payment 一笔总付 yībǐ zǒngfù
luxury goods 奢侈品 shēchǐpǐn
mail *n* 信件 xìnjiàn

Mail or Telephone Order Rule 邮购或电话订购规则
yóugòu huò diànhuà dìnggòu guīzé

management *n* 管理 guǎnlǐ, 资方 zīfāng

manager *n* 经理 jīnglǐ

managing director 董事总经理 dǒngshì zǒngjīnglǐ

manufacturer *n* 制造商 zhìzàoshāng

market *n* 市场 shìchǎng

market rate 市场利率 shìchǎng lìlǜ, 市场汇率 shìchǎng huìlǜ

maturity *n* 到期 dàoqī

medical expenses 医药费用 yīyào fèiyòng

Medicare tax 医疗保健税 yīliáo bǎojiàn shuì

meeting of the minds 合意 héyì, 意见一致 yìjiàn yīzhì

merchandise *n* 商品 shāngpǐn

merchant *n* 商人 shāngrén

merchant bank 商人银行 shāngrén yínháng

merchantable *adj* 适合销售的 shìhé xiāoshòu de

mergers and acquisitions (M&A) 并购 bìnggòu

minimum payment due 最低应付金额 zuìdī yīngfù jīn'é

monetary compensation 金钱赔偿 jīnqián péicháng

money laundering 洗钱 xǐqián

money market 货币市场 huòbì shìchǎng

money market account 货币市场账户 huòbì shìchǎng zhànghù

money order 汇票 huìpiào

money transfer 转账 zhuǎnzhàng

moneylender 放债人 fàngzhài rén

municipal bond 市政债券 shìzhèng zhàiquàn

mutual fund 共同基金 gòngtóng jījīn

National Commission on Consumer Finance
全美消费金融委员会 quánměi xiāofèi jīnróng wěiyuánhuì

negotiable instrument 可转让票据 kě zhuǎnràng piàojù,
　　流通票据 liútōng piàojù
net *adj* 净的 jìng de; *n* 净额 jìng'é; *v* 净得 jìngdé
net earnings 净收益 jìngshōuyì
net profit 净利 jìnglì
net sales 销货净额 xiāohuò jìng'é
net worth 净值 jìngzhí
night deposit 夜间存款 yèjiān cúnkuǎn
no-competition clause 不竞争条款 bùjìngzhēng tiáokuǎn
non-compliance 违约行为 wéiyuē xíngwéi, 不遵守
　　bùzūnshǒu, 不合规 bùhéguī
nonprofit *adj* 非营利的 fēi yínglì de
nonwage payment 非工资性支付 fēi gōngzī xìng zhīfù
note *n* 票据 piàojù
offer *n* 要约 yāoyuē, 发盘 fāpán
offeree *n* 被要约人 bèi yāoyuērén
offering circular 发行说明书 fāxíng shuōmíngshū
offeror *n* 要约人 yāoyuērén
offshoring *n* 离岸外包 lí'àn wàibāo
online banking 网上银行业务 wǎngshàng yínháng yèwù
oral contract 口头合同 kǒutóu hétong
ordinary dividends 普通红利 pǔtōng hónglì
outsourcing *n* 外包 wàibāo
outstanding balance 未清余额 wèiqīng yú'é
overbilling *n* 超额计费 chāo'é jìfèi
overdraft *n* 透支 tòuzhī
overdraft checking account 透支保护支票账户 tòuzhī
　　bǎohù zhīpiào zhànghù
overdraw *v* 透支 tòuzhī
overlimit charge 超限费 chāo xiàn fèi
owe *v* 欠 qiàn
ownership *n* 所有权 suǒyǒuquán

par value 票面价值 piàomiàn jiàzhí, 面值 miànzhí

parent company 母公司 mǔgōngsī

partner *n* 合伙人 héhuǒrén

partnership *n* 合伙 héhuǒ

partnership business 合伙企业 héhuǒ qǐyè, 合伙生意 héhuǒ shēngyì

passive activity 被动经营 bèidòng jīngyíng

password *n* 密码 mìmǎ

patent *n* 专利 zhuānlì

pay by check 支票支付 zhīpiào zhīfù

pay in cash 现金支付 xiànjīn zhīfù

pay off 付清 fùqīng

payable *adj* 应付 yīngfù

payable at sight 见票即付 jiàn piào jí fù

paycheck *n* 工资支票 gōngzī zhīpiào

payee *n* 收款人 shōukuǎnrén

payment *n* 付款 fùkuǎn, 支付 zhīfù

payment due date 付款到期日 fùkuǎn dàoqī rì

payor (payer) *n* 付款人 fùkuǎnrén

PayPal 贝宝 bèibǎo

payroll *n* 员工工资表 yuángōng gōngzī biǎo

payroll tax 雇用税 gùyòngshuì

penalty *n* 罚款 fákuǎn

pension *n* 养老金 yǎnglǎojīn

pension fund 养老基金 yǎnglǎo jījīn

permit *n* 许可证 xǔkězhèng

personal check 个人支票 gèrén zhīpiào

personal identification number (PIN) 个人识别号 gèrén shíbié hào

phishing *n* 网络钓鱼 wǎngluò diàoyú (*scam using e-mail for information or identity theft* / 利用电子邮件进行的诈骗行为)

PIN 见 personal identification number

pirated copyright goods 盗版商品 dàobǎn shāngpǐn

poison pill 毒丸 dúwán (*tactic by a company to avoid a hostile takeover* / 一种反兼并策略)

preferred *adj* 优先的 yōuxiān de

premature withdrawal 期满前提款 qīmǎn qián tíkuǎn

prepackaged *adj* 预先包装的 yùxiān bāozhuāng de

president *n* 总裁 zǒngcái

previous balance 上期结余 shàngqī jiéyú

price *n* 价格 jiàgé, 价款 jiàkuǎn

price catalog 价目表 jiàmùbiǎo

price gouging 哄抬物价 hōngtái wùjià

prime rate 最优惠利率 zuì yōuhuì lìlǜ

principal *n* 本金 běnjīn, 委托人 wěituōrén

privacy policy 隐私政策 yǐnsī zhèngcè

private company 非上市公司 fēi shàngshì gōngsī

pro forma 预计的 yùjì de, 假定的 jiǎdìng de

pro rata 按比例 ànbǐlì

proceeds *n* 收益 shōuyì

produce *n* 农产品 nóngchǎnpǐn; *v* 生产 shēngchǎn

product *n* 产品 chǎnpǐn

product liability 产品责任 chǎnpǐn zérèn

product mark 产品标记 chǎnpǐn biāojì

production *n* 生产 shēngchǎn, 产量 chǎnliàng

productivity *n* 生产力 shēngchǎnlì, 生产率 shēngchǎnlǜ

profit *n* 利润 lìrùn

profit sharing 利润分成 lìrùn fēnchéng

profit tax 利润税 lìrùnshuì

progressive tax 累进税 lěijìnshuì

promissory note 本票 běnpiào, 期票 qīpiào

prorate *v* 按比例摊派 ànbǐlì tānpài

prospectus *n* 计划书 jìhuàshū, 说明书 shuōmíngshū

Commercial Law

proxy statement 代表权申明书 dàibiǎoquán
    shēnmíngshū, 股东委托书 gǔdōng wěituōshū
public company 上市公司 shàngshì gōngsī
publicity *n* 宣传 xuānchuán
publicly traded company 见 public company
purchase *n/v* 购买 gòumǎi
purchase price 购买价 gòumǎijià
rate of return 回报率 huíbàolǜ
raw material 原料 yuánliào
realized loss or profit 已实现损益 yǐ shíxiàn sǔnyì
recall *n/v* 召回 zhàohuí
receipt *n* 收据 shōujù
receivables *n* 应收款 yīngshōu kuǎn
recipient *n* 收受者 shōushòu zhě
recovery *n* 追回 zhuīhuí, 补偿 bǔcháng, 回升 huíshēng
refund *n/v* 退款 tuìkuǎn, 退税 tuìshuì
registration *n* 注册 zhùcè, 登记 dēngjì
reimburse *v* 偿还 chánghuán, 报销 bàoxiāo
reimbursement *n* 偿还 chánghuán, 报销 bàoxiāo
release note 收讫单 shōuqì dān
renewal of contract 续订合同 xùdìng hétong
rental expenses 租金支出 zūjīn zhīchū
repayment *n* 偿还 chánghuán
repayment period 偿还期 chánghuánqī
replenish *v* 补充 bǔchōng
repossess *v* 收回 shōuhuí
restructuring *n* 重组 chóngzǔ
retail *n/v* 零售 língshòu
retire *v* 退休 tuìxiū, 清偿 (债务) qīngcháng (*zhàiwù*)
retirement plan 退休计划 tuìxiū jìhuà
return *n* 税表 shuìbiǎo, 收益 shōuyì, 回报 huíbào;
    n/v 退货 tuìhuò; *v* 申报 shēnbào

return preparer 报税代理人 bàoshuì dàilǐrén

revolving account 循环帐户 xúnhuán zhànghù

Roth IRA 罗斯个人退休金账户 luósī gèrén tuìxiūjīn zhànghù

sale *n* 出售 chūshòu

sale price 售价 shòujià

sales law 销售法 xiāoshòufǎ

sales tax 销售税 xiāoshòushuì

save *v* 节省 jiéshěng, 积蓄 jīxù

savings *n* 储蓄 chǔxù, 存款 cúnkuǎn

savings account 储蓄账户 chǔxù zhànghù

savings bond 储蓄公债 chǔxù gōngzhài

SBA 见 Small Business Administration

scam *n* 诈骗 zhàpiàn

schedule *n* (税表的) 附表 (shuìbiǎo de) fùbiǎo

secured party 被担保方 bèi dānbǎofāng

secured transactions 担保交易 dānbǎo jiāoyì

securitization *n* 证券化 zhèngquànhuà

security *n* 证券 zhèngquàn, 担保物 dānbǎowù

self-employment tax 自雇税 zì gù shuì

seller 卖方 màifāng

sender *n* 发件人 fājiànrén

service contract 服务合同 fúwù hétong

share *n* 股份 gǔfèn

shareholder *n* 股东 gǔdōng

Sherman Antitrust Act 谢尔曼反托拉斯法 xiè'ěrmàn fǎn tuōlāsī fǎ

ship *v* 交运 jiāoyùn, 运送 yùnsòng

shipment *n* 装运 zhuāngyùn

shipping *n* 货运 huòyùn, 运输 yùnshū

short selling; shorting 卖空 màikōng

small business 小企业 xiǎo qǐyè

Commercial Law

Small Business Administration (SBA) 小企业管理署
xiǎo qǐyè guǎnlǐshǔ

small claims 小额索赔 xiǎo'é suǒpéi

Social Security benefits 社会保障金 shèhuì bǎozhàngjīn

Social Security income 社会保障收入 shèhuì bǎozhàng shōurù

Social Security tax 社会保障税 shèhuì bǎozhàngshuì, 社会安全税 shèhuì ānquánshuì

solvent *adj* 有偿债能力的 yǒu chángzhài nénglì de

state tax 州税 zhōushuì

statement *n* 报表 bàobiǎo, 声明 shēngmíng

stock *n* 股票 gǔpiào

stock exchange 证券交易所 zhèngquàn jiāoyìsuǒ

stock market 股市 gǔshì

stop payment 停止付款 tíngzhǐ fùkuǎn

strict products liability 严格产品责任 yángé chǎnpǐn zérèn

subsidiary *n* 子公司 zǐgōngsī

supplier *n* 供应商 gōngyìngshāng

supply *v* 供应 gōngyìng

surcharge *n* 附加税 fùjiāshuì

takeover *n* 接管 jiēguǎn, 收购 shōugòu

tariffs *n* 关税 guānshuì

tax *n* 税 shuì; *v* 征税 zhēngshuì

tax assessment 估定税额 gūdìng shuì'é

tax credit 抵税 dǐshuì, 抵扣额 dǐkòu'é
(直接从应纳税额中扣除 / *direct dollar-for-dollar reduction of an individual's tax liability*)

tax deduction 减税 jiǎnshuì, 减除额 jiǎnchú'é
(从应纳税所得额中扣除 / *subtracted from adjusted gross income when calculating taxable income*)

tax deferred 延迟纳税 yánchí nàshuì

tax exempt 免税的 miǎnshuì de
tax exemption 免税 miǎnshuì
tax law 税法 shuìfǎ
tax liability 应纳税额 yīng nàshuì'é
tax preparer 报税代理人 bàoshuì dàilǐrén
tax rate 税率 shuìlǜ
tax return 纳税申报表 nàshuì shēnbàobiǎo, 报税表
  bàoshuìbiǎo
tax shelter 避税手段 bìshuì shǒuduàn
tax treaty 税务条约 shuìwù tiáoyuē
taxable *adj* 应纳税的 yīng nàshuì de
taxpayer *n* 纳税人 nàshuìrén
TeleTax 税务热线电话 shuìwù rèxiàn diànhuà
teller's check 本票 běnpiào
term life insurance 定期人寿保险 dìngqī rénshòu bǎoxiǎn
termination of contract 合同终止 hétong zhōngzhǐ
thrift institution 储蓄机构 chǔxù jīgòu
time deposit 定期存款 dìngqī cúnkuǎn
tip *n* 小费 xiǎofèi; *v* 给小费 gěi xiǎofèi
trade secret 商业机密 shāngyè jīmì
trader *n* 交易人 jiāoyìrén
trades *n* 交易 jiāoyì, 买卖 mǎimài
trading volume 交易量 jiāoyì liàng
traditional IRA 传统个人退休金帐户 chuántǒng gèrén
  tuìxiūjīn zhànghu
transaction *n* 交易 jiāoyì
transaction fees 交易费 jiāoyì fèi
traveler's check 旅行支票 lǚxíng zhīpiào
treasury bill 长期国库债券 chángqī guókù zhàiquàn
trust fund 信托基金 xìntuō jījīn
Truth in Lending Act (TILA) 诚实借贷法 chéngshí
  jièdài fǎ

Commercial Law

turnaround *n* 扭转 niǔzhuǎn

unauthorized withdrawal 未经许可提取 wèijīng xǔkě tíqǔ

underwriter *n* (证券) 承销人 (*zhèngquàn*) chéngxiāorén, (保险) 承保人 (*bǎoxiǎn*) chéngbǎorén

unfair competition 不公平竞争 bùgōngpíng jìngzhēng

Uniform Commercial Code (UCC) 统一商法典 tǒngyī shāngfǎdiǎn

Uniform Fraudulent Transfers Act (UFTA) 统一反欺诈性转移法 tǒngyī fǎn qīzhàxìng zhuǎnyí fǎ

United States Tax Court 美国税务法院 měiguó shuìwù fǎyuàn

unlawful gains 非法收益 fēifǎ shōuyì

unrealized loss or profit 未实现损益 wèi shíxiàn sǔnyì

value *n* 价值 jiàzhí

value added tax (VAT) 增值税 zēngzhíshuì

VAT 见 value added tax

vending machine 自动销售机 zìdòng xiāoshòujī

vendor *n* 卖方 màifāng, 供应商 gōngyìngshāng

verbal contract 口头合同 kǒutóu hétong

vishing *n* 网络钓语 wǎngluò diàoyǔ (*a VoIP scam to gain access to private personal and financial information from the public for the purpose of financial reward* / 利用网络电话诈骗钱财的不法行为)

voice mail 语音邮件 yǔyīn yóujiàn

void *adj* 无效的 wúxiào de; *v* 使无效 shǐ wúxiào, 废止 fèizhǐ

voluntary compliance 自愿遵守 zìyuàn zūnshǒu

W-2 见 Form W-2

W-4 见 Form W-4

warranty *n* 保用 bǎoyòng, 保用期 bǎoyòngqī

whole life insurance 终生人寿保险 zhōngshēng rénshòu bǎoxiǎn

wholesale *n* 批发 pīfā

winding up 清盘 qīngpán

wire transfer 电汇 diànhuì

wireless *adj* 无线的 wúxiàn de

withdraw *v* 提款 tíkuǎn

withdrawal *n* 提款 tíkuǎn

withholding *n* 预扣所得税 yùkòu suǒdéshuì

worth *n* 值 zhí, 价值 jiàzhí

write off *v* 注销 zhùxiāo

write-off account 冲销帐户 chōngxiāo zhànghù

written contract 书面合同 shūmiàn hétong

written notice 书面通知 shūmiàn tōngzhī

Commercial Law

Criminal Law
刑法词汇

Criminal law, also known as penal law, deals with acts which society treats as punishable offenses. According to an ancient principle, *nulla poena sine lege* ("there is no penalty without a law"), acts are not punishable until a law has been passed making them so. Under provisions against double jeopardy a person who has been acquitted (found innocent) cannot be tried again for the same crime. The accused facing prosecution generally enjoys certain safeguards in mounting his defense under criminal procedure codes, and if convicted (found guilty) will be punished according to the seriousness of the crime, with penalties ranging from fines for misdemeanors (minor offenses) to sentences of imprisonment or even death for felonies (serious offenses). In the United States, criminal matters are governed by both state and federal laws.

5K letter 5k信件 wǔ k xìnjiàn
abduct *v* 诱拐 yòuguǎi, 绑架 bǎngjià, 劫持 jiéchí
abduction *n* 诱拐 yòuguǎi, 绑架 bǎngjià, 劫持 jiéchí
abductor *n* 诱拐者 yòuguǎizhě, 绑架者 bǎngjiàzhě,
    劫持者 jiéchízhě
abstract of judgment 判决书摘要 pànjuéshū zhāiyào
acceptance of responsibility 承担责任 chéngdān zérèn
accessory *n* 从犯 cóngfàn
accessory after the fact 事后从犯 shìhòu cóngfàn
accomplice *n* 共犯 gòngfàn

accused *n* 被告 bèigào, 被检控人 bèi jiǎnkòng rén
accuser *n* 原告 yuángào, 控告人 kònggàorén
acquit *v* 裁定无罪 cáidìng wúzuì
acquittal *n* 无罪裁定 wúzuì cáidìng
acquitted *adj* 被裁定无罪 bèi cáidìng wúzuì
adjusted offense level 调整后的罪行级别 tiáozhěng hòu de zuìxíng jíbié
admission *n* 供认 gòngrèn
adverse witness 敌对证人 díduì zhèngrén
affirmative defense 积极抗辩 jījí kàngbiàn
aggravated *adj* 严重的 yánzhòng de
aggravated felony 有加重情节的重罪 yǒu jiāzhòng qíngjié de zhòngzuì
aggravating circumstances 加重情节 jiāzhòng qíngjié
aiding and abetting 帮助和教唆 bāngzhù hé jiàosuō
alibi *n* 不在犯罪现场的抗辩 bùzài fànzuì xiànchǎng de kàngbiàn
allegation *n* 指控 zhǐkòng, 主张 zhǔzhāng
alleged offense 指控的罪行 zhǐkòng de zuìxíng
allocution *n* 判决前被告自白 pànjué qián bèigào zìbái
alternative sentence 非监禁刑 fēi jiānjìn xíng
amnesty *n* 赦免 shèmiǎn, 大赦 dàshè
armed career criminal 持械职业罪犯 chíxiè zhíyè zuìfàn
arraign *v* 堂讯 tángxùn
arraignment *n* 堂讯 tángxùn
arrest *n/v* 逮捕 dàibǔ
arrest history; arrest record 逮捕记录 dàibǔ jìlù
arrest warrant 逮捕证 dàibǔzhèng
arresting officer 执行逮捕的警员 zhíxíng dàibǔ de jǐngyuán
arson *n* 纵火罪 zònghuǒzuì

assault *n* 攻击 gōngjī, 强奸 qiángjiān, 企图伤害 qǐtú shānghài

assault and battery 攻击和殴打 gōngjī hé ōudǎ

assault with a deadly weapon 使用致命武器攻击 shǐyòng zhìmìng wǔqì gōngjī

attempt *n* 未遂罪 wèisuì zuì, 企图犯罪罪 qǐtú fànzuì zuì; *v* 企图 qǐtú, 图谋 túmóu

attempted murder 谋杀未遂罪 móushā wèisuìzuì, 企图谋杀罪 qǐtú móushāzuì

auto stripping; auto tampering 拆盗破坏汽车罪 chāi dào pòhuài qìchē zuì

bail *n* 保释 bǎoshì, 保释金 bǎoshìjīn, 保释人 bǎoshìrén

bail bondsman 保释担保人 bǎoshì dānbǎorén

bail hearing 保释听证会 bǎoshì tīngzhènghuì

bail package 一揽子保释条件 yīlǎnzi bǎoshì tiáojiàn

Bail Reform Act 保释改革法 bǎoshì gǎigé fǎ

bailiff *n* 法警 fǎjǐng

base offense level 基本罪行级别 jīběn zuìxíng jíbié

battery *n* 殴打 ōudǎ

beyond a reasonable doubt 排除合理怀疑 páichú hélǐ huáiyí

bigamy *n* 重婚 chónghūn, 重婚罪 chónghūnzuì

bill of particulars 书面详细说明 shūmiàn xiángxì shuōmíng

bind over 具结候审 jùjié hòushěn

blackmail *n* 敲诈 qiāozhà, 勒索 lèsuǒ

book *v* 记录在册 jìlù zàicè

BOP 见 Federal Bureau of Prisons

breaking and entering 破门入室罪 pòmén rùshì zuì

bribe *n/v* 行贿 xínghuì, 贿赂 huìlù

bribery *n* 贿赂 huìlù

brothel *n* 妓院 jìyuàn

bug *n* 窃听器 qiètīngqì; *v* 窃听 qiètīng
burden of proof 举证责任 jǔzhèng zérèn
burglar *n* 入室盗窃者 rùshì dàoqiè zhě
burglar's tools 入室行盗工具 rùshì xíngdào gōngjù
burglary *n* 入室盗窃罪 rùshì dàoqièzuì
capital offense 死罪 sǐzuì
capital punishment 死刑 sǐxíng
carrying a firearm 携带枪支 xiédài qiāngzhī
cell *n* 单人囚房 dānrén qiúfáng
challenge a decision 对判决提出异议 duì pànjué tíchū yìyì
charge *n/v* 控告 kònggào
charged *adj* 被告 bèigào
civil collections 民事催收 mínshì cuī shōu
clemency *n* 宽大 kuāndà
co-conspirator *n* 共谋者 gòngmóu zhě
code of criminal procedure 刑事诉讼法 xíngshì sùsòngfǎ
coercion *n* 强制 qiángzhì, 胁迫 xiépò
collateral for bail 保释担保物 bǎoshì dānbǎowù
collection of evidence 取证 qǔzhèng
commission (of crime) *n* 实施 (犯罪) shíshī (fànzuì)
commit (crime) *v* 实施 (犯罪) shíshī (fànzuì)
commitment order 收监令 shōujiān lìng, 押交令 yājiāo lìng
community service 社区服务 shèqū fúwù
complaint (civil) *n* 民事自诉状 mínshì zìsùzhuàng
complaint (criminal) *n* 刑事自诉状 xíngshì zìsùzhuàng
concurrent sentence 合并处刑 hébìng chǔxíng
conditional plea of guilty 有条件认罪 yǒutiáojiàn rènzuì
conditional release 假释 jiǎshì, 有条件释放 yǒutiáojiàn shìfàng
conditions of release 释放条件 shìfàng tiáojiàn

confession *n* 供认 gòngrèn

confine *v* 禁闭 jìnbì, 限制 xiànzhì

confinement *n* 监禁 jiānjìn, 限制 xiànzhì

confiscate *v* 没收 mòshōu, 查抄 cháchāo

consecutive sentences 连续判决 liánxù pànjué

consolidation of proceedings 合并诉讼 hébìng sùsòng

conspiracy *n* 阴谋 yīnmóu, 共谋 gòngmóu

conspirator *n* 阴谋者 yīnmóuzhě, 共谋者 gòngmóuzhě

conspire *v* 共谋 gòngmóu, 密谋 mìmóu

contraband *n* 违禁品 wéijìnpǐn

contributing to the delinquency of a minor
    教唆未成年人犯罪 jiàosuō wèichéngniánrén fànzuì

convict *n* 已决犯 yǐjuéfàn, 囚犯 qiúfàn; *v* 宣判有罪
    xuānpàn yǒuzuì, 定罪 dìngzuì

convicted *adj* 已判罪的 yǐ pànzuì de

conviction *n* 判罪 pànzuì, 定罪 dìngzuì

cooperation agreement 合作协议 hézuò xiéyì

cooperation with the prosecution 与检方合作 yǔ
    jiǎnfāng hézuò

correctional center 教养中心 jiàoyǎng zhōngxīn

corrupt *adj* 贪腐的 tānfǔde; *v* 贪腐 tānfǔ

corruption *n* 贪腐 tānfǔ

count (*of indictment*) *n* (起诉书列举的) 罪项 (qǐsùshū
    lièjǔ de) zuì xiàng

counterfeit *adj* 伪造的 wěizào de, 假冒的 jiǎmào de

counterfeiter *n* 伪造者 wěizàozhě

counterfeiting *n* 伪造货币罪 wěizào huòbì zuì, 伪造罪
    wěizàozuì

crime *n* 犯罪 fànzuì, 罪行 zuìxíng

crime of moral turpitude 道德堕落罪 dàodé duòluò zuì

crime of passion 激情犯罪 jīqíng fànzuì

crime of violence 暴力罪 bàolì zuì

criminal history category 犯罪记录类别 fànzuì jìlù lèibié

criminal negligence 刑事疏忽罪 xíngshì shūhū zuì, 过失罪 guòshī zuì

criminal possession of a weapon 非法拥有武器 fēifǎ yōngyǒu wǔqì

criminal record (*history*) 犯罪记录 fànzuì jìlù

criminal trespass 非法侵入罪 fēifǎ qīnrù zuì

culpable *adj* 有罪的 yǒuzuì de, 应受惩处的 yīngshòu chéngchǔ de

custody (*of person*) *n* 拘禁 jūjìn, 扣押 kòuyā

date rape 约会强奸 yuēhuì qiángjiān

deadly force 致命力 zhìmìng lì

deadly weapon 致命武器 zhìmìng wǔqì

death penalty 死刑 sǐxíng

defense *n* 辩护 biànhù, 辩方 biànfāng

defense attorney 辩护律师 biànhù lǜshī

defense preparation period 辩护准备时间 biànhù zhǔnbèi shíjiān

defraud *v* 诈骗 zhàpiàn

deportation *n* 驱逐出境 qūzhú chūjìng

detective *n* 侦探 zhēntàn

detention *n* 羁押 jīyā

determinate sentence 定期刑 dìngqī xíng

disciplinary proceedings 纪律诉讼 jìlù sùsòng

dismissal of charges 驳回控告 bóhuí kònggào

disorder (*physical or mental*) (身心) 障碍 (shēnxīn) zhàng'ài

disqualification *n* 取消资格 qǔxiāo zīgé

disturbing the peace 扰乱治安 rǎoluàn zhì'ān

double jeopardy 一罪二审 yī zuì èr shěn

dragnet *n* 法网 fǎwǎng, 罗网 luówǎng

drug dealer; drug trafficker 贩毒者 fàndúzhě, 毒贩 dúfàn

drug trafficking offense 贩毒罪 fàndúzuì

duress *n* 胁迫 xiépò

electronic monitoring; electronic surveillance
电子监视 diànzǐ jiānshì

embezzlement *n* 盗用 dàoyòng, 侵吞 qīntūn

enter a plea 表示 biǎoshì

entrapment *n* 警察圈套 jǐngchá quāntào, 官诱民犯 guān yòu mín fàn

escape *n/v* 逃走 táozǒu, 逃脱 táotuō

escapee *n* 逃犯 táofàn

evidentiary hearing 举证听证会 jǔzhèng tīngzhènghuì

excessive bail 过高保释金 guò gāo bǎoshìjīn

exculpatory evidence 开脱证据 kāituō zhèngjù,
免责证据 miǎnzé zhèngjù

exonerate *v* 证明无罪 zhèngmíng wúzuì

expunge *v* 删除 shānchú, 销毁 xiāohuǐ

extenuating circumstances 减轻情节 jiǎnqīng qíngjié

extortion *n* 敲诈 qiāozhà, 勒索 lèsuǒ

eyewitness *n* 目击证人 mùjī zhèngrén

face charges 面临起诉 miànlín qǐsù, 被起诉 bèi qǐsù

false imprisonment 非法拘禁 fēifǎ jūjìn

false pretenses 诈骗罪 zhàpiànzuì

fear *n* 恐惧 kǒngjù, 害怕 hàipà

Federal Bureau of Prisons (BOP) 联邦监狱局 liánbāng jiānyù jú

federal offense 联邦罪 liánbāng zuì

Federal Rules of Evidence 联邦证据规则 liánbāng zhèngjù guīzé

felon *n* 重罪犯 zhòngzuìfàn

felony *n* 重罪 zhòngzuì

felony murder 重大谋杀罪 zhòngdà móushāzuì

Criminal Law

Fifth Amendment right against self-incrimination 第五修正案所赋不自证其罪的权利 dì-wǔ xiūzhèng'àn suǒ fù bù zì zhèng qí zuì de quánlì

fight *n/v* 斗殴 dòu'ōu

final sentence 终审判决 zhōngshěn pànjué

fingerprints *n* 指纹 zhǐwén

firearm *n* 火器 huǒqì, 枪支 qiāngzhī

first degree murder 一级谋杀罪 yījí móushāzuì

first offense 初犯 chūfàn

flee *v* 逃走 táozǒu

flight *n* 逃跑 táopǎo, 畏罪潜逃 wèizuì qiántáo

force *n* 武力 wǔlì, 暴力 bàolì

forfeit bail 没收保释金 mòshōu bǎoshì jīn

forfeiture *n* 没收 mòshōu

forger *n* 伪造者 wěizàozhě

forgery *n* 伪造 wěizào, 伪造罪 wěizàozuì, 伪造品 wěizàopǐn

fraud *n* 欺诈 qīzhà

fraudulent *adj* 欺诈的 qīzhà de

frisk *v* 搜身 sōushēn

fugitive *n* 逃犯 táofàn

gambling *n* 赌博 dǔbó

gang *n* 团伙 tuánhuǒ, 帮派 bāngpài

gang assault 团伙攻击罪 tuánhuǒ gōngjīzuì

gang rape 轮奸 lúnjiān

general intent 一般故意 yībān gùyì

go to trial 受审 shòushěn, 开审 kāishěn

good behavior time 因表现良好而减刑期 yīn biǎoxiàn liánghǎo ér jiǎn xíngqī

grand jury 大陪审团 dà péishěntuán

grand larceny 重大盗窃罪 zhòngdà dàoqièzuì

guilty *adj* 有罪的 yǒuzuì de

gun *n* 手枪 shǒuqiāng

gunman *n* 持枪歹徒 chíqiāng dǎitú, 职业杀手 zhíyè
　　shāshǒu

habitual offender 惯犯 guànfàn

handcuffs *n* 手铐 shǒukào

harassment *n* 骚扰 sāorǎo

harmful *adj* 有损害的 yǒu sǔnhài de, 不利的 bùlì de

hate crime 仇恨犯罪 chóuhèn fànzuì

hazing *n* 欺凌 qīlíng

Hobbs Act 霍布斯法 huòbùsī fǎ

holding cell 法院拘留所 fǎyuàn jūliúsuǒ

home detention 家庭监禁 jiātíng jiānjìn

homicide *n* 他杀 tāshā, 杀人 shārén

hooker *n* 妓女 jìnǚ

hostage *n* 人质 rénzhì

hostage taking 劫持人质 jiéchí rénzhì

house arrest 软禁 ruǎnjìn

hung jury 悬案陪审团 xuán àn péishěntuán

identity theft 盗用身份 dàoyòng shēnfèn

ill-treatment *n* 虐待 nüèdài

impossibility *n* 不可能性 bùkěnéngxìng

imprisonment *n* 监禁 jiānjìn, 徒刑 túxíng

in absentia 缺席 quēxí

inadmissible (*evidence*) *adj* (证据) 不可采信的
　　(zhèngjù) bùkě cǎixìn de

inadmissible (*to the U.S.*) *adj* (人员) 不允许入境的
　　(rényuán) bùyǔnxǔ rùjìng de

incest *n* 乱伦 luànlún

inchoate crime 不完整罪 bùwánzhěng zuì

indecent exposure 猥亵性暴露罪 wěixièxìng bàolùzuì

independent evidence 独立证据 dúlì zhèngjù

indeterminate sentence 不定期刑 bùdìngqī xíng

indictment *n* 刑事起诉 xíngshì qǐsù, 刑事起诉书 xíngshì qǐsùshū

infancy *n* 幼年 yòunián

informant *n* 举报人 jǔbào rén, 告密者 gàomì zhě, 线民 xiànmín

information *n* 公诉书 gōngsùshū

infraction *n* 违规 wéiguī

injured party 受损方 shòusǔnfāng

inmate *n* 监狱囚犯 jiānyù qiúfàn

innocence *n* 无罪 wúzuì, 无辜 wúgū

innocent *adj* 无罪的 wúzuì de, 清白的 qīngbái de

insufficient evidence 证据不足 zhèngjù bùzú

intent *n* 故意 gùyì, 意向 yìxiàng

intentional *adj* 故意的 gùyì de

intercept *v* 窃听 qiètīng, 截取 jiéqǔ

intermittent sentence 断续监禁判决 duànxù jiānjìn pànjué

intoxication *n* 中毒 zhòngdú

　alcohol intoxication 酒精中毒 jiǔjīng zhòngdú

　narcotic intoxication 毒品中毒 dúpǐn zhòngdú

investigate *v* 调查 diàochá, 侦查 zhēnchá

investigation *n* 调查 diàochá, 侦查 zhēnchá

investigator *n* 调查员 diàocháyuán, 侦查员 zhēncháyuán

involuntary manslaughter 过失杀人罪 guòshī shārénzuì

irresistible impulse 不可抗拒的冲动 bùkě kàngjù de chōngdòng

jail *n* 监狱 jiānyù (*jails are operated by city or county governments to house prisoners who are being detained before trial or serving sentences less than one year* / 市和县级监狱叫 *jail*)

Jencks Act 詹克斯法 zhānkèsī fǎ

joinder of offenses 罪行合并 zuìxíng hébìng
juvenile offender 少年犯 shàoniánfàn
kidnapping *n* 绑架 bǎngjià
knowingly *adv* 故意地 gùyì de
larceny *n* 盗窃罪 dàoqièzuì, 非法侵占他人财产罪 fēifǎ
   qīnzhàn tārén cáichǎn zuì
law enforcement methods 执法方式 zhífǎ fāngshì
law enforcement official (officer) 执法人员 zhífǎ rényuán
leniency *n* 宽大 kuāndà
lenient *adj* 宽大的 kuāndà de
life sentence 终身监禁 zhōngshēn jiānjìn, 无期徒刑
   wúqī túxíng
light sentence 轻判 qīng pàn
lineup *n* 列队辨认 lièduì biànrèn
loan sharking 放高利贷 fàng gāolìdài
long-arm jurisdiction 长臂管辖权 chángbì guǎnxiáquán
   (*legal provision that permits one state to claim*
   jurisdiction over someone who lives in another state /
   对外州居民的司法管辖权)
looting *n* 抢掠 qiǎnglüè
malice *n* 恶意 èyì
malicious *adj* 恶意的 èyì de
malicious mischief 恶意破坏他人财产 èyì pòhuài tārén
   cáichǎn
maliciously *adv* 恶意地 èyì de
mandatory minimum sentence 法定最低刑期 fǎdìng
   zuìdī xíngqī
manslaughter *n* 杀人罪 shārénzuì
mastermind *n* 主谋 zhǔmóu
mayhem *n* 致残罪 zhìcánzuì
menacing *n* 恐吓罪 kǒnghèzuì

minimal participant 作用最小的参与者 zuòyòng zuìxiǎo de cānyùzhě

minor participant 起次要作用的参与者 qǐ cìyào zuòyòng de cānyùzhě

Miranda warnings 米兰达告诫 mǐlándá gàojiè

misconduct *n* 不当行为 bùdàng xíngwéi

misconduct before the court 法庭上的不当行为 fǎtíng shàng de bùdàng xíngwéi

misdemeanor *n* 轻罪 qīngzuì

misdemeanor court 轻罪法院 qīngzuì fǎyuàn

Model Penal Code 示范刑法典 shìfàn xíngfǎ diǎn

money laundering 洗钱 xǐqián

morgue *n* 陈尸所 chénshīsuǒ

motion after trial 审后动议 shěn hòu dòngyì

motion to limit the use of evidence 限制使用证据动议 xiànzhì shǐyòng zhèngjù dòngyì

motion to suppress evidence 排除证据动议 páichú zhèngjù dòngyì

mugger *n* 抢劫者 qiǎngjiézhě

murder *n* 谋杀罪 móushāzuì

necessity defense 紧急避险辩护 jǐnjí bìxiǎn biànhù

no contest 不抗辩 bùkàngbiàn

nolo contendere 不争辩 bùzhēngbiàn

non-jail sentence 非监禁刑 fēi jiānjìn xíng

not guilty 无罪 wúzuì

obstruction of justice 妨碍司法 fáng'ài sīfǎ

offender *n* 罪犯 zuìfàn, 违法者 wéifǎzhě

offense *n* 犯罪 fànzuì, 违法行为 wéifǎ xíngwéi

offense level 罪行级别 zuìxíng jíbié

operating a business of prostitution 经营淫业 jīngyíng yínyè

organized crime 有组织犯罪 yǒuzǔzhī fànzuì

outcry witness 哭诉证人 kūsù zhèngrén (*the first adult to whom a child victim told about the abuse* / 第一个听到受虐儿童诉说的成年人)

pandering *n* 拉皮条 lāpítiáo

pardon *n* 赦免 shèmiǎn, 宽恕 kuānshù

parole *n* 假释 jiǎshì, 有条件释放 yǒutiáojiàn shìfàng

parole board 假释委员会 jiǎshì wěiyuánhuì

parole hearing 假释听证会 jiǎshì tīngzhènghuì

parole officer 假释官 jiǎshìguān

PATRIOT Act 反恐法 fǎnkǒng fǎ (又译爱国法 *a.k.a.* àiguó fǎ)

penal *adj* 刑事的 xíngshì de

penalty *n* 刑罚 xíngfá, 处罚 chǔfá

penitentiary *n* 教养中心 jiàoyǎng zhōngxīn, 监狱 jiānyù

peremptory challenge 绝对回避 juéduì huíbì

perjury *n* 伪证 wěizhèng

perpetrator (perp) *n* 罪犯 zuìfàn

persistent offender 惯犯 guànfàn, 累犯 lěifàn

petit jury 小陪审团 xiǎo péishěntuán

petition *n* 请求 qǐngqiú, 诉状 sùzhuàng; *v* 提出申请 tíchū shēnqǐng

physical injury 人身伤害 rénshēn shānghài

physical restraint 身体强制 shēntǐ qiángzhì

pick a pocket 扒窃 páqiè

pickpocket *n* 扒手 páshǒu

pimp *n* 皮条客 pítiáokè

pimping *n* 拉皮条 lā pítiáo

plea agreement; plea bargain; plea-bargaining 辩诉协议 biàn sù xiéyì, 辩诉协让 biàn sù xié ràng

police blotter 逮捕记录 dàibǔ jìlù

possession *n* 占有 zhànyǒu, 所有物 suǒyǒuwù

post bail 交保 jiāobǎo, 取保 qǔbǎo

post-release supervision 释后监督 shì hòu jiāndū

precedent *n* 先例 xiānlì

prejudicial *adj* 有损害的 yǒu sǔnhài de, 不利的 bùlì de

premeditated *adj* 预谋的 yùmóu de

preponderance of the evidence 证据的优势 zhèngjù de yōushì

pre-sentence investigation report 量刑前调查报告 liàngxíng qián diàochá bàogào

presumption *n* 推定 tuīdìng

presumption of innocence 无罪推定 wúzuì tuīdìng

pretrial detention 审前羁押 shěn qián jīyā

pretrial services department 审前服务部 shěn qián fúwù bù

pretrial statements 审前陈述 shěn qián chénshù

prior conviction 前科 qiánkē

prior juvenile offense 少年犯罪前科 shàonián fànzuì qiánkē

prison *n* 监狱 jiānyù (*prisons are operated by the federal and state governments* / 联邦和州一级的监狱叫 *prison*)

prison guard 监狱看守 jiānyù kānshǒu

prisoner *n* 犯人 fànrén, 囚犯 qiúfàn

probable cause 合理根据 hélǐ gēnjù, 合理怀疑 hélǐ huáiyí

probation *n* 缓刑 huǎnxíng

probation hearing 缓刑听证会 huǎnxíng tīngzhènghuì

probation officer 缓刑官 huǎnxíngguān

procurer *n* 皮条客 pítiáokè

procuress *n* 老鸨 lǎobǎo

procuring *n* 拉皮条 lā pítiáo

proffer *n* 提供证据 tígōng zhèngjù

profiling *n* 以貌取人 yǐmàoqǔrén

prohibit *v* 禁止 jinzhǐ

刑法词汇

prohibited *adj* 被禁止的 bèi jìnzhǐ de
prosecute *v* 起诉 qǐsù, 检控 jiǎnkòng
prosecuting officer 公诉人 gōngsùrén
prosecution *n* 起诉 qǐsù, 检方 jiǎnfāng
prosecution witness 检方证人 jiǎnfāng zhèngrén
prosecutor *n* 公诉人 gōngsùrén, 检察官 jiǎncháguān
prostitute *n* 妓女 jìnǚ, 娼妓 chāngjì
prostitution *n* 卖淫 màiyín
proximate cause 近因 jìnyīn
public defender 公设辩护人 gōng shè biànhùrén
punitive *adj* 惩罚性的 chéngfáxìng de
qualified immunity 有条件豁免 yǒutiáojiàn huòmiǎn
questioning of witness 诘问证人 jiéwèn zhèngrén
racial slur 种族蔑称 zhǒngzú mièchēng
Racketeer Influenced and Corrupt Organizations Act (RICO) 反诈骗、操纵和贿赂组织法 fǎn zhàpiàn cāozòng hé huìlù zǔzhī fǎ (又译反黑连坐法 *a.k.a.* fǎn hēi liánzuò fǎ)
racketeering *n* 敲诈勒索 qiāozhà-lèsuǒ
ransom *n* 赎金 shújīn
rap sheet 犯罪档案 fànzuì dàng'àn
rape *n/v* 强奸 qiángjiān
reasonable basis 合理根据 hélǐ gēnjù
reasonable doubt 合理怀疑 hélǐ huáiyí
rebuttable presumption 可反驳的推定 kě fǎnbó de tuīdìng
rebuttal *n* 反证 fǎnzhèng, 反驳 fǎnbó
receiving stolen property 接受脏物 jiēshòu zāngwù
recidivist *n* 惯犯 guànfàn, 累犯 lěifàn
reckless endangerment 莽撞危及他人人身罪 mǎngzhuàng wēijí tārén rénshēn zuì

Criminal Law

recklessly *adv* 莽撞地 mǎngzhuàng de, 不顾后果地 bùgù hòuguǒ de

recklessness *n* 莽撞 mǎngzhuàng

record of convictions 犯罪记录 fànzuì jìlù

record of questioning 询问笔录 xúnwèn bǐlù

record on appeal 上诉案卷 shàngsù ànjuàn

recusal *n* 回避 huíbì

recuse *v* 回避 huíbì, 要求回避 yāoqiú huíbì

reformatory *n* 少年犯管教所 shàoniánfàn guǎnjiàosuǒ

release *n/v* 释放 shìfàng

release on bail 保释 bǎoshì

relevant conduct 有关行为 yǒuguān xíngwéi

remanding order 还押令 huán yā lìng

remove *v* 驱逐出境 qūzhú chūjìng

renunciation *n* 放弃 fàngqì

reparation *n* 补救 bǔjiù, 赔偿 péicháng

repeat offender 惯犯 guànfàn, 累犯 lěifàn

re-sentencing *n* 重新量刑 chóngxīn liàngxíng

respondent on appeal 被上诉人 bèi shàngsùrén

restitution *n* 归还 guīhuán, 恢复原状 huīfù yuánzhuàng, 赔偿 péicháng

reversal *n* 撤销原判 chèxiāo yuánpàn

review *n/v* 复查 fùchá, 复审 fùshěn

right to trial 被告接受审判的权利 bèigào jiēshòu shěnpàn de quánlì

robbery *n* 抢劫 qiǎngjié

Rosario rule 罗萨里奥规则 luósàlǐ'ào guīzé

Rules of Criminal Procedure 刑事诉讼规则 xíngshì sùsòng guīzé

safety valve 安全阀 ānquánfá

sanction *n/v* 制裁 zhìcái, 处罚 chǔfá

sealed indictment 密封的大陪审团起诉书 mìfēng de dà péishěntuán qǐsùshū

search *n/v* 搜查 sōuchá

search and seizure 搜查和没收 sōuchá hé mòshōu

search warrant 搜查证 sōucházhèng

second degree murder 二级谋杀罪 èrjí móushāzuì

security classification 安全等级 ānquán děngjí

seize *v* 逮捕 dàibǔ, 查封 cháfēng, 扣押 kòuyā

seizure *n* 捕获 bǔhuò, 扣押 kòuyā, 没收 mòshōu

self-defense *n* 自卫 zìwèi, 正当防卫 zhèngdāng fángwèi

self-incrimination *n* 自证其罪 zì zhèng qí zuì

self-surrender *n* 自动投案 zìdòng tóu'àn

sentence *n/v* 判决 pànjué, 判刑 pànxíng, 量刑 liàngxíng

sentence above the guideline range
        高于量刑指南规定的刑罚 gāoyú liàngxíng zhǐnán guīdìng de xíngfá

sentence below the guideline range
        低于量刑指南规定的刑罚 dīyú liàngxíng zhǐnán guīdìng de xíngfá

sentencing guidelines 量刑指南 liàngxíng zhǐnán

sentencing hearing 量刑听证会 liàngxíng tīngzhènghuì

serious bodily injury 严重人身伤害 yánzhòng rénshēn shānghài

serve a sentence 服刑 fúxíng

severance of proceedings 分离诉讼 fēnlí sùsòng

sexual abuse 性侵犯 xìng qīnfàn

sexual predator 性侵犯者 xìng qīnfànzhě

sheriff *n* 县治安官 xiàn zhì'ānguān

shoot *v* 开枪 kāiqiāng, 射击 shèjī

shoot to kill 开枪射杀 kāiqiāng shèshā

shoplifter *n* 商店扒手 shāngdiàn páshǒu

shoplifting *n* 商店行窃 shāngdiàn xíngqiè

smuggle *v* 走私 zǒusī

smuggler *n* 走私者 zǒusīzhě

smuggling *n* 走私 zǒusī

sodomy *n* 鸡奸 jījiān

solicitation *n* 勾引 gōuyǐn, 拉客 lākè

specialized skill 专门技巧 zhuānmén jìqiǎo

specific intent 特定故意 tèdìng gùyì

Speedy Trial Act 迅速审理法 xùnsù shěnlǐ fǎ

stab *v* 刺伤 cìshāng

state *n* 状况 zhuàngkuàng

state of mind 精神状况 jīngshén zhuàngkuàng,
心境 xīnjìng

state trooper 州警 zhōujǐng

statement *n* 声明 shēngmíng, 主张 zhǔzhāng,
陈述 chénshù

status *n* 状况 zhuàngkuàng, 地位 dìwèi, 身份 shēnfèn

statute *n* 制定法 zhìdìngfǎ

statute of limitations 诉讼时效法 sùsòng shíxiàofǎ

statutory rape 法定强奸罪 fǎdìng qiángjiānzuì

stay enforcement of the judgment 暂缓执行判决
zànhuǎn zhíxíng pànjué

strict liability 严格责任 yángé zérèn

subpoena *n* 传票 chuánpiào; *v* 传票传唤 chuánpiào
chuánhuàn

substantial assistance to the government
向政府提供重要协助 xiàng zhèngfǔ tígōng
zhòngyào xiézhù

sufficient reason to suspect 合理根据 hélǐ gēnjù,
合理怀疑 hélǐ huáiyí

suicide *n* 自杀 zìshā

summons *n* 传票 chuánpiào, 传唤 chuánhuàn

supervening cause 介入原因 jièrù yuányīn

suppression hearing 排除证据听证会 páichú zhèngjù tīngzhènghuì

suppression of evidence 排除证据 páichú zhèngjù

surrender *v* 投案 tóu'àn, 交回 jiāohuí

surveillance *n* 监视 jiānshì

surveillance tape 监视录像带 jiānshì lùxiàngdài

suspect *n* 犯罪嫌疑人 fànzuì xiányírén; *v* 怀疑 huáiyí

swear *v* 宣誓 xuānshì

sworn *adj* 宣过誓的 xuān guò shì de

tamper with *v* 篡改 cuàngǎi, 干扰 gānrǎo

tampering with jury 非法影响陪审团 fēifǎ yǐngxiǎng péishěntuán

tax evasion 逃税 táoshuì

Temporary Protection Status (TPS) 临时保护身份 línshí bǎohù shēnfèn

terrorism *n* 恐怖主义 kǒngbùzhǔyì

terrorist *n* 恐怖分子 kǒngbù fēnzǐ

theft *n* 盗窃罪 dàoqièzuì

three-strikes statute 三振出局法 sān zhèn chūjú fǎ

time in prison 监禁期 jiānjìnqī

time off for good behavior 因表现良好而减刑期 yīn biǎoxiàn liánghǎo ér jiǎn xíngqī

time served 已服刑期 yǐ fú xíngqī

tip off *v* 告密 gàomì

TPS 见 Temporary Protection Status

traffic infraction 交通违规 jiāotōng wéiguī

transfer of proceedings 诉讼转移 sùsòng zhuǎnyí

try *v* 审判 shěnpàn, 审理 shěnlǐ

uncorroborated *adj* 未经证实的 wèi jīng zhèngshí de

undercover operation 秘密行动 mìmì xíngdòng

Criminal Law

undercover police officer 便衣警官 biànyī jǐngguān
underworld *n* 黑社会 hēishèhuì
undocumented *adj* 无证件的 wú zhèngjiàn de
United States Code 美国联邦法典 měiguó liánbāng
    fǎdiǎn
United States Sentencing Commission
    美国量刑委员会 měiguó liàngxíng wěiyuánhuì
unpunished *adj* 未受处罚的 wèi shòu chǔfá de
usury 高利贷 gāolìdài
vandalism *n* 肆意破坏财产 sìyì pòhuài cáichǎn
vehicular manslaughter 驾车致人死命罪 jiàchē zhìrén
    sǐmìng zuì
verdict *n* (陪审团的) 裁决 *(péishěntuán de)* cáijué
victim *n* 受害人 shòuhàirén
victim and witness assistance program
    受害人和证人援助计划 shòuhàirén hé zhèngrén
    yuánzhù jìhuà
victim impact statement 受害人影响陈述 shòuhàirén
    yǐngxiǎng chénshù
Victims of Crime Act (VOCA) 犯罪受害人法 fànzuì
    shòuhàirén fǎ
victims' rights 受害人的权利 shòuhàirén de quánlì
voluntary manslaughter 故意杀人罪 gùyì shārénzuì
voluntary surrender 自动投案 zìdòng tóu'àn
vulnerable victim 弱势受害人 ruòshì shòuhàirén
warden *(of prison)* *n* 监狱长 jiānyùzhǎng
warrant *n* 令状 lìngzhuàng
weapon *n* 武器 wǔqì
willful *adj* 蓄意的 xùyì de
willfully *adv* 蓄意地 xùyì de
wire *n* 窃听器 qiètīngqì

wiretap *n* 窃听 qiètīng

wiretap recording 窃听录音 qiètīng lùyīn

withdraw (*from a conspiracy*) *v* 退出 (共谋) tuìchū (gòngmóu)

witness protection plan 证人保护计划 zhèngrén bǎohù jìhuà

Family Law
家事法词汇

Family law deals with family events and relationships such as birth and marriage, or its dissolution (separation or divorce), laying down rules to ensure support for dependents and protecting the interests of children. A judgment of divorce may contain provisions on custody and visitation regulating the divorced parents' duties and rights with respect to minor children. Laws may also exist defining requirements for marriage, such as reaching a marriageable age, or setting conditions under which a marriage may be annulled or under which a pre-nuptial agreement between spouses may be enforced.

abandonment (*of marital domicile*) *n* 弃家 qìjiā
abortion *n* 堕胎 duòtāi
absolute divorce 绝对离婚 juéduì líhūn
actual separation 实际分居 shíjì fēnjū
administrator (*of estate*) *n* (遗产) 管理人 (*yíchǎn*) guǎnlǐrén
adolescent *n* (青春期) 青少年 (*qīngchūnqī*) qīngshàonián
adopt *v* 收养 shōuyǎng
adoption *n* 收养 shōuyǎng
adoption tax credit 收养抵税额 shōuyǎng dǐshuì'é
adoptive *adj* 收养的 shōuyǎng de, 有收养关系的 yǒu shōuyǎng guānxì de

adulterer *n* 通奸男子 tōngjiān nánzǐ, 奸夫 jiānfū

adulteress *n* 通奸女子 tōngjiān nǚzǐ, 奸妇 jiānfù

adultery *n* 通奸 tōngjiān

AFDC 见 Aid to Families With Dependent Children

age of majority 法定成年人年龄 fǎdìng chéngniánrén niánlíng

Aid to Families With Dependent Children (AFDC) 失依子女家庭援助 shī yī zǐnǚ jiātíng yuánzhù

alimony *n* (配偶之间) 扶养费 (pèi'ǒu zhījiān) fúyǎngfèi

annulment of marriage 宣告婚姻无效 xuāngào hūnyīn wúxiào

artificial insemination 人工授精 réngōng shòujīng

assignment of support rights 转让子女抚养费权利 zhuǎnràng zǐnǚ fúyǎngfèi quánlì

aunt *n*
　　姑 gū (*father's sister*)
　　姨 yí (*mother's sister*)
　　婶母 shěnmǔ (*wife of father's younger brother*)
　　伯母 bómǔ (*wife of father's elder brother*)
　　舅母 jiùmǔ (*wife of mother's brother*)

beneficiary *n* 受益人 shòuyìrén

best interests of the child *n* 子女最佳利益 zǐnǚ zuìjiā lìyì

bigamist *n* 犯重婚罪者 fàn chónghūnzuì zhě

bigamy *n* 重婚罪 chónghūnzuì

biological parent 生身父母 shēngshēn fùmǔ

birth *n* 出生 chūshēng

birth certificate 出生证 chūshēngzhèng

birth control 节制生育 jiézhì shēngyù

born *adj* 出生 chūshēng

brother *n* 兄弟 xiōngdì

brother-in-law *n*

连襟 liánjīn (*husband of sister*)

姐夫 jiěfu (*husband of elder sister*)

妹夫 mèifu (*husband of younger sister*)

内兄 nèixiōng (*wife's elder brother*)

内弟 nèidì (*wife's younger brother*)

大伯子 dàbǎizi (*husband's elder brother*)

小叔子 xiǎoshūzi (*husband's younger brother*)

child *n* 子女 zǐnǚ, 儿童 értóng

child care center 托儿中心 tuō'er zhōngxīn

child support 子女抚养费 zǐnǚ fǔyǎngfèi

child support enforcement agency (office) 子女抚养费强制执行机构 zǐnǚ fǔyǎngfèi qiángzhì zhíxíng jīgòu

child support guidelines 子女抚养费指导方针 zǐnǚ fǔyǎngfèi zhǐdǎo fāngzhēn

childbirth *n* 分娩 fēnmiǎn

civil union 法定结合 fǎdìng jiéhé

common law marriage 普通法婚姻 pǔtōngfǎ hūnyīn

community property 夫妻共同财产 fūqī gòngtóng cáichǎn

competency *n* 能力 nénglì

competency hearing 能力听证会 nénglì tīngzhènghuì

condom *n* 安全套 ānquántào

condonation *n* 宽恕 kuānshù

consanguinity *n* 血亲 xuèqīn, 同宗 tóngzōng

consent *n* 同意 tóngyì

contraception *n* 避孕 bìyùn

contraceptive *n* 避孕药具 bìyùn yàojù

counseling *n* 辅导 fǔdǎo, 咨询 zīxún

couple *n* 夫妻 fūqī

Family Law

cousin *n*

堂兄 tángxiōng (*father's brother's son who is older than you*)

堂弟 tángdì (*father's brother's son who is younger than you*)

堂姐 tángjiě (*father's brother's daughter who is older than you*)

堂妹 tángmèi (*father's brother's daughter who is younger than you*)

表兄 biǎoxiōng (*father's sister's son who is older than you; mother's sibling's son who is older than you*)

表弟 biǎodì (*father's sister's son who is younger than you; mother's sibling's son who is younger than you*)

表姐 biǎojiě (*father's sister's daughter who is older than you; mother's sibling's daughter who is older than you*)

表妹 biǎomèi (*father's sister's daughter who is younger than you; mother's sibling's daughter who is younger than you*)

cruelty *n* 虐待 nüèdài

custodial abduction 监护诱拐 jiānhù yòuguǎi

custodial parent 有监护权的父亲或母亲 yǒu jiānhùquán de fùqīn huò mǔqīn

custody *n* 监护 jiānhù, 监护权 jiānhùquán

daughter *n* 女儿 nǚ'ér

daughter-in-law *n* 媳妇 xífù, 儿媳 érxí

deadbeat dad 不付抚养费的父亲 bùfù fǔyǎngfèi de fùqīn

death certificate 死亡证明书 sǐwáng zhèngmíngshū

deceased *adj* 死去的 sǐqù de

decedent *n* 死者 sǐzhě

Department of Social Services 社会服务局 shèhuì
   fúwù jú
dependent *adj* 受养的 shòuyǎng de; *n* 受养人
   shòuyǎngrén (指配偶和子女)
dissolution of marriage 解除婚姻 jiěchú hūnyīn
distributee *n* 遗产继承人 yíchǎn jìchéngrén
divorce *n/v* 离婚 líhūn
divorce decree 离婚判决 líhūn pànjué
divorced *adj* 离了婚的 lí le hūn de
divorcee *n* 离了婚的人 lí le hūn de rén
domestic *adj* 家庭的 jiātíng de
domestic partner 同居伴侣 tóngjū bànlǚ
domestic relations 家庭关系 jiātíng guānxì
domestic violence 家庭暴力 jiātíng bàolì
duty to support
   扶养义务 fúyǎng yìwù (*refers to spousal support /*
      指配偶之间)
   抚养义务 fǔyǎng yìwù (*refers to parent-to-child
      support /* 指父母对子女)
earnings assignment 收入拨付 shōurù bōfù
earnings withholding order 收入代扣令 shōurù dàikòu
   lìng
emancipate *v* 解脱 jiětuō
emancipated minor 取得独立生活资格的未成年人
   qǔdé dúlì shēnghuó zīgé de wèichéngniánrén
engagement (*to marry*) *n* 订婚 dìnghūn
estate *n* 遗产 yíchǎn
estate tax 遗产税 yíchǎnshuì
executor *n* 遗嘱执行人 yízhǔ zhíxíngrén
ex-husband *n* 前夫 qiánfū
ex-wife *n* 前妻 qiánqī
faithful *adj* 忠实的 zhōngshí de

Family Law

family *n* 家庭 jiātíng

family court 家事法院 jiāshì fǎyuàn

family court judge 家事法院法官 jiāshì fǎyuàn fǎguān

family law 家事法 jiāshìfǎ

family planning 计划生育 jìhuà shēngyù

family reunification 家庭团聚 jiātíng tuánjù

father *n* 父亲 fùqīn

father-in-law *n*

  公公 gōnggong (*husband's father*)

  岳父 yuèfù (*wife's father*)

FCR 见 Federal Case Registry

Federal Case Registry (FCR) 联邦子女抚养案登记处 liánbāng zǐnǚ fǔyǎng àn dēngjìchù

Federal Parent Locator Service (FPLS)
  联邦查找父母服务网 liánbāng cházhǎo fùmǔ fúwù wǎng

fertile *adj* 有生育能力的 yǒu shēngyù nénglì de

fiancé *n* 未婚夫 wèihūnfū

fiancée *n* 未婚妻 wèihūnqī

fidelity *n* 忠实 zhōngshí

final decree of divorce 终局离婚判决 zhōngjú líhūn pànjué

foreign marriage 涉外婚姻 shèwài hūnyīn

foster care 寄养 jìyǎng

foster parent 养父 yǎngfù, 养母 yǎngmǔ

FPLS 见 Federal Parent Locator Service

GAL 见 guardian ad litem

garnishment *n* 扣付债务人工资令 kòu fù zhàiwùrén gōngzī lìng

gay marriage 同性婚姻 tóngxìng hūnyīn

gift tax 赠与税 zèngyǔshuì

grandchild *n*
　　孙子女 sūnzǐnǚ (*son's children*)
　　外孙子女 wàisūnzǐnǚ (*daughter's children*)
granddaughter *n*
　　孙女 sūnnǚ (*son's daughter*)
　　外孙女 wàisūnnǚ (*daughter's daughter*)
grandfather *n*
　　祖父 zǔfù (*father's father*)
　　外祖父 wàizǔfù (*mother's father*)
grandmother *n*
　　祖母 zǔmǔ (*father's mother*)
　　外祖母 wàizǔmǔ (*mother's mother*)
grandparents *n*
　　祖父母 zǔfùmǔ (*father's parents*)
　　外祖父母 wàizǔfùmǔ (*mother's parents*)
grandson *n*
　　孙子 sūnzi (*son's son*)
　　外孙 wàisūn (*daughter's son*)
grounds for divorce 离婚的理由 líhūn de lǐyóu
guardian *n* 监护人 jiānhùrén
guardian ad litem (GAL) 诉讼监护人 sùsòng jiānhùrén
guardianship *n* 监护 jiānhù, 监护权 jiānhùquán
guidance *n* 咨询 zīxún
guidance counselor 咨询顾问 zīxún gùwèn, 辅导员
　　fǔdǎoyuán
guidelines *n* 指导方针 zhǐdǎo fāngzhēn, 准则 zhǔnzé
head of household 户主 hùzhǔ
heterosexual *adj* 异性恋的 yìxìngliàn de; *n* 异性恋者
　　yìxìngliànzhě
home *n* 家 jiā, 家庭 jiātíng, 住所 zhùsuǒ
homosexual *adj* 同性恋的 tóngxìngliàn de; *n* 同性恋者
　　tóngxìngliànzhě

husband *n* 丈夫 zhàngfu

illegitimate *adj* 非法的 fēifǎ de, 非婚生的 fēi hūnshēng de

immediate family 直系家庭 zhíxì jiātíng

impediment to marriage 法定婚姻障碍 fǎdìng hūnyīn
zhàng'ài

impotence *n* 阳痿 yángwěi

impotent *adj* 阳痿的 yángwěi de

in vitro fertilization (IVF) 试管受精 shìguǎn shòujīng

incapacitated *adj* 丧失行为能力的 sàngshī xíngwéi
nénglì de

income withholding 收入代扣 shōurù dài kòu

incompetent person 无行为能力者 wú xíngwéi
nénglì zhě

infertile *adj* 不育的 bùyù de

infertility *n* 不育症 bùyùzhèng

infidelity *n* (夫妻间) 不忠实 (fūqī jiān) bù zhōngshí

injunction against molestation 禁止骚扰令 jìnzhǐ
sāorǎo lìng

in-laws *n* 姻亲 yīnqīn

intestate *adj* 未留遗嘱的 wèi liú yízhǔ de

irreconcilable differences 不能和解的分歧 bùnéng
héjiě de fēnqí

IVF 见 in vitro fertilization

joint custody 共同监护权 gòngtóng jiānhùquán

judgment *n* 判决 pànjué

juvenile *adj* 少年的 shàonián de, 未成年的
wèichéngnián de; *n* 少年 shàonián, 未成年人
wèichéngniánrén

Keeping Children and Families Safe Act
保护儿童和家庭安全法 bǎohù értóng hé jiātíng
ānquán fǎ

kinship *n* 亲属关系 qīnshǔ guānxì

legal custody 法律监护权 fǎlǜ jiānhùquán

legal separation 判决分居 pànjué fēnjū

legitimate *adj* 合法的 héfǎ de, 婚生的 hūnshēng de

lesbian *n* 女同性恋者 nǚ tóngxìngliànzhě

living separate and apart 分居 fēnjū

lover *n* 情人 qíngrén

maintenance (*a.k.a.* **alimony, spousal support**) *n* 扶养费 fúyǎngfèi

marital asset 婚姻资产 hūnyīn zīchǎn

marital debt 婚姻债务 hūnyīn zhàiwù

marital property 婚姻财产 hūnyīn cáichǎn

marital rape 婚内强奸 hūnnèi qiángjiān

marital settlement agreement 婚姻财产协议 hūnyīn cáichǎn xiéyì

marriage *n* 结婚 jiéhūn, 婚姻 hūnyīn

marriage ceremony 婚礼 hūnlǐ

marriage certificate 结婚证书 jiéhūn zhèngshū

marriage counseling 婚姻咨询 hūnyīn zīxún

marriage counselor 婚姻咨询员 hūnyīn zīxúnyuán

marriageable age 法定结婚年龄 fǎdìng jiéhūn niánlíng

married *adj* 已婚的 yǐhūn de

marry *v* 结婚 jiéhūn, 娶 qǔ, 嫁 jià

maternity leave 产假 chǎnjià

maternity ward 产科病房 chǎnkē bìngfáng

matrimonial *adj* 婚姻的 hūnyīn de

matrimony *n* 婚姻关系 hūnyīn guānxì

medical certificate 健康证明 jiànkāng zhèngmíng

midwife *n* 助产士 zhùchǎnshì

minor *adj* 未成年的 wèichéngnián de; *n* 未成年人 wèichéngniánrén

miscarriage *n* 小产 xiǎochǎn

monetary award 赔偿金裁定额 péichángjīn cáidìng'é
mother *n* 母亲 mǔqīn
mother-in-law *n*
    婆母 pómǔ (*husband's mother*)
    岳母 yuèmǔ (*wife's mother*)
neglect of child 忽视儿童 hūshì értóng
nephew *n*
    侄子 zhízi (*brother's son*)
    外甥 wàisheng (*sister's son*)
niece *n*
    侄女 zhínǚ (*brother's daughter*)
    外甥女 wàishēngnǚ (*sister's daughter*)
no-fault divorce 无过错离婚 wú guòcuò líhūn
nursery *n* 托儿所 tuō'érsuǒ
OCSE 见 Office of Child Support Enforcement
Office of Child Support Enforcement (OCSE)
    子女抚养费强制执行处 zǐnǚ fǔyǎngfèi qiángzhì zhíxíngchù
offspring *n* 后代 hòudài, 子孙 zǐsūn
orphan *n* 孤儿 gū'ér; *v* 成为孤儿 chéngwéi gū'ér
paramour *n* 情夫 qíngfū, 情妇 qíngfù
parent *n*
    父亲 fùqīn (*father*)
    母亲 mǔqīn (*mother*)
parental *adj* 父母的 fùmǔ de
parental abduction 父母诱拐 fùmǔ yòuguǎi
parental rights 父母权利 fùmǔ quánlì
parents *n* 父母 fùmǔ
paternity *n* 生父关系 shēngfù guānxi
paternity proceeding; paternity suit 确认生父的诉讼 quèrèn shēngfù de sùsòng

pendente lite 诉讼待决期间 sùsòng dàijué qījiān
physical custody 人身监护权 rénshēn jiānhùquán
pregnancy *n* 怀孕 huáiyùn, 妊娠 rènshēn
pregnant *adj* 怀孕的 huáiyùn de, 妊娠的 rènshēn de
premature birth 早产 zǎochǎn
pre-nuptial agreement 婚前协议 hūnqián xiéyì
probate *n* 遗嘱检验 yízhǔ jiǎnyàn
puberty *n* 青春期 qīngchūnqī
putative father 推定的父亲 tuīdìng de fùqīn
putative spouse 自认的配偶 zìrèn de pèi'ǒu
reconciliation *n* 和解 héjiě
relief *n* 救济 jiùjì
remarry *v* 再婚 zàihūn
retirement *n* 退休 tuìxiū
right of election by surviving spouse 未亡配偶选择权
    wèiwáng pèi'ǒu xuǎnzéquán
same-sex marriage 同性婚姻 tóngxìng hūnyīn
separate property 个人财产 gèrén cáichǎn
    (*in contrast to community property* /
    与夫妻共同财产相对)
separated *adj* 分居的 fēnjū de
separation agreement 分居协议 fēnjū xiéyì
settlement *n* 解决 jiějué, 转让 zhuǎnràng, 清偿 qīngcháng,
    授予 shòuyǔ
shared custody 共同监护权 gòngtóng jiānhùquán
sibling *n* (同父母的) 兄弟姐妹 (*tong fùmǔ de*) xiōngdì
    jiěmèi
single *adj* 单身的 dānshēn de, 未婚的 wèihūn de
sister *n*
    姐 jiě (*elder sister*)
    妹 mèi (*younger sister*)

sister-in-law *n*
  妯娌 zhóuli (*brother's wife*)
  嫂子 sǎozi (*elder brother's wife*)
  弟媳 dìxí (*younger brother's wife*)
  姑子 gūzi (*husband's sister*)
  大姑子 dàgūzi (*husband's elder sister*)
  小姑子 xiǎogūzi (*husband's younger sister*)
  姨子 yízi (*wife's sister*)
  大姨子 dàyízi (*wife's elder sister*)
  小姨子 xiǎoyízi (*wife's younger sister*)
sole custody 单方监护权 dānfāng jiānhùquán
solemnize *(marriage)* *v* 举行婚礼 jǔxíng hūnlǐ
son *n* 儿子 érzi
son-in-law *n* 女婿 nǚxù
spousal abuse 虐待配偶 nüèdài pèi'ǒu
spousal support 配偶扶养费 pèi'ǒu fúyǎngfèi
spouse *n* 配偶 pèiǒu
stepfather *n* 继父 jìfù
stepmother *n* 继母 jìmǔ
stillborn *adj* 死产的 sǐchǎn de
support payment *(child)* 抚养费 fúyǎngfèi
surrogate court proceeding 遗产法院程序 yíchǎn
    fǎyuàn chéngxù
surrogate mother 代孕母亲 dàiyùn mǔqīn
TANF 见 temporary aid for needy families
teenage *adj* 青少年的 qīngshàonián de
temporary aid for needy families (TANF)
    贫困家庭临时救济 pínkùn jiātíng línshí jiùjì
temporary custody 临时监护权 línshí jiānhùquán
temporary order 临时命令 línshí mìnglìng
temporary restraining order (TRO) 临时禁止令 línshí
    jìnzhǐ lìng

TRO 见 temporary restraining order
twins *n* 双胞胎 shuāngbāotāi
uncle *n*
   伯父 bófù (*father's elder brother*)
   叔父 shūfù (*father's younger brother*)
   姑父 gūfu (*father's sister's husband*)
   舅父 jiùfù (*mother's brother*)
   姨父 yífù (*mother's sister's husband*)
uncontested divorce 无争议离婚 wú zhēngyì líhūn
underage *adj* 未成年的 wèichéngnián de,
   未达法定年龄的 wèidá fǎdìng niánlíng de
unfaithful *adj* 不忠实的 bùzhōngshí de
use and possession 使用与占用 shǐyòng yǔ zhànyòng
visitation *n* 探视 tànshì
visitation rights 探视权 tànshìquán
wage withholding 工资代扣 gōngzī dài kòu
waiting period (离婚) 等待期 (*líhūn*) děngdàiqī
wellbeing *n* 福祉 fúzhǐ
wetnurse *n* 奶妈 nǎimā
widow *n* 寡妇 guǎfù
widower *n* 鳏夫 guānfū
wife *n* 妻子 qīzi

Health-Care Law
保健法词汇

Health-care laws deal with injuries, diseases and other medical conditions that require medical treatment, how insurance coverage is obtained and provided for such treatment under public and private plans, and how the practice of medicine and the sale of medicines are regulated to protect the public against risks to health and malpractice.

access *n/v* 获得 huòdé

accident *n* 意外事件 yìwài shìjiàn, 事故 shìgù

accidental death and dismemberment 意外死亡和伤残 yìwài sǐwán hé shāngcán

acquired immunodeficiency syndrome (AIDS) 艾滋病 àizībìng (又译爱滋病 *a.k.a.* àizībìng)

acupuncture *n* 针灸 zhēnjiǔ

acute *adj* 急性的 jíxìng de

acute care 急性病护理 jíxìngbìng hùlǐ

addiction *n* 瘾 yǐn

addiction to alcohol 酒瘾 jiǔyǐn

addiction to drugs 毒瘾 dúyǐn

additional coverage 附加保险范围 fùjiā bǎoxiǎn fànwéi

adequate care 适当护理 shìdàng hùlǐ

adult daycare center 成人日间护理中心 chéngrén rìjiān hùlǐ zhōngxīn

adult day service 见 adult daycare center

AIDS 见 acquired immunodeficiency syndrome

allowance *n* 给付额 jǐfù'é

alternative medicine 替代医学 tìdài yīxué

ambulance *n* 救护车 jiùhùchē

ambulatory *adj* 不需卧床的 bùxū wòchuáng de

appeal process 申诉程序 shēnsù chéngxù

appointment *n* 预约 yùyuē

asbestos *n* 石棉 shímián

assisted living 辅助生活 fǔzhù shēnghuó

at-home nursing care 居家护理 jūjiā hùlǐ

attorney's fee 律师费 lǜshīfèi

behavioral health 行为健康 xíngwéi jiànkāng

beneficiary *n* 受益人 shòuyìrén

beneficiary designation 指定受益人 zhǐdìng shòuyìrén

benefit *n* 给付 jǐfù, 福利 fúlì

benign *adj* 良性的 liángxìng de

cancer care 癌症护理 áizhèng hùlǐ

capitation *n* 按人包干制 ánrén bāogān zhì

carcinogen *n* 致癌物 zhì'áiwù

cardiac care 心脏病护理 xīnzàngbìng hùlǐ

cardiovascular disease 心血管病 xīnxuèguǎnbìng

care *n* 护理 hùlǐ

care management 护理管理 hùlǐ guǎnlǐ

caregiver; caretaker *n* 护理员 hùlǐyuán

cavity *n* 龋洞 qǔdòng

childhood disease 小儿疾病 xiǎo'ér jíbìng

chronic *adj* 慢性的 mànxìng de

chronic disease 慢性病 mànxìngbìng

claim *n* 索赔 suǒpéi, 报销申请 bàoxiāo shēnqǐng

claim form 索赔表 suǒpéibiǎo

clinic *n* 诊所 zhěnsuǒ

collect *v* 领取 lǐngqǔ

compensation *n* 补偿 bǔcháng, 赔偿 péicháng

compensation system 补偿制度 bǔcháng zhìdù

comprehensive coverage 全保 quánbǎo
consent to treatment 同意治疗 tóngyì zhìliáo
contact lenses 隐形镜片 yǐnxíng jìngpiàn
controlled substance 受管制物质 shòu guǎnzhì wùzhì
co-payment *n* 共付费 gòngfùfèi
coverage *n* 保险范围 bǎoxiǎn fànwéi
covered benefit 给付范围内的福利 jǐfù fànwéi nèi de fúlì
cure *n* 治疗 zhìliáo, 治愈 zhìyù
deductible *n* 扣除额 kòuchú'é
denial *n* 拒赔 jùpéi, 拒绝 jùjué
dental *adj* 牙科的 yákē de
dentist *n* 牙医 yáyī
deny *v* 拒赔 jùpéi, 拒绝 jùjué
dependability *n* 可靠性 kěkàoxìng
diabetes *n* 糖尿病 tángniàobìng
disability *n* 残疾 cánjí
disability benefit 残疾福利 cánjí fúlì
disabled *adj* 残疾的 cánjí de
disease *n* 疾病 jíbìng
disease control 疾病控制 jíbìng kòngzhì
disease prevention 疾病预防 jíbìng yùfáng
doctor *n* 医生 yīshēng
domestic violence 家庭暴力 jiātíng bàolì
drug *n* 药品 yàopǐn
drug rehabilitation 戒毒 jièdú
drug-resistant *adj* 抗药的 kàngyào de
easy access 容易获得 róngyì huòdé
elder *n* 老年人 lǎoniánrén
elder care 老年保健 lǎonián bǎojiàn
elder law 老年法律 lǎonián fǎlǜ
elderly *adj* 老年的 lǎonián de

eligible *adj* 合格的 hégé de, 合乎条件的 héhū tiáojiàn de

emergency room 急诊室 jízhěnshì

entitled (*to benefits*) 应享 (福利) yīngxiǎng (*fúlì*)

excluded risk 除外风险 chúwài fēngxiǎn

exclusion (*policy*) *n* 除外 chúwài

expertise *n* 专门技能 zhuānmén jìnéng

exposure and disappearance benefit
遭遇天灾与失踪给付 zāoyù tiānzāi yǔ shīzōng jǐfù

eyeglasses *n* 眼镜 yǎnjìng

family *n* 家庭 jiātíng

fertility services 辅助生殖中心 fǔzhù shēngzhí zhōngxīn

fitness *n* 健康 jiànkāng

free *adj* 免费的 miǎnfèi de

free access 免费使用 miǎnfèi shǐyòng, 免费获得 miǎnfèi
huòdé

gastric carcinoma 胃癌 wèi'ái

general practitioner 普通医生 pǔtōng yīshēng,
全科医生 quánkē yīshēng

grievance *n* 冤情 yuānqíng, 申诉 shēnsù

handicap *n* 残障 cánzhàng

handicapped *adj* 残障的 cánzhàng de

health *n* 健康 jiànkāng, 卫生 wèishēng

health care 保健 bǎojiàn

health-care management 保健管控 bǎojiàn guǎnkòng

health-care proxy 保健委托书 bǎojiàn wěituōshū

health maintenance organization (HMO) 保健组织
bǎojiàn zǔzhī

healthy *adj* 健康的 jiànkāng de

high blood pressure; hypertension *n* 高血压 gāoxuèyā

HIV 见 human immunodeficiency virus

HMO 见 health maintenance organization

home attendant 家庭护理员 jiātíng hùlǐyuán

hospital *n* 医院 yīyuàn

hospitalization *n* 住院 zhùyuàn

human avian influenza; human bird flu 人禽流感 rén qín liúgǎn

human immunodeficiency virus (HIV) 艾滋病毒 àizībìngdú

ill *adj* 有病的 yǒubìng de

illness *n* 疾病 jíbìng

impotence *n* 阳痿 yángwěi

incapacity *n* 无行为能力 wú xíngwéi nénglì

infection *n* 传染 chuánrǎn, 感染 gǎnrǎn

infectious disease 传染病 chuánrǎnbìng

informed consent 知情的同意 zhīqíng de tóngyì

injury *n* 受伤 shòushāng, 伤害 shānghài

inpatient *n* 住院病人 zhùyuàn bìngrén

insurance *n* 保险 bǎoxiǎn

insurance carrier 承保人 chéngbǎorén

insurance policy 保险单 bǎoxiǎndān

insured *n* 被保险人 bèi bǎoxiǎnrén

insurer *n* 保险人 bǎoxiǎnrén

intensive care 特别护理 tèbié hùlǐ

lead paint 含铅油漆 hán qiān yóuqī

legal access 获得法律服务 huòdé fǎlǜ fúwù

legally blind 法定盲人 fǎdìng mángrén

legally incapacitated 法定丧失行为能力者 fǎdìng sàngshī xíngwéi nénglì zhě

leukemia *n* 白血病 báixuèbìng

life-threatening *adj* 危及生命的 wēijí shēngmìng de

liver cancer 肝癌 gān'ái

living will 维生预嘱 wéishēng yù zhǔ

loss *n* 丧失 sàngshī, 失去 shīqù, 损失 sǔnshī

loss of both hands and feet 失去双手和双脚 shīqù shuāngshǒu hé shuāngjiǎo

loss of entire sight 完全失明 wánquán shīmíng

loss of hearing 失去听力 shīqù tīnglì

loss of life 生命损失 shēngmìng sǔnshī

loss of speech 失去语言能力 shīqù yǔyán nénglì

loss of thumb and index finger of the same hand 失去同一只手的拇指和食指 shīqù tóng yīzhīshǒu de mǔzhǐ hé shízhǐ

lung cancer 肺癌 fèi'ái

malignant *adj* 恶性的 èxìng de

malpractice *n* 过失 guòshī

malpractice case 过失案件 guòshī ànjiàn

malpractice claim 过失索赔 guòshī suǒpéi

managed care 有管控的保健 yǒu guǎnkòng de bǎojiàn

managed care organization 管控保健组织 guǎnkòng bǎojiàn zǔzhī

Medicaid 医疗补助计划 yīliáo bǔzhù jìhuà

medical *adj* 医疗的 yīliáo de, 医学的 yīxué de

medically necessary treatment 医学上必要的治疗 yīxué shàng bìyào de zhìliáo

Medicare 医疗保健计划 yīliáo bǎojiàn jìhuà

medicine *n* 药品 yàopǐn, 医学 yīxué

mental *adj* 精神的 jīngshén de, 心理的 xīnlǐ de

mental handicap 智障 zhìzhàng

mental health 精神健康 jīngshén jiànkāng

mental retardation 智力迟钝 zhìlì chídùn

minimum standards 最低标准 zuìdī biāozhǔn

NADSA 见 National Adult Day Services Association

National Adult Day Services Association (NADSA) 全国成人日间护理协会 quánguó chéngrén rìjiān hùlǐ xiéhuì

neglect *n/v* 忽视 hūshì
non-traditional medicine 非传统医学 fēi chuántǒng yīxué
notice of claim 索赔通知 suǒpéi tōngzhī
nurse *n* 护士 hùshi
nursing care 护理 hùlǐ
nursing home 护理之家 hùlǐ zhī jiā
obesity *n* 肥胖症 féipàngzhèng
occupational health 职业健康 zhíyè jiànkāng
operating room 手术室 shǒushùshì
optometrist *n* 验光师 yànguāngshī
organ transplant 器官移植 qìguān yízhí
out-of-network; out-of-plan 计划外 jìhuà wài
out-of-pocket maximum 自付限额 zìfù xiàn'é
outpatient *n* 门诊病人 ménzhěn bìngrén
over-the-counter drug 非处方药 fēi chǔfāngyào
overweight *adj* 超重的 chāozhòng de
payment of claim 索赔给付 suǒpéi jǐfù
pending claim 待决索赔 dàijué suǒpéi
permanent disability 永久残疾 yǒngjiǔ cánjí
permanent partial disability 永久局部残疾 yǒngjiǔ júbù cánjí
permanent total disability 永久完全残疾 yǒngjiǔ wánquán cánjí
physical handicap 身体残障 shēntǐ cánzhàng
physical injury 身体伤害 shēntǐ shānghài
physical therapy 理疗 lǐliáo
physician *n* 医生 yīshēng
plan *n* 计划 jìhuà
plan allowance 计划给付额 jìhuà jǐfù'é
policy *n* 保单 bǎodān
policy benefit 保险给付 bǎoxiǎn jǐfù
policy limit 保单限额 bǎodān xiàn'é

policyholder 保单持有人 bǎodān chíyǒurén

practitioner *n* 开业医生 kāiyè yīshēng

pre-admission certification 住院前核准 zhùyuàn qián hézhǔn

pre-admission review 住院前审核 zhùyuàn qián shěnhé

premium *n* 保险费 bǎoxiǎnfèi

pre-natal health 产前健康 chǎnqián jiànkāng

prescription *n* 处方 chǔfāng

prescription drug 处方药 chǔfāngyào

prescription drug benefit 处方药给付 chǔfāngyào jǐfù

prevent *v* 预防 yùfáng

prevention *n* 预防 yùfáng

preventive *adj* 预防的 yùfáng de

preventive medicine 预防医学 yùfáng yīxué

preventive screening 预防性筛查 yùfángxìng shāichá

private insurance 私人保险 sīrén bǎoxiǎn

professional *adj* 专业的 zhuānyè de

proof of loss 损失证明 sǔnshī zhèngmíng

prostatitis *n* 前列腺炎 qiánlièxiànyán

provider *n* 医疗服务提供者 yīliáo fúwù tígōngzhě

provider-patient relationship 医患关系 yīhuàn guānxì

psychiatrist *n* 精神病医生 jīngshénbìng yīshēng

psychiatry *n* 精神病学 jīngshénbìngxué

quality of life 生活质量 shēnghuó zhìliàng

recovery room 恢复室 huīfùshì

referral *n* 转诊 zhuǎnzhěn

referral line 转诊电话 zhuǎnzhěn diànhuà

referral service 转诊服务 zhuǎnzhěn fúwù

rehabilitation *n* 康复 kāngfù

retirement *n* 退休 tuìxiū

senior citizen 老人 lǎorén

senior services 老人服务 lǎorén fúwù

sexually transmitted disease 性传染病 xìng chuán jíbìng

sick *adj* 有病的 yǒubìng de

standard *n* 标准 biāozhǔn

standard of care 护理标准 hùlǐ biāozhǔn

stomach cancer 胃癌 wèi'ái

subscriber *n* 投保人 tóubǎorén

substandard care 不达标准的护理 bùdá biāozhǔn de hùlǐ

surgeon *n* 外科医生 wàikē yīshēng

surgery *n* 手术 shǒushù

survivor *n* 幸存者 xìngcúnzhě

temporary disability 暂时残疾 zànshí cánjí

terminate *v* 终止 zhōngzhǐ

terminations and denials 终止和拒绝 zhōngzhǐ hé jùjué

test *n* 化验 huàyàn, 检验 jiǎnyàn

therapy *n* 治疗 zhìliáo, 疗法 liáofǎ

tonsilitis *n* 扁桃体炎 biǎntáotǐyán

toxic *adj* 有毒的 yǒudú de

traditional medicine 传统医学 chuántǒng yīxué

trans fats; trans fatty acids 反式脂肪酸 fǎnshì
    zhīfángsuān

treatment *n* 治疗 zhìliáo

unemployment *n* 失业 shīyè

unemployment compensation 失业补偿金 shīyè
    bǔchángjīn, 失业救济金 shīyè jiùjìjīn

utilization review 使用情况审核 shǐyòng qíngkuàng
    shěnhé

waive *v* 放弃 fàngqì, 免除 miǎnchú

weight *n* 体重 tǐzhòng

weight loss 减肥 jiǎnféi, 体重减轻 tǐzhòng jiǎnqīng

weight management 控制体重 kòngzhì tǐzhòng

保健法词汇

welfare *n* 福利 fúlì

will *n* 遗嘱 yízhǔ

workman's compensation 工人补偿金 gōngrén
　　bǔchángjīn

written notice of claim 书面索赔通知 shūmiàn suǒpéi
　　tōngzhī

Housing Law
住房法词汇

Housing law deals with the rules that govern real property, how housing units such as apartments must be used and maintained, rental agreements, leases, mortgages, and the rights and duties of landlords and tenants. In the United States, state and local laws govern most housing-law issues.

abandon *v* 遗弃 yíqì

abandonment of premises 弃产 qì chǎn, 弃屋 qì wū

acceleration clause 加速条款 jiāsù tiáokuǎn

access to premises 房地进入权 fángdì jìnrùquán

accessory *adj* 附属的 fùshǔ de

accessory apartment 附属单元 fùshǔ dānyuán

accessory uses (土地) 附属用途 (tǔdì) fùshǔ yòngtú

active adult community 活跃成人社区 huóyuè chéngrén shèqū

adjustable rate mortgage (ARM) 可调利率按揭 kětiáo lìlǜ ànjiē

administrator's deed 遗产管理人契据 yíchǎn guǎnlǐrén qìjù

adverse possession 反向占有 fǎnxiàng zhànyǒu, 时效占有 shíxiào zhànyǒu

apartment *n* 公寓 gōngyù

apartment building *n* 公寓楼 gōngyù lóu

appraisal *n* 估价 gūjià

appraiser *n* 估价员 gūjiàyuán

ARM 见 adjustable rate mortgage
assessed value 计税估价 jìshuì gūjià
assessor *n* 估价员 gūjiàyuán
assignment of lease 租约转让 zūyuē zhuǎnràng
balloon mortgage 气球式按揭 qìqiúshì ànjiē
bargain and sale deed 房地产转让契据 fángdìchǎn
    zhuǎnràng qìjù
base rent 基本租金 jīběn zūjīn
bathroom *n* 卫生间 wèishēngjiān
beach home; beach house 海滨住宅 hǎibīn zhùzhái
bedroom *n* 卧室 wòshì
blockbusting *n* 制造街区恐慌 zhìzào jiēqū kǒnghuāng
    (*a practice by real estate agents to frighten
    white homeowners into selling their houses at
    a low price by telling them that minorities are
    moving into their neighborhood and driving down
    property values; afterwards the agents resell the
    houses at a much higher price, often to minorities* /
    指在白人住区散布谣言称少数族裔将大举迁入,
    致使屋主低价出售其产业)
broker *n* 经纪人 jīngjìrén
builder *n* 建筑商 jiànzhùshāng
building *n* 建筑物 jiànzhùwù, 楼房 lóufáng
bungalow *n* 平房 píngfáng
buydown *n* 买低 mǎidī (*a cash payment made to the
    lender by the seller, builder or buyer to reduce
    the buyer's mortgage rate, usually for the first
    one to five years of loan* / 卖方或买方付点数,
    换取低于市场的按揭利率, 常见的有2/1计划和
    3/2/1计划)
cession deed 转让契据 zhuǎnràng qìjù
closing *n* 过户会 guòhùhuì, 交割会 jiāogēhuì

commercial lease 商用租赁 shāngyòng zūlìn
commercial property 商用不动产 shāngyòng bùdòngchǎn
commission *n* 佣金 yòngjīn
common elements (康斗) 公用区 (kāngdǒu) gōngyòngqū
condominium *n* 共有公寓 gòngyǒu gōngyù, 康斗 kāngdǒu
constructive eviction 推定逐客 tuīdìng zhúkè
　　(when rented premises becomes uninhabitable
　　due to the landlord's action or inaction /
　　房东修缮不周致使房屋不适合居住,
　　又称变相逐客)
convey *v* 转让 zhuǎnràng
conveyance *n* 转让 zhuǎnràng
co-operative; co-op *n* 合作公寓 hézuò gōngyù
cost approach 成本法 chéngběn fǎ
court-ordered eviction 法院下令逐客 fǎyuàn xiàlìng zhúkè
covenant *n* 专约 zhuānyuē
covenant against encumbrances 无负担专约 wú fùdān zhuānyuē
covenant of quiet enjoyment 安宁享受专约 ānníng xiǎngshòu zhuānyuē
deed *n* 契据 qìjù, 文书 wénshū
deed of correction 改正契据 gǎizhèng qìjù
deed of gift 赠与契据 zèngyǔ qìjù
deed of trust 信托契据 xìntuō qìjù
Department of Housing and Urban Development (HUD) 联邦住房和城市发展部 liánbāng zhùfáng hé chéngshì fāzhǎn bù
deposit *n* 押金 yājīn
developer *n* 开发商 kāifāshāng
dining room 餐厅 cāntīng
direct costs 直接费用 zhíjiē fèiyòng

easement *n* 地役权 dìyìquán

equity *n* 净值 jìngzhí

estate *n* 房地产 ángdìchǎn, 房地产权 fángdìchǎnquán

estate at sufferance 见 holdover tenant

estate at will 随意租约 suíyì zūyuē

estate for years 限期租约 xiànqī zūyuē

evict *v* 驱逐房客 qūzhú fángkè

eviction *n* 驱逐房客 qūzhú fángkè

exclusive agency listing 独家代理契约 dújiā dàilǐ qìyuē

exclusive right to sell listing 独家销售权契约 dújiā xiāoshòuquán qìyuē

executor's deed 遗产执行人契据 yíchǎn zhíxíngrén qìjù

expiration of lease term 租约期满 zūyuē qīmǎn

fair housing 公平住房 gōngpíng zhùfáng

family room 家庭厅 jiātíng tīng

Federal Home Loan Mortgage Corporation (Freddie Mac) 联邦住房抵押贷款公司 liánbāng zhùfáng dǐyā dàikuǎn gōngsī

Federal Housing Administration (FHA) 联邦住房管理局 liánbāng zhùfáng guǎnlǐ jú

fee simple absolute 无条件产权 wútiáojiàn chǎnquán

fee simple defeasible 有条件产权 yǒutiáojiàn chǎnquán

fence *n* 栅栏 zhàlan

FHA 见 Federal Housing Administration

financing *n* 贷款 dàikuǎn

first refusal right 见 right of first refusal

fixed-date estate 见 estate for years

fixture *n* 固定附着物 gùdìng fùzhuówù

foreclose *v* 取消赎回权 qǔxiāo shúhuíquán, 法拍 fǎ pāi

foreclosure *n* 赎回权的取消 shúhuíquán de qǔxiāo

Freddie Mac 见 Federal Home Loan Mortgage Corporation

free-hold estate 自主持有地产权 zìzhǔ chíyǒu dìchǎnquán

front room 客厅 kètīng

full covenant and warranty deed 完全担保契据
wánquán dānbǎo qìjù

garage *n* 车库 chēkù

general warranty deed 全权契据 quánquán qìjù,
无债权契据 wúzhàiquán qìjù

graduated lease 浮动租金租约 fúdòng zūjīn zūyuē

grant *n* 转让 zhuǎnràng

grantee *n* 受让人 shòuràngrén

grantor *n* 转让人 zhuǎnràngrén

ground lease 土地租约 tǔdì zūyuē

habitable *adj* 适于居住的 shìyú jūzhù de

heating *n* 供暖 gōngnuǎn

holding period 持有期间 chíyǒu qījiān

holdover tenant 逾期房客 yúqī fángkè (*a tenant who
fails to leave the leased premises after the term of
lease has expired* / 指租约到期而不搬走的房客)

home *n* 住房 zhùfáng

home equity line of credit 房屋净值信贷额度 fángwū
jìngzhí xìndài édù

home equity loan 房屋净值贷款 fángwū jìngzhí dàikuǎn

house *n* 房屋 fángwū, 住宅 zhùzhái

housing *n* 住房 zhùfáng

housing court 房屋法院 fángwū fǎyuàn

housing project 住房工程 zhùfáng gōngchéng

HUD 见 Department of Housing and Urban Development

inspection *n* 检查 jiǎnchá

insured value 保险价值 bǎoxiǎn jiàzhí

involuntary lien 非自愿留置权 fēizìyuàn liúzhìquán

joint tenancy 联权共有 liánquán gòngyǒu, 联名房产权
liánmíng fángchǎnquán

judicial deed 法院契据 fǎyuàn qìjù

junior mortgage 二级按揭 èrjí ànjiē

kitchen *n* 厨房 chúfáng

landlord *n* 房东 fángdōng

laundry room 洗衣室 xǐyīshì

lease *n* 租赁 zūlìn; *v* 出租 chūzū, 租得 zūdé

lease agreement 租约 zūyuē

lease expiration 租约期满 zūyuē qīmǎn

lease term 租赁条件 zūlìn tiáojiàn

lease-hold estate 租赁持有地产权 zūlìn chíyǒu dìchǎnquán

lessee *n* 承租人 chéngzūrén

lessor *n* 出租人 chūzūrén

lien *n* 留置权 liúzhìquán

life estate 终身地产权 zhōngshēn dìchǎnquán

listed property 上市房地产 shàngshì fángdìchǎn

listing contract 房屋销售合同 fángwū xiāoshòu hétong

littoral rights 海滨产权 hǎibīn chǎnquán

living room 客厅 kètīng

loan-to-value ratio 贷款价值比 dàikuǎn jiàzhí bǐ

log home; log house 原木房 yuánmùfáng

lot *n* 地块 dìkuài

low-income housing 低收入者住房 dīshōurùzhě zhùfáng

luxury home 豪华住宅 háohuá zhùzhái

maintain *v* 维护 wéihù

maintenance *n* 维护 wéihù

manufactured home 预制房 yùzhì fáng

market value 市场价值 shìchǎng jiàzhí

materialman's lien 建材供应商留置权 jiàncái gōngyìngshāng liúzhìquán

mechanic's lien 技工留置权 jìgōng liúzhìquán

metes and bounds 边界线 biānjièxiàn

mobile home 活动房 huódòng fáng

modular home 模块房 mókuài fáng

mortgage *n* 按揭 ànjiē, 房屋抵押贷款 fángwū dǐyā dàikuǎn

mortgagee *n* 按揭权人 ànjiēquánrén (*The lender in a mortgage agreement* / 指放款方)

mortgagor *n* 按揭 人 ànjiērén (*The borrower in a mortgage agreement* / 指借款方)

multi-family housing 多家庭住房 duō jiātíng zhùfáng

negative covenant 消极专约 xiāojí zhuānyuē

notice to quit 搬迁通知 bānqiān tōngzhī

occupancy *n* 居住 jūzhù

open house 公开展示 gōngkāi zhǎnshì

open-end mortgage 不封口按揭 bùfēngkǒu ànjiē (*mortgage in which the borrower is allowed to re-borrow against principal that has been paid* / 让借款人用已偿本金作抵押再借款)

open-ended estate 见 estate at will

open-listing agreement 公开销售契约 gōngkāi xiāoshòu qìyuē

option to renew 续签选择 xùqiān xuǎnzé

owner *n* 所有人 suǒyǒurén, 业主 yèzhǔ

partition *n* 隔间 géjiān; *v* 分割 fēngē

party wall 共用墙 gòngyòng qiáng

permit *n* 许可证 xǔkězhèng

plat *n* 地籍图 dìjítú

plottage *n* 组合地块 zǔhé dìkuài

points *n* 点数 diǎnshù

positive covenant 积极专约 jījí zhuānyuē

possession *n* 占有 zhànyǒu

premises *n* 房地 fángdì (*land and the buildings on it* / 指宅基地和宅基地上的房屋)

prepayment clause 提前清偿条款 tíqián qīngcháng tiáokuǎn

primary mortgage 一级按揭 yījí ànjiē

principal residence 主要居所 zhǔyào jūsuǒ

principal uses 主要用途 zhǔyào yòngtú

property *n* 财产 cáichǎn, 财产权 cáichǎnquán

property interest 财产权益 cáichǎn quányì

property tax 财产税 cáichǎnshuì

proprietary lease 产权租赁 chǎnquán zūlìn

purchase-money mortgage 售方按揭 shòufāng ànjiē
   (*home-financing technique in which the buyer borrows from the seller* / 卖方向买方提供的抵押贷款)

quiet enjoyment 安宁享受 ānníng xiǎngshòu

quiet title 产权归属诉讼 chǎnquán guīshǔ sùsòng

quitclaim deed 弃权契据 qìquán qìjù, 放弃权利证书 fàngqì quánlì zhèngshū

radon inspection 氡检查 dōng jiǎnchá

ratification *n* 认可 rènkě

real estate 房地产 fángdìchǎn, 不动产 bùdòngchǎn

real estate broker 房地产经纪人 fángdìchǎn jīngjìrén

realtor *n* 会员经纪人 huìyuán jīngjìrén

redeem *v* 赎回 shúhuí, 偿清 chángqīng

redemption *n* 赎回 shúhuí, 偿清 chángqīng

redlining *n* 拒绝发放按揭 jùjué fāfàng ànjiē

referee's deed 见 sheriff's deed

refinancing *n* 重新贷款 chóngxīn dàikuǎn

rent *n* 租金 zūjīn

rent control 租金控制 zūjīn kòngzhì

rent regulation 租金管制 zūjīn guǎnzhì

rent stabilization 租金稳定 zūjīn wěndìng

repossession *n* 收回 shōuhuí, 重新占有 chóngxīn zhànyǒu

residence *n* 居所 jūsuǒ

resident *n* 居民 jūmín

residential *adj* 居住的 jūzhù de, 居民的 jūmín de

residential market 住宅市场 zhùzhái shìchǎng

residential market analysis 住宅市场分析 zhùzhái shìchǎng fēnxī

residential property 住宅用不动产 zhùzhái yòng bùdòngchǎn

restrictive covenant 限制性专约 xiànzhìxìng zhuānyuē

retirement community 退休社区 tuìxiū shèqū

retirement home 退休房 tuìxiū fáng

reversion *n* 复归 fùguī

reversionary interest 复归权益 fùguī quányì

revocation *n* 撤销 chèxiāo

RHS 见 Rural Housing Service

rider *n* 附件 fùjiàn, 附加条款 fùjiā tiáokuǎn

right of first refusal 先购权 xiāngòuquán

right of survivorship 生存者取得权 shēngcúnzhě qǔdé quán

riparian rights 河岸权 hé'ànquán

rooming house 寄宿舍 jìsùshè

Rural Housing Service (RHS) 农村住房服务局 nóngcūn zhùfáng fúwù jú

sales agent 销售代理 xiāoshòu dàilǐ

school district 学区 xuéqū

secondary mortgage 二级按揭 èrjí ànjiē

secondary mortgage market 二级按揭市场 èrjí ànjiē shìchǎng

security deposit 押金 yājīn

shelter *n* 住房 zhùfáng

sheriff's deed 执法官契据 zhífǎguān qìjù

single-family home 一家庭住房 yī jiātíng zhùfáng

special use permit 特别用途许可证 tèbié yòngtú xǔkězhèng

special warranty deed 特别担保契据 tèbié dānbǎo qìjù

squatter *n* 非法占用者 fēifǎ zhànyòngzhě

steering *n* 操引 cāoyǐn (*illegal practice of directing home buyers to different neighborhoods according to their race* / 按购房人或租房人的种族、肤色将其带到不同地区的非法做法)

storage room 储存室 chǔcúnshì

straight term mortgage 分期付息到期还本的按揭 fēnqī fùxī dàoqī huánběn de ànjiē

studio apartment 一室公寓房 yīshì gōngyù fáng

sublease *v* 转租 zhuǎnzū, 分租 fēnzū

sublessee; subtenant *n* 转租承租人 zhuǎnzū chéngzūrén, 转租房客 zhuǎnzū fángkè, 二房客 èrfángkè

sublet *v* 转租 zhuǎnzū, 分租 fēnzū

subprime mortgage 次级按揭 cìjí ànjiē

subsidized housing 补贴住房 bǔtiē zhùfáng

tax deed 税契 shuìqì

tax lien 税收留置权 shuìshōu liúzhìquán

tenancy by the entirety 完全共有 wánquán gòngyǒu

tenancy in common 分权共有 fēnquán gòngyǒu

tenant *n* 房客 fángkè, 承租人 chéngzūrén

termite inspection 白蚁检查 báiyǐ jiǎnchá

title *n* 产权 chǎnquán

title insurance 产权保险 chǎnquán bǎoxiǎn

title search 产权调查 chǎnquán diàochá

trespass *v* 擅自进入 shànzì jìnrù

two-family home 二家庭住房 èr jiātíng zhùfáng

uninhabitable *adj* 不适宜居住的 bùshìyí jūzhù de

utilities *n* 公用事业 gōngyòng shìyè

vacate *v* 搬出 bānchū
valuation *n* 估价 gūjià
wall *n* 墙 qiáng
warranty deed 担保契据 dānbǎo qìjù
waste *n* 废物 fèiwù
wear and tear 磨损 mósǔn
wraparound mortgage 包裹按揭 bāoguǒ ànjiē
zoning *n* 区划 qūhuà

Immigration Law
移民法词汇

Immigration law deals with the conditions under which foreign persons are admitted to the United States as temporary visitors or permanent residents and how they become U.S. citizens. These rules are now administered by the Department of Homeland Security.

A-1 Visa A-1 签证 a-yī qiānzhèng (*for diplomats* / 外交人员签证)

A-2 Visa A-2 签证 a-èr qiānzhèng (*for official business* / 公务人员签证)

A-3 Visa A-3 签证 a-sān qiānzhèng (*for attendants, servants and personal employees of A-1 and A-2 visa holders* / A-1、A-2 签证持有者的私人随行人员签证)

AAO 见 Administrative Appeals Office

abused alien 受虐外国人 shòu nuè wàiguórén

abused immigrant spouse 受虐移民配偶 shòu nuè yímín pèi'ǒu

accompanying relative 偕行亲属 xiéxíng qīnshǔ

accompanying visa 陪伴签证 péibàn qiānzhèng

acquired citizenship 依血统取得的公民身份 yī xuètǒng qǔdé de gōngmín shēnfèn

adjust *v* 调整 tiáozhěng

adjustment of status 调整身份 tiáozhěng shēnfèn

Administrative Appeals Office (AAO) 行政上诉办公室 xíngzhèng shàngsù bàngōngshì

admission *n* 入境 rùjìng

advance parole 预先入境许可 yùxiān rùjìng xǔkě (俗称回美证 *a.k.a* huíměizhèng)

advisal of rights 告知权利 gàozhī quánlì

AEDPA 见 Antiterrorism and Effective Death Penalty Act

Affidavit of Support (I-864) 经济担保书 (I-864 表) jīngjì dānbǎoshū

affiliation *n* 从属关系 cóngshǔ guānxì

affirmation *n* 确认 quèrèn

affirmative asylum process 主动庇护程序 zhǔdòng bìhù chéngxù

agricultural worker 农工 nónggōng

alien *adj* 外国的 wàiguó de; *n* 外国人 wàiguórén, 外侨 wàiqiáo

alien labor certification 外国人劳工证 wàiguórén láogōngzhèng, 劳工纸 láogōngzhǐ

alien of extraordinary ability (EB-1(a)) 杰出人才 jiéchū réncái

alien registration number 外国人登记号码 wàiguórén dēngjì hàomǎ, 绿卡号码 lǜkǎ hàomǎ

alien registration receipt card (Form I-551; green card) 外国人登记收据卡 wàiguórén dēngjì shōujù kǎ (即 *I-551* 表, 也就是绿卡)

alternate chargeability 替代记入 tìdài jìrù

alternate order of removal 替代驱逐出境令 tìdài qūzhú chūjìng lìng

annual limit 年度限额 niándù xiàn'é

ANSIR 见 Automated Nationwide System for Immigration Review

Antiterrorism and Effective Death Penalty Act (AEDPA) 反恐和有效死刑法 fǎnkǒng hé yǒuxiào sǐxíng fǎ

applicant *n* 申请人 shēnqǐngrén

applicant for admission 入境申请人 rùjìng shēnqǐngrén

applicant for political asylum 政治庇护申请人 zhèngzhì bìhù shēnqǐngrén

application *n* 申请 shēnqǐng, 申请书 shēnqǐngshū

application for adjustment of status 申请调整身份 shēnqǐng tiáozhěng shēnfèn

application for admission 申请入境 shēnqǐng rùjìng

application for cancellation of removal 申请撤销驱逐出境 shēnqǐng chèxiāo qūzhú chūjìng

application support center (ASC) 申请协助中心 shēnqǐng xiézhù zhōngxīn (*of USCIS, offering fingerprint and other services* / 移民局下设机构, 提供打指印等服务)

apply for a visa 申请签证 shēnqǐng qiānzhèng

appointment package 面谈需携带资料 miàntán xū xiédài zīliào

approval notice 批准通知 pīzhǔn tōngzhī

arrival category 入境类别 rùjìng lèibié

arrival date 入境日期 rùjìng rìqī

Arrival-Departure Card (I-94) 入境-出境卡 rùjìng-chūjìng kǎ (*I-94表 i-jiǔ sì biǎo*)

arriving alien 入境外国人 rùjìng wàiguórén

ASC 见 application support center

Asian American 亚裔美国人 yàyì měiguórén

asylee *n* 受庇护者 shòu bìhù zhě, 寻求庇护者 xúnqiú bìhù zhě

asylee application 庇护申请 bìhù shēnqǐng

asylee status 受庇护者身份 shòu bìhù zhě shēnfèn

asylum *n* 庇护 bìhù

asylum officer 庇护官 bìhùguān

asylum seeker 寻求庇护者 xúnqiú bìhù zhě

asylum-only hearing 只关庇护听证会 zhǐ guān bìhù tīngzhènghuì

attestation *n* 见证 jiànzhèng

Automated Nationwide System for Immigration Review (ANSIR) 全国自动化移民审查系统 quánguó zìdònghuà yímín shěnchá xìtǒng

B-1 Visa B-1 签证 b-yī qiānzhèng (*for business-related activities* / 商务签证)

B-2 Visa B-2 签证 b-èr qiānzhèng (*for tourists* / 旅游签证)

bar to asylum 禁止庇护 jìnzhǐ bìhù

bar to readmission 禁止再入境 jìnzhǐ zài rùjìng

battered *adj* 受到殴打的 shòudào ōudǎ de

battered child 被殴儿童 bèi ōu értóng

battered spouse 被殴配偶 bèi ōu pèi'ǒu

battered spouse/child relief 对被殴配偶和儿童的法律救济 duì bèi ōu pèi'ǒu hé értóng de fǎlǜ jiùjì

battered spouse waiver 被殴配偶豁免 bèi ōu pèi'ǒu huòmiǎn

biographical (biographic) information 个人简历 gèrén jiǎnlì

BIS 见 Board of Immigration Appeals

Board of Immigration Appeals (BIS) 移民上诉委员会 yímín shàngsù wěiyuánhuì

border crosser 跨界往来者 kuàjiè wǎnglái zhě (*an alien resident of the United States reentering the country after an absence of less than six months in Canada or Mexico; or a nonresident alien entering the United States across the Canadian border for stays of no more than six months or across the Mexican border for stays of no more than 72 hours* / 指从美加和美墨边界进境的居民或非居民外国人)

border patrol 边境巡逻 biānjìng xúnluó

Border Patrol Sector 边境巡逻区 biānjìng xúnluóqū

business non-immigrant 商务非移民 shāngwù fēi yímín

cancellation of removal 撤销驱逐出境 chèxiāo qūzhú chūjìng

cancelled without prejudice 无害注销 wúhài zhùxiāo

case number 个案编号 gè'àn biānhào

central address file 通信地址总录 tōngxìn dìzhǐ zǒnglù

certificate of citizenship 公民证书 gōngmín zhèngshū

certificate of naturalization 归化证书 guīhuà zhèngshū

change of status 改变身份 gǎibiàn shēnfèn

changed circumstances 情事变更 qíngshì biàngēng

charge *v* 记入 jìrù (*to count an immigrant towards a given country's numerical limit* / 指申请人使用某一国家或地区的移民配额)

chargeable *adj* 可记入 kě jìrù

China's mainland 中国大陆 zhōngguó dàlù

Chinese American 美籍华人 měijí huárén, 华裔美国人 huáyì měiguórén

citizenship *n* 公民身份 gōngmín shēnfèn, 公民资格 gōngmín zīgé

clear, convincing, and unequivocal evidence 清楚、可信、无疑的证据 qīngchǔ kěxìn wúyí de zhèngjù

clearly and beyond a doubt 清楚无疑 qīngchǔ wúyí

co-applicant *n* 共同申请人 gòngtóng shēnqǐngrén

conditional grant 有条件准予 yǒutiáojiàn zhǔnyǔ

conditional residence visa 有条件居留签证 yǒutiáojiàn jūliú qiānzhèng

conditional resident 有条件居民 yǒutiáojiàn jūmín

consequence *n* 后果 hòuguǒ

consular officer 领事官 lǐngshìguān

consulate *n* 领事馆 lǐngshìguǎn

Immigration Law

consulate general 总领事馆 zǒnglǐngshìguǎn

continuous physical presence 连续实际住在 liánxù shíjì zhùzài

continuous residence 连续居住 liánxù jūzhù

country of birth 出生国 chūshēng guó

country of chargeability 记入国 jìrù guó

crewman *n* 机组人员 jīzǔ rényuán, 海员 hǎiyuán

criminal alien 犯罪的外国人 fànzuì de wàiguórén

criminal removal 因刑事犯罪驱逐出境 yīn xíngshì fànzuì qūzhú chūjìng

current *adj* 轮到 lúndào, 有名额 yǒu míng'é
    (*One's case is current when one's **priority date** is earlier than the **cut-off date** according to the monthly **Visa Bulletin**. This means one's immigrant visa case can now be processed. /* 指优先日期早于截止日期, 轮到办理签证手续。)

current status 当前身份 dāngqián shēnfèn

custody redetermination hearing 重新设定担保金数额听证会 chóngxīn shèdìng dānbǎojīn shù'é tīngzhènghuì

cut-off date 截止日期 jiézhǐ rìqī

danger to the community 对社区的威胁 duì shèqū de wēixié

defensive asylum process 被动庇护程序 bèidòng bìhù chéngxù

deferred sentence 暂缓执行的判决 zànhuǎn zhíxíng de pànjué

Department of Homeland Security (DHS) 国土安全部 guótǔ ānquán bù

Department of Labor (DOL) 劳工部 láogōngbù

departure under safeguards 监督离境 jiāndū líjìng

移民法词汇

dependent *n* 家属 jiāshǔ (*spouse and/or children under 21* / 指配偶和不满21岁的子女)

deport *v* 递解出境 dìjiè chūjìng

deportable alien 应递解出境的外国人 yīng dìjiè chūjìng de wàiguórén

deportation *n* 递解出境 dìjiè chūjìng

deportation hearing 递解出境听证会 dìjiè chūjìng tīngzhènghuì

derivative beneficiary 派生受益人 pàishēng shòuyìrén

derivative citizenship 派生公民身份 pàishēng gōngmín shēnfèn

derivative status 派生身份 pàishēng shēnfèn

discretion *n* 酌情裁量权 zhuóqíng cáiliàngquán

discretionary relief 酌情救济 zhuóqíng jiùjì

district office *(of USCIS)* 支局 zhījú (*USCIS has 26 district offices* / 移民局设有26个支局)

diversity country 多元化国家 duōyuánhuà guójiā (*a country that has a low rate of immigration to the United States* / 指对美移民率低的国家)

diversity immigrant (DV) 多元化移民 duōyuánhuà yímín

Diversity Immigrant Visa Program 多元化移民签证计划 duōyuánhuà yímín qiānzhèng jìhuà

Diversity Visa Lottery 多元化签证抽签 duōyuánhuà qiānzhèng chōuqiān

documentarily qualified 材料合格的 cáiliào hégé de

DOL 见 Department of Labor

domicile *n* 住所 zhùsuǒ

domiciled *adj* 定居的 dìngjū de

duration of status 身份有效期 shēnfèn yǒuxiàoqī

DV 见 diversity immigrant

DV Lottery 见 Diversity Visa Lottery

education level 教育水平 jiàoyù shuǐpíng, 文化程度 wénhuà chéngdù

eligibility *n* 合格 hégé

embassy *n* 大使馆 dàshǐguǎn

emigrant *n* 移民 yímín (*an immigrant from the perspective of the country of origin* / 指离境移民)

employment authorization 工作许可 gōngzuò xǔkě (俗称工卡 *a.k.a* gōngkǎ)

employment-based first (second, third, fourth, fifth) preference 职业第一 (第二、第三、第四、第五) 优先 zhíyè dì-yī (dì-èr, dì-sān, dì-sì, dì-wǔ) yōuxiān

English proficiency 英语水平 yīngyǔ shuǐpíng

entitled to be admitted 应予入境的 yīng yǔ rùjìng de

establish eligibility as a refugee 确定难民资格 quèdìng nànmín zīgé

exceptional circumstances 例外情况 lìwài qíngkuàng

exchange alien 交换学者 jiāohuàn xuézhě

exchange visitor 交换学者 jiāohuàn xuézhě

excludable alien 禁止入境的外国人 jìnzhǐ rùjìng de wàiguórén

exclusion *n* 禁止入境 jìnzhǐ rùjìng

expedited hearing 速办听证会 sùbàn tīngzhènghuì

expedited removal proceeding 加速驱逐程序 jiāsù qūzhú chéngxù

expiration date 过期日 guòqīrì

expulsion *n* 驱逐 qūzhú

extension of stay 延期停留 yánqī tíngliú

extreme cruelty 极端残酷 jíduān cánkù

extreme hardship 极端困难 jíduān kùnnan

failure to appear 不出庭 bùchūtíng, 逃庭 táotíng

failure to depart 不离境 bùlíjìng

failure to surrender 不投案 bùtóu'àn

false marriage 假结婚 jiǎ jiéhūn

Family Unity Program 家庭团聚计划 jiātíng tuánjù jìhuà

family-sponsored first (second, third, fourth)
    preference 家庭第一 (第二、第三、第四) 优先
    jiātíng dì-yī (dì-èr, dì-sān, dì-sì) yōuxiān

Federal Poverty Guidelines 联邦贫穷线指导方针
    liánbāng pínqióngxiàn zhǐdǎo fāngzhēn

field office 地方办事处 dìfāng bànshìchù (*of USCIS /*
    移民支局下设机构)

filing fee 申请费 shēnqǐngfèi

final order of removal 最终驱逐令 zuìzhōng qūzhú lìng

fingerprint *n* 指印 zhǐyìn; *v* 打指印 dǎ zhǐyìn

firmly resettled (*refugees*) 已永久安置 yǐ yǒngjiǔ ānzhì

first (second, third, fourth, fifth) preference 第一
    (第二、第三、第四、第五) 优先 dì-yī (dì-èr,
    dì-sān, dì-sì, dì-wǔ) yōuxiān

following to join 随后团聚 suíhòu tuánjù

forensic document laboratory 文件法证实验室 wénjiàn
    fǎzhèng shíyànshì

frivolous application 琐屑性申请 suǒxièxìng shēnqǐng

full-time student 全日学生 quánrì xuéshēng

gender-related persecution 性别迫害 xìngbié pòhài

genuine fear of persecution 对迫害的真切恐惧 duì
    pòhài de zhēnqiè kǒngjù

green card 绿卡 lǜkǎ

green card lottery 绿卡抽签 lǜkǎ chōuqiān

homeless *adj* 无家的 wújiā de

Hong Kong SAR 香港特别行政区 xiānggǎng tèbié
    xíngzhèngqū

household income 家庭收入 jiātíng shōurù

I-551 见 alien registration receipt card

ICE 见 Immigration and Customs Enforcement

identification card 身份证 shēnfènzhèng

illegal entry 偷渡 tōudù

Illegal Immigration Reform and Immigrant Responsibility Act 非法移民改革和移民责任法 fēifǎ yímín gǎigé hé yímín zérèn fǎ

immediate family 直系家庭 zhíxì jiātíng (*generally used to refer to the smallest unit of a family that an individual lives with, which usually includes a father, a mother and siblings /* 一般指父母和子女组成的小家庭)

immediate relative 直系亲属 zhíxì qīnshǔ (*spouse, widow(er) and unmarried children under the age of 21 of an American citizen; a parent is an immediate relative if the American citizen is 21 years of age or older /* 美国公民的直系亲属包括其配偶、其21岁以下未婚子女以及21岁以上美国公民的父母)

immigrant *n* 移民 yímín (指入境移民)

immigrant petition 移民申请 yímín shēnqǐng

immigrant visa 移民签证 yímín qiānzhèng

immigration *n* 移民 yímín

Immigration and Customs Enforcement (ICE) 移民与海关执行局 yímín yǔ hǎiguān zhíxíng jú

Immigration and Nationality Act (INA) 移民与国籍法 yímín yǔ guójí fǎ

Immigration and Naturalization Service (INS) 移民与归化局 yímín yǔ guīhuà jú (*INS changed its name in 2003 to the* **United States Citizenship and Immigration Services (USCIS)** / 移民与归化局 2003年改称美国公民与移民服务局, 中文仍简称 移民局)

immigration hold 移民扣留令 yímín kòuliú lìng

immigration judge 移民法官 yímín fǎguān

移民法词汇

immigration lawyer (attorney) 移民律师 yímín lǜshī

immigration officer 移民官 yímínguān

immigration record 移民记录 yímín jìlù

INA 见 Immigration and Nationality Act

inadmissible alien 禁止入境的外国人 jìnzhǐ rùjìng de wàiguórén

ineligible *adj* 无资格的 wú zīgé de, 不合格的 bùhégé de

instruction package 指南材料袋 zhǐnán cáiliào dài

intention to rescind 撤销身份的意向 chèxiāo shēnfèn de yìxiàng

interview *n* 面试 miànshì

intracompany transferee 跨国公司调派人员 kuàguógōngsī diàopài rényuán

joint sponsor 共同担保人 gòngtóng dānbǎorén

K-1 Visa K-1 签证 k-yī qiānzhèng (*nonimmigrant visa for fiancé(e) to travel to the United States for marriage* / 未婚夫 (妻) 签证)

labor certification 劳工证 láogōngzhèng, 劳工纸 láogōngzhǐ

Labor Condition Application (LCA) 劳工情况申请表 láogōng qíngkuàng shēnqǐngbiǎo

last residence 上一个住所 shàng yīgè zhùsuǒ

lawful permanent resident (LPR) 合法永久居民 héfǎ yǒngjiǔ jūmín

lawful permanent resident alien (LPRA) 合法永久居民 héfǎ yǒngjiǔ jūmín

lawfully admitted 合法入境 héfǎ rùjìng

lay worker 平信徒杂役 píngxìntú záyì

LCA 见 Labor Condition Application

Legal Immigration Family Equity Act 合法移民家庭公平法 héfǎ yímín jiātíng gōngpíng fǎ

legalized alien 取得合法居留身份的外国人 qǔdé héfǎ jūliú shēnfèn de wàiguórén

legitimated *adj* 合法化的 héfǎhuà de

level of education 教育水平 jiàoyù shuǐpíng, 文化程度 wénhuà chéngdù

LIFE Act 见 Legal Immigration Family Equity Act

lottery *n* 抽签 chōuqiān

LPR 见 lawful permanent resident

LPRA 见 lawful permanent resident alien

Macao SAR 澳门特别行政区 àomén tèbié xíngzhèngqū

machine-readable passport (MRP) 机器可读护照 jīqì kědú hùzhào

machine-readable visa (MRV) 机器可读签证 jīqì kědú qiānzhèng

maintenance of status and departure bond 保持身份和离境担保金 bǎochí shēnfèn hé líjìng dānbǎojīn

Managers and Executive Transferees (EB-1(c)) 跨国公司经理 kuàguógōngsī jīnglǐ

mandatory detention 强制羁押 qiángzhì jīyā

marital status 婚姻状况 hūnyīn zhuàngkuàng

marriage certificate 结婚证书 jiéhūn zhèngshū

marriage fraud 婚姻欺诈 hūnyīn qīzhà

medical waiver 健康豁免 jiànkāng huòmiǎn

migrant farm (or agricultural) worker 流动农工 liúdòng nónggōng

moral turpitude 道德堕落 dàodé duòluò

motion for termination 终止动议 zhōngzhǐ dòngyì

MRP 见 machine-readable passport

MRV 见 machine-readable visa

National Benefit Center (NBC) 全国服务中心 quánguó fúwù zhōngxīn (*of USCIS* / 移民局所属机构)

national interest 国家利益 guójiā lìyì

national interest waiver (NIV) 国家利益豁免 guójiā lìyì huòmiǎn

nationality *n* 国籍 guójí

naturalization *n* 归化 guīhuà, 入籍 rùjí

naturalization application 归化申请 guīhuà shēnqǐng

naturalization ceremony 归化仪式 guīhuà yíshì

naturalization court 归化法院 guīhuà fǎyuàn

naturalization papers 归化文件 guīhuà wénjiàn

naturalized citizen 归化公民 guīhuà gōngmín

NBC 见 National Benefit Center

negative factor 负面因素 fùmiàn yīnsù

NIV 见 national interest waiver

no-match letter 身份不符通知 shēnfèn bùfú tōngzhī
(*letter from the Social Security Administration to an employer stating that an employee's reported Social Security number does not match SSA records* / 社会保障署给雇主的信件，指出雇员的社会保障号码与社会保障署的记录不符)

nonacademic student (M-1 Visa) 非学位学生 fēi xuéwèi xuéshēng (*M-1*签证*m-yī qiānzhèng*)

noncurrent *adj* 未轮到 wèi lúndào, 无名额 wú míng'é
(*One's case is non-current when one's priority date is later than the cut-off date according to the monthly Visa Bulletin. This means one will need to wait until one's priority date is reached.* / 指优先日期晚于截止日期，需要继续等待。)

nondisclosure *n* 不披露 bùpīlù

nonimmigrant *n* 非移民 fēi yímín

nonimmigrant visa 非移民签证 fēi yímín qiānzhèng

nonresident alien 非居民外国人 fēi jūmín wàiguórén

notice to appear (NTA) 出庭通知 chūtíng tōngzhī

NTA 见 notice to appear
numerical limit 数量限制 shùliàng xiànzhì
oath *n* 宣誓 xuānshì
occupation *n* 职业 zhíyè
Office of Immigration Litigation (OIL) 移民诉讼局
　　yímín sùsòng jú
OIL 见 Office of Immigration Litigation
one-year filing deadline 见 one-year rule
one-year rule 一年规则 yīnián guīzé
out of status 丧失合法身份 sàngshī héfǎ shēnfèn
Outstanding Professor 杰出教授 jiéchū jiàoshòu
Outstanding Researcher (EB-1(b)) 杰出研究员 jiéchū
　　yánjiūyuán
overstay 逾期逗留 yúqī dòuliú
panel physician 指定移民医生 zhǐdìng yímín yīshēng
parole *n* 权宜入境许可 quányí rùjìng xǔkě
parole someone into the U.S. 权宜许可入境美国
　　quányí xǔkě rùjìng měiguó
paroled aliens 权宜入境的外国人 quányí rùjìng de
　　wàiguórén
parolee *n* 权宜入境者 quányí rùjìng zhě
particularly serious crime 特别严重的罪行 tèbié
　　yánzhòng de zuìxíng
part-time student 非全日学生 fēi quánrì xuéshēng
passport *n* 护照 hùzhào
people smuggling 人口走私 rénkǒu zǒusī
people-smuggling syndicate 偷渡集团 tōudù jítuán
per-country limit 各国签证限额 gèguó qiānzhèng xiàn'é
permanent resident 永久居民 yǒngjiǔ jūmín
permanent resident card (PRC) 永久居民卡 yǒngjiǔ
　　jūmín kǎ
petition for review 复核申请 fùhé shēnqǐng

petitioner *n* 申请人 shēnqǐngrén

place of last entry 最后一次入境地点 zuìhòu yícì rùjìng dìdiǎn

plausible in light of country conditions 根据国家情况 (证言) 似乎可信 gēnjù guójiā qíngkuàng (zhèngyán) sìhū kěxìn

POCR 见 post order custody review

political asylum 政治庇护 zhèngzhì bìhù

port of entry 入境口岸 rùjìng kǒu'àn

post order custody review (POCR) 驱逐令下达后扣押 审查 qūzhúlìng xiàdá hòu kòuyā shěnchá

PRC 见 permanent resident card

preclude *v* 防止 fángzhǐ, 阻止 zǔzhǐ, 排除 páichú

preference category 优先类别 yōuxiān lèibié

preference immigrant 优先移民 yōuxiān yímín

preference system 优先制度 yōuxiān zhìdù

pre-inspection *n* 事先检查 shìxiān jiǎnchá

prima facie eligibility 初看合格 chūkàn hégé

primary beneficiary 主要受益人 zhǔyào shòuyìrén

principal alien 主要外国人 zhǔyào wàiguórén

priority date 优先日期 yōuxiān rìqī

public charge 公共负担 gōnggòng fùdān

qualifying family relationship 合乎规定的家庭关系 héhū guīdìng de jiātíng guānxì

quota *n* 配额 pèi'é

record of proceeding (ROP) 听证记录 tīngzhèng jìlù

records check 检查记录 jiǎnchá jìlù

re-entry permission 再入境许可 zài rùjìng xǔkě

refugee *n* 难民 nànmín

refugee approvals 难民批准人数 nànmín pīzhǔn rénshù

refugee arrivals 难民入境人数 nànmín rùjìng rénshù

Immigration Law

refugee authorized admissions 核准难民入境人数 hézhǔn nànmín rùjìng rénshù

refugee status 难民身份 nànmín shēnfèn

regional office 分局 fēnjú (*of USCIS; USCIS has 4 regional offices* / 移民局设有四个分局)

    Central Regional Office 中区分局 zhōngqū fēnjú

    Northeast Regional Office 东北区分局 dōngběiqū fēnjú

    Southeast Regional Office 东南区分局 dōngnánqū fēnjú

    Western Regional Office 西区分局 xīqū fēnjú

registry date 登记日期 dēngjì rìqī

removable 应驱逐出境的 yīng qūzhú chūjìng de

removable alien 应驱逐出境的外国人 yīng qūzhú chūjìng de wàiguórén

removal *n* 驱逐出境 qūzhú chūjìng

removal hearing 驱逐出境听证会 qūzhú chūjìng tīngzhènghuì

removal of inadmissible and deportable aliens 将禁止入境和应递解的人驱逐出境 jiāng jìnzhǐ rùjìng hé yīng dìjiè de rén qūzhú chūjìng

removal proceeding 驱逐程序 qūzhú chéngxù

remove *v* 驱逐 qūzhú

remove at government expense 政府负担驱逐费用 zhèngfǔ fùdān qūzhú fèiyòng

renewal application 展期申请 zhǎnqī shēnqǐng

required departure 规定离境 guīdìng líjìng

rescission process 撤销身份的程序 chèxiāo shēnfèn de chéngxù

reserved decision 延后决定 yánhòu juédìng

resettlement *n* 重新安置 chóngxīn ānzhì

residence *n* 住所 zhùsuǒ, 居住地 jūzhùdì

resident alien 居民外国人 jūmín wàiguórén

returning resident alien 回美的居民外国人 huíměi de jūmín wàiguórén

ROP 见 record of proceeding

safe haven 庇护所 bìhùsuǒ

safe third country 安全第三国 ānquán dì-sān guó

sanctions for contemptuous conduct 对藐视行为的惩罚 duì miǎoshì xíngwéi de chéngfá

SAW 见 special agricultural worker

service center 服务中心 fúwù zhōngxīn *(of USCIS /* 移民局设有四个服务中心)

  California Service Center 加利福尼亚州服务中心 jiālìfúníyà zhōu fúwù zhōngxīn

  Nebraska Service Center 内布拉斯加州服务中心 nèibùlāsījiā zhōu fúwù zhōngxīn

  Texas Service Center 得克萨斯州服务中心 dékèsàsī zhōu fúwù zhōngxīn

  Vermont Service Center 佛蒙特州服务中心 fóméngtè zhōu fúwù zhōngxīn

significant possibility 很高的可能性 hěn gāo de kěnéngxìng

smuggler *(of people)* n 人口走私者 rénkǒu zǒusī zhě, 蛇头 shétóu

special agricultural worker (SAW) 特别农工 tèbié nónggōng

special immigrant 特别移民 tèbié yímín

special naturalization provisions 特别归化规定 tèbié guīhuà guīdìng

specialty occupation 特殊专业 tèshū zhuānyè

sponsor n 担保人 dānbǎorén

State Department response 国务院的批复 guówùyuàn de pīfù

stateless *adj* 无国籍的 wú guójí de

status review 身份审查 shēnfèn shěnchá

stowaway *n* 偷渡者 tōudùzhě, 偷渡客 tōudùkè

student *n* 学生 xuéshēng

suboffice 办事处 bànshìchù (*of a district office, USCIS /* 移民支局下设机构)

supplemental asylum application 补充庇护申请 bǔchōng bìhù shēnqǐng

supporting document 支持性文件 zhīchíxìng wénjiàn, 证明文件 zhèngmíng wénjiàn

surrender for removal 为执行驱逐出境而到案 wéi zhíxíng qūzhú chūjìng ér dào'àn

swear in citizens 入籍宣誓 rùjí xuānshì

swearing-in ceremony 宣誓仪式 xuānshì yíshì

swearing-in session 宣誓仪式 xuānshì yíshì

Temporary Protection Status (TPS) 临时保护身份 línshí bǎohù shēnfèn

temporary resident 临时居民 línshí jūmín

temporary worker 临时工人 línshí gōngrén

terrorist activity 恐怖主义活动 kǒngbùzhǔyì huódòng

TPS 见 Temporary Protection Status

transit alien 过境外国人 guòjìng wàiguórén

Transit Without Visa (TWOV) 无签证过境 wú qiānzhèng guòjìng

Transition Period Custody Rules 过渡期扣押规则 guòdùqī kòuyā guīzé

treaty investor (E-2 Visa) 条约国投资人 tiáoyuē guó tóuzīrén (*E-2* 签证 *e-èr qiānzhèng*)

treaty trader (E-1 Visa) 条约国商人 tiáoyuē guó shāngrén (*E-1* 签证 *e-yī qiānzhèng*)

TWOV 见 Transit Without Visa

two-year rule 两年规则 liǎngnián guīzé (*two-year home country physical presence requirement for J-1 exchange visitors and their J-2 dependents / J-1* 交换学者须回国服务两年)

unaccompanied minor 孤身未成年人 gūshēn wèichéngniánrén

undocumented aliens 无证外国人 wú zhèng wàiguórén, 非法移民 fēifǎ yímín

United States Citizenship and Immigration Services (USCIS) 美国公民与移民服务局 měiguó gōngmín yǔ yímín fúwù jú

unlawful stay 非法逗留 fēifǎ dòuliú

unlawfully present 非法居留 fēifǎ jūliú

USCIS 见 United States Citizenship and Immigration Services

visa *n* 签证 qiānzhèng

Visa Bulletin 签证公报 qiānzhèng gōngbào, 移民排期表 yímín páiqī biǎo

visa extension 签证延期 qiānzhèng yánqī

Visa Waiver Program (VWP) 签证豁免计划 qiānzhèng huòmiǎn jìhuà

vocational student (M-1 Visa) 职业培训学生 zhíyè péixùn xuéshēng (*M-1* 签证 *m-yī qiānzhèng*)

voluntary departure 自动离境 zìdòng líjìng

voluntary departure at the conclusion of proceedings 诉讼程序结束后自动离境 sùsòng chéngxù jiéshù hòu zìdòng líjìng

voluntary departure bond 自动离境担保金 zìdòng líjìng dānbǎojīn

voluntary departure order 自动离境令 zìdòng líjìng lìng

**voluntary departure prior to completion of
    proceedings** 诉讼程序结束前自动离境 sùsòng
    chéngxù jiéshù qián zìdòng líjìng
voluntary removal 自动离境 zìdòng líjìng
VWP 见 Visa Waiver Program
well-founded fear of persecution 有充分理由害怕受到
    迫害 yǒu chōngfèn lǐyóu hàipà shòudào pòhài
withdrawal *n* 撤回 chèhuí, 撤销 chèxiāo
withholding of deportation 暂缓递解出境 zànhuǎn dìjiè
    chūjìng
withholding of removal 暂缓驱逐出境 zànhuǎn qūzhú
    chūjìng

移民法词汇

Traffic Law
交通法词汇

Traffic law deals with the rules governing the use of motor vehicles on public highways, the requirements for obtaining a driver's license, requirements concerning insurance, penalties for breaking traffic rules, and methods of enforcing safety measures such as seat-belt requirements and the ban against driving while intoxicated. In the United States, state law governs most traffic-law matters.

accident *n* 事故 shìgù
accident report 事故报告 shìgù bàogào
accumulation of points 累积记分 lěijī jìfēn
aggravated unlicensed operation (AUO) 严重无照驾驶 yánzhòng wúzhào jiàshǐ (指驾照被扣留或吊销期间开车)
aggressive driver program 攻击性驾驶辅导班 gōngjīxìng jiàshǐ fǔdǎobān
aggressive driving 攻击性驾驶 gōngjīxìng jiàshǐ
alcoholic beverage 酒精饮料 jiǔjīng yǐnliào
alternate-side parking 换边泊车 huànbiān bóchē
ambulance *n* 救护车 jiùhùchē
answer a ticket 答复罚单 dáfù fádān
at-fault states 实行过失制的州 shíxíng guòshīzhì de zhōu
AUO 见 aggravated unlicensed operation
BAC 见 blood alcohol concentration
basic speed rule 基本速度规则 jīběn sùdù guīzé

blood alcohol concentration (BAC) 血液酒精浓度 xuèyè jiǔjīng nóngdù

breath test 呼吸测试 hūxī cèshì

bridge *n* 桥 qiáo

buckle up 系安全带 jì ānquándài

cancel *v* 撤销 chèxiāo

careless driving 粗心驾驶 cūxīn jiàshǐ

case number 案件编号 ànjiàn biānhào

cell phone law 手机法 shǒujī fǎ

chemical test refusal 拒绝接受化学测试 jùjué jiēshòu huàxué cèshì

child restraint law 儿童保护措施法 értóng bǎohù cuòshī fǎ

citation *n* 传讯 chuánxùn, 传票 chuánpiào

claim trial 请求庭审 qǐngqiú tíngshěn

clean driving record 无不良驾驶记录 wú bùliáng jiàshǐ jìlù

collateral *n* 担保 dānbǎo, 抵押 dǐyā

collision *n* 碰撞 pèngzhuàng

conditional license 有条件的驾照 yǒutiáojiàn de jiàzhào

confiscated license 被没收驾照 bèi mòshōu jiàzhào

contest *v* 抗辩 kàngbiàn

contributory negligence 原告过失 yuángào guòshī

conviction *n* 判罪 pànzuì

court appearance date 出庭日 chūtíng rì

court appearance violations 需出庭的违规行为 xū chūtíng de wéiguī xíngwéi

court trial 庭审 tíngshěn

courtesy notice 礼节性通知 lǐjiéxìng tōngzhī

crash *n/v* 撞车 zhuàngchē

crossing guard 过路护卫 guòlù hùwèi

cutting 抢道超车 qiǎngdào chāochē

DDL 见 digital driver license

DDP 见 drinking driver program

death *n* 死亡 sǐwáng

default conviction 缺席判罪 quēxí pànzuì

defensive driving 防御性驾驶 fángyùxìng jiàshǐ

Department of Transportation (DOT) 交通部
　　jiāotōngbù

digital driver license (DDL) 数码驾照 shùmǎ jiàzhào

dismiss *v* 撤销 chèxiāo, 不受理 bùshòulǐ

disregard of the rights or safety of others
　　不顾他人权利或安全 bùgù tārén quánlì huò ānquán

DLC 见 Driver's License Compact

DOT 见 Department of Transportation

double parking 双重泊车 shuāngchóng bóchē

drinking and driving offenses 酒后开车 jiǔhòu kāichē

drinking driver program (DDP) 酒后开车辅导班
　　jiǔhòu kāichē fǔdǎobān

driver *n* 驾驶人 jiàshǐrén, 司机 sījī

driver improvement program 改善驾驶辅导班 gǎishàn
　　jiàshǐ fǔdǎobān

driver record 驾驶记录 jiàshǐ jìlù

driver's license 驾照 jiàzhào

Driver's License Compact (DLC) 驾照公约 jiàzhào
　　gōngyuē (各州之间交换交通违规信息的公约)

driving privilege 驾驶特权 jiàshǐ tèquán

driving through safety zone 穿行安全岛 chuānxíng
　　ānquándǎo

driving under the influence (DUI) 酒后开车 jiǔ hòu
　　kāichē, 吸毒后开车 xīdú hòu kāichē

driving while ability impaired (DWAI)
　　驾驶能力受损后开车 jiàshǐ nénglì shòusǔn hòu
　　kāichē

driving while intoxicated (DWI) 酒后开车 jiǔ hòu kāichē, 吸毒后开车 xīdú hòu kāichē

driving while suspended 驾照被扣留期间开车 jiàzhào bèi kòuliú qījiān kāichē

driving with an expired license 驾照过期开车 jiàzhào guòqī kāichē

DUI 见 driving under the influence

DWAI 见 driving while ability impaired

DWI 见 driving while intoxicated

emergency stop 紧急停车 jǐnjí tíngchē

emergency vehicles 紧急车辆 jǐnjí chēliàng

exceeding maximum speed limit 超过最高限速 chāoguò zuìgāo xiànsù

expressway *n* 快速公路 kuàisù gōnglù

failure to obey traffic control device 不遵守交通控制装置 bùzūnshǒu jiāotōng kòngzhì zhuāngzhì

failure to pay fine (FTP) 不付罚款 bùfù fákuǎn

failure to stop for traffic light 闯交通灯 chuǎng jiāotōngdēng

failure to use turn signals 转弯不打灯 zhuǎnwān bùdǎdēng

failure to yield right of way 不让路 bùrànglù

failure to yield to pedestrian in crosswalk 不给人行横道上的行人让路 bùgěi rénxíng héngdào shàng de xíngrén rànglù

falsify *v* 窜改 cuàngǎi, 伪造 wěizào

fatal accident 致命事故 zhìmìng shìgù

fatality *n* 致命事故 zhìmìng shìgù, 致命性 zhìmìngxìng

fault *n* 过失 guòshī

fight a traffic ticket 对交通罚单提出抗辩 duì jiāotōng fádān tíchū kàngbiàn

financial responsibility 财务责任 cáiwù zérèn
fine *n/v* 罚款 fákuǎn
first offense 第一次违规 dì-yīcì wéiguī
fix-it-ticket 修车罚单 xiūchē fádān
following distance 跟车距离 gēnchē jùlí
following too closely 跟车过近 gēnchē guò jìn
freeway *n* 高速公路 gāosù gōnglù
frontal impact 正面碰撞 zhèngmiàn pèngzhuàng
front-seat occupants 前排乘客 qiánpái chéngkè
FTP 见 failure to pay fine
green light 绿灯 lùdēng
hazard *n* 危险 wēixiǎn
head-on collision 迎面相撞 yíngmiàn xiāngzhuàng
highway *n* 高速公路 gāosù gōnglù
highway patrol 高速公路巡警 gāosù gōnglù xúnjǐng
hit and run 肇事逃逸 zhàoshì táoyì
honk *v* 鸣喇叭 míng lǎba
identity *n* 身份 shēnfèn, 身份证 shēnfènzhèng
impact *n* 碰撞 pèngzhuàng
impeding traffic 阻碍交通 zǔ'ài jiāotōng
implied consent 默示同意 mòshì tóngyì
impound *v* 扣押车辆 kòuyā chēliàng
impound lot *n* 扣车场 kòuchē chǎng
impounded vehicle 被扣押车辆 bèi kòuyā chēliàng
imprisonment *n* 监禁 jiānjìn
improper *adj* 不当的 bùdàng de
improper passing 不当超车 bùdàng chāochē
improper turn at traffic light 交通路口不当转弯
　　　jiāotōng lùkǒu bùdàng zhuǎnwān
in excess of 超出 chāochū
infraction *n* 轻微违规 qīngwēi wéiguī
injury *n* 伤害 shānghài

inspection *n* 车检 chējiǎn

inspection sticker 车检标签 chējiǎn biāoqiān

insurance identification card 保险卡 bǎoxiǎnkǎ

insurance premium 保险费 bǎoxiǎnfèi

insurance settlement 保险理赔 bǎoxiǎn lǐpéi

insurance violation 保险违规 bǎoxiǎn wéiguī

intersection *n* 道路交叉口 dàolù jiāochākǒu

interstate highway 州际高速公路 zhōujì gāosù gōnglù

intoxication *(alcohol; drug)* *n* 中毒 zhòngdú

    alcohol intoxication 酒精中毒 jiǔjīng zhòngdú

    narcotic intoxication 毒品中毒 dúpǐn zhòngdú

issuing officer 开罚单的警官 kāi fádānde jǐngguān

jaywalk *v* 违规过马路 wéiguī guò mǎlù

junction *n* 交叉口 jiāochākǒu

lane violation 车道违规 chēdào wéiguī

law enforcement 执法 zhífǎ, 执法部门 zhífǎ bùmén

leaving the scene of an accident 擅离事故现场 shànlí
    shìgù xiànchǎng

liability insurance 责任保险 zérèn bǎoxiǎn

license plate 车牌 chēpái

local road 地方道路 dìfāng dàolù

loss of driving privileges 失去驾驶特权 shīqù jiàshǐ
    tèquán

making unsafe lane changes 不当换车道 bùdàng huàn
    chēdào

mandatory *adj* 法定的 fǎdìng de, 强制性的
    qiángzhìxìng de

mandatory appearance violations
    法定出庭的交通违规行为 fǎdìng chūtíng de
    jiāotōng wéiguī xíngwéi

mechanical violation 设备违规 shèbèi wéiguī

miles per hour (mph) 时速 shísù

minimum speed rule 最低速度规则 zuìdī sùdù guīzé

motor vehicle 机动车 jīdòngchē

motor vehicle authority 机动车辆管理局 jīdòng
     chēliàng guǎnlǐ jú

motorist *n* 机动车驾驶人 jīdòngchē jiàshǐrén

moving against traffic 逆行 nìxíng

moving violation 行车违规 xíngchē wéiguī

mph 见 miles per hour

**National Highway Traffic Safety Administration
     (NHTSA)** 国家高速公路交通安全局 guójiā gāosù
     gōnglù jiāotōng ānquán jú

no contest plea 不抗辩 bùkàngbiàn

no parking 禁止泊车 jìnzhǐ bóchē

no standing 禁止停留 jìnzhǐ tíngliú

no stopping 禁止停车 jìnzhǐ tíngchē

no-fault state 实行无过失制的州 shíxíng wú guòshīzhì
     de zhōu

non-compliance *n* 违规 wéiguī

non-mandatory appearance violations 非法定出庭的
     违规行为 fēi fǎdìng chūtíngde wéiguī xíngwéi

non-moving violation 非行车违规 fēi xíngchē wéiguī

Nonresident Violator Compact (NRVC)
     非居民违规公约 fēi jūmín wéiguī gōngyuē

notice of revocation *(of driver's license)* 吊销驾照通知
     diàoxiāo jiàzhào tōngzhī

notice of suspension *(of driver's license)* 扣留驾照通知
     kòuliú jiàzhào tōngzhī

NRVC 见 Nonresident Violator Compact

obey *v* 遵守 zūnshǒu

offense *n* 违规 wéiguī

Traffic Law

open container law 开封法 kāifēngfǎ (*law that prohibits the possession of any open alcoholic beverage container and the consumption of any alcoholic beverage in the passenger area of any motor vehicle that is located on a public highway or right-of-way* / 禁止在汽车客舱携带打开盖子的酒精饮料或饮用酒精饮料)

overtaking and passing 超车 chāochē

overturn *v* 翻车 fānchē

paid parking permit 预付费停车证 yùfùfèi tíngchēzhèng

parking ticket 泊车罚单 bóchē fádān

parking violations 泊车违规 bóchē wéiguī

parkway *n* 公园路 gōngyuán lù

passing a stopped school bus 超停着的校车 chāo tíngzhe de xiàochē

passing on the right 右边超车 yòubian chāochē

passing on the shoulder 路肩超车 lùjiān chāochē

pay by mail 邮寄支付 yóujì zhīfù

PBJ 见 probation before judgment

penalty *n* 处罚 chǔfá

personal injury protection (PIP) 人身伤害保护险 rénshēn shānghài bǎohù xiǎn

PIP 见 personal injury protection

point *n* 记分 jìfēn

point system 记分制度 jìfēn zhìdù

police report 警察报告 jǐngchá bàogào

posted speed limit 标志限速 biāozhì xiànsù

privilege *n* 特权 tèquán

probation *n* 查看 chákàn, 缓刑 huǎnxíng

probation before judgment (PBJ) 判决前查看 pànjué qián chákàn

probationary driver program 见习驾驶人辅导班
jiànxí jiàshǐrén fǔdǎobān

proof of identity 身份证明 shēnfèn zhèngmíng

proof of insurance 保险证明 bǎoxiǎn zhèngmíng

property damage 财产损失 cáichǎn sǔnshī

provisional driver's license 见习驾照 jiànxí jiàzhào

pull over 靠边停车 kàobiān tíngchē (*police instruction to a motorist to bring his or her vehicle to a stop at a curb or at the side of a road* / 警察命令驾驶人靠路边停车)

race *n* 赛车 sàichē

racing on the highway 高速公路赛车 gāosù gōnglù sàichē

radar detector 雷达探测器 léidá tàncèqì

ramp *n* 匝道 zādào

reaction distance 反应距离 fǎnyìng jùlí

reaction time 反应时间 fǎnyìng shíjiān

rear-end collision 追尾 zhuīwěi

reckless driving 野蛮驾驶 yěmán jiàshǐ, 鲁莽驾驶
lǔmǎng jiàshǐ

red light 红灯 hóngdēng

reduction in points 减分 jiǎnfēn

refusing to submit to a breath test 拒绝接受呼吸测试
jùjué jiēshòu hūxī cèshì

registration *n* 登记 dēngjì

reinstatement *n* 恢复驾驶特权 huīfù jiàshǐ tèquán

respond *v* 回应 huíyìng

restoration *n* 恢复驾驶特权 huīfù jiàshǐ tèquán

restriction *n* 限制 xiànzhì

revocation *n* 吊销驾照 diàoxiāo jiàzhào

right of way 先行权 xiānxíngquán, 路权 lùquán

road *n* 道路 dàolù

road rage 公路斗气 gōnglù dòuqì

Traffic Law

roll-over *n* 翻车 fānchē

run a red light 闯红灯 chuǎng hóngdēng

run a stop sign 闯停车标志 chuǎng tíngchē biāozhì

safety responsibility hearing 安全责任听证会 ānquán zérèn tīngzhènghuì

Safety Responsibility Law 安全责任法 ānquán zérèn fǎ

sanction *n* 惩罚 chéngfá

scene of an accident 事故现场 shìgù xiànchǎng

school bus 校车 xiàochē

school zone 校区 xiàoqū

scofflaw *n* 拒付罚款的交通违规者 jùfù fákuǎn de jiāotōng wéiguīzhě

seat belt law 安全带法 ānquándài fǎ

second offense 第二次违规 dì-èrcì wéiguī

serious physical injury 严重人身伤害 yánzhòng rénshēn shānghài

shoulder harness 肩带 jiāndài

side collision 侧面碰撞 cèmiàn pèngzhuàng

signal for help 求助示意 qiúzhù shìyì

siren *n* 警报器 jǐngbàoqì

slow down 减速 jiǎnsù

slow speed blocking traffic 车速太慢阻碍交通 chēsù tàimàn zǔ'ài jiāotōng

speed contest 赛车 sàichē

speed limit 速度限制 sùdù xiànzhì

speeding *n* 超速 chāosù

speeding ticket 超速罚单 chāosù fádān

stalling on railroad tracks 汽车在铁路道口熄火 qìchē zài tiělù dàokǒu xīhuǒ

standing violation 停留违规 tíngliú wéiguī

statutory speed limit 法定限速 fǎdìng xiànsù

交通法词汇

stop *v* 停止 tíngzhǐ, 停车 tíngchē
stop sign 停车标志 tíngchē biāozhì
stopping violations 停车违规 tíngchē wéiguī
summary offense 即决违规行为 jíjué wéiguī xíngwéi
surcharge *n* 附加费 fùjiāfèi
suspension *n* 扣留驾照 kòuliú jiàzhào
suspension termination fee 发还扣留驾照手续费
    fāhuán kòuliú jiàzhào shǒuxùfèi
tailgate *v* 跟车过近 gēnchē guò jìn
third offense 第三次违规 dì-sāncì wéiguī
ticket *n* 罚单 fádān; *v* 开罚单 kāi fádān
tire blowout 爆胎 bàotāi
toll *adj/n/v* 收费 shōufèi
toll booth 收费站 shōufèi zhàn
toll bridge 收费桥 shōufèi qiáo
toll road 收费路 shōufèi lù
traffic court 交通法庭 jiāotōng fǎtíng
traffic offenses 交通违规 jiāotōng wéiguī
traffic school 交通违规学校 jiāotōng wéiguī xuéxiào
traffic sign 交通标志 jiāotōng biāozhì, 道路标志 dàolù
    biāozhì
traffic tickets 交通罚单 jiāotōng fádān
traffic violations bureau 交通违规事务处 jiāotōng
    wéiguī shìwù chù
traffic violations reciprocity 交通违规的对等处理
    jiāotōng wéiguī de duìděng chǔlǐ
traffic violator school 违规驾驶人学校 wéiguī jiàshǐrén
    xuéxiào
traveling in excess of the speed limit 超速行驶 chāosù
    xíngshǐ
tunnel *n* 隧道 suìdào
turn in a license 上交驾照 shàngjiāo jiàzhào

turnpike *n* 坦派克收费高速公路 tǎn pài kè shōufèi gāosù gōnglù

unattended motor vehicle 驾驶人不在场的机动车辆 jiàshǐrén bùzàichǎng de jīdòng chēliàng

uninsured vehicle 未保险车辆 wèi bǎoxiǎn chēliàng

unlawful use of median strip 非法使用隔离带 fēifǎ shǐyòng gélídài

vehicle code 交通法规 jiāotōng fǎguī

vehicular assault 车辆伤害罪 chēliàng shānghài zuì

vehicular homicide 车祸致人死命罪 chēhuò zhìrén sǐmìng zuì

violation *n* 违规 wéiguī

violator *n* 违规者 wéiguīzhě

wear *(seat belt)* *v* 系 jì (安全带 ānquándài)

weaving *n* 迂回穿行 yūhuí chuānxíng

whiplash *n* 鞭打式损伤 biāndǎshì sǔnshāng

window tint 车窗贴膜 chēchuāng tiēmó

yellow light 黄灯 huángdēng

yield *v* 让路 rànglù

zero tolerance law 零容忍法 língróngrěn fǎ

交通法词汇

Appendices

(附录)

Appendix I
附录一

Useful Phrases
常用短语

Are you choking?
你卡着了？ nǐ qiǎzhe le?

Are you hurt?
你受伤了吗？ nǐ shòushāngle ma?

Are you lost?
你迷路了吗？ nǐ mílùle ma?

Come out with your hands up!
举手出来！ jǔshǒu chūlái!

Cover this person with a blanket.
给他 (她) 盖条毯子。gěi tā gài tiáo tǎnzi.

Do not move this person.
不要动他 (她)。bùyào dòng tā.

Do you know how to read?
你会读吗？ nǐ huì dú ma?

Do you know how to write?
你会写吗？ nǐ huì xiě ma?

Do you need a doctor?
你需要医生吗？ nǐ xūyào yīshēng ma?

282

Do you speak Chinese?
你说中文吗？ nǐ shuō zhōngwén ma?

Do you speak English?
你说英文吗？ nǐ shuō yīngwén ma?

Do you understand me?
你懂我的话吗？ nǐ dǒng wǒ de huà ma?

Do you wish to make a statement?
你有话要说吗？ nǐ yǒu huà yào shuō ma?

Don't shoot!
别开枪！ bié kāiqiāng!

Drop the weapon!
放下武器！ fàngxià wǔqì!

Exit the building!
从楼房出来！ cóng lóufáng chūlái!

Fire!
火！ huǒ!

Get out of the car!
下车！ xiàchē!

Help!
救命！ jiùmìng!

I am a police officer!
我是警察！ wǒ shì jǐngchá!

I am going to give you first aid.
我马上给你做急救。 wǒ mǎshàng gěi nǐ zuò jíjiù.

I was robbed.
我被抢了。 wǒ bèi qiǎng le.

Is there a doctor here?
这里谁是医生？ zhèlǐ shuí shì yīshēng?

Is there anyone else here?
还有人吗？ háiyǒu rén ma?

Is there anyone here?
有人吗？ yǒu rén ma?

Lie down on the floor (face down)!
趴下！脸朝下！ pā xià! liǎn cháo xià!

Open the door, I have a search warrant!
开门，我有搜查证！ kāimén, wǒ yǒu sōucházhèng!

Please come with me.
请随我来。 qǐng suí wǒ lái.

Please fill out this form.
请填这张表。 qǐng tián zhè zhāng biǎo.

Please read this.
请过目。 qǐng guòmù.

Please repeat.
请再说一遍。 qǐng zài shuō yībiàn.

Please sign this.
请签名。 qǐng qiānmíng.

Please speak more slowly.
请再说慢点儿。 qǐng zài shuō màndiǎnr.

Please tell me what happened.
告诉我出了什么事。 gàosù wǒ chūle shénme shì.

Please wait here.
请在这里等。 qǐng zài zhèlǐ děng.

Pull over and stop!
靠边停车！ kào biān tíngchē!

Put your hands against the car!
双手扶车！ shuāngshǒu fú chē!

Put your hands against the wall!
双手扶墙！shuāngshǒu fú qiáng!

Put your hands behind your head!
双手放在脑后！shuāngshǒu fang zài nǎohòu!

Release that person!
放那人走！fàng nàrén zǒu!

Show me your ID / driver's license / car registration / passport.
请出示身份证 / 驾照 / 车辆登记卡 / 护照。qǐng chūshì shēnfènzhèng / jiàzhào / chēliàng dēngjìkǎ / hùzhào.

Stand still and don't move!
站着别动！zhànzhe biédòng!

Stop!
站住！zhàn zhù!

Stop or I'll shoot!
站住，不站住我开枪了！zhànzhù, bù zhànzhù wǒ kāiqiāng le!

Thank you.
谢谢。xièxiè.

This woman is in labor.
这位妇女要生了。zhèwèi fùnǚ yào shēng le.

What country are you from?
你是哪国人？nǐ shì nǎ guó rén?

What is your name?
你叫什么名字？nǐ jiào shénme míngzì?

What language do you speak?
你说哪国话？nǐ shuō nǎ guó huà?

Where are your parents?
你家长在哪里? nǐ jiāzhǎng zài nǎli?

Where do you live?
你住哪里? nǐ zhù nǎli?

You are free to go.
你可以走了。nǐ kěyǐ zǒu le.

You are under arrest!
你被逮捕了！nǐ bèi dàibǔ le!

You may call a lawyer.
你可以给律师打电话。nǐ kěyǐ gěi lùshī dǎ diànhuà.

You may contact your consulate.
你可以跟领事馆联系。nǐ kěyǐ gēn lǐngshìguǎn liánxì.

You may make a telephone call.
你可以打电话。nǐ kěyǐ dǎ diànhuà.

Appendix II
附录二

Miranda Warnings
米兰达告诫

You have the right to remain silent. If you give up that right, anything you say can and will be used against you in a court of law. You have the right to an attorney and to have an attorney present during questioning. If you cannot afford an attorney, one will be provided to you at no cost. During any questioning, you may decide at any time to exercise these rights, not answer any questions or make any statements.

你有权保持沉默。如果你放弃这项权利，你说的任何话可当做对你不利的供词提交法庭。你有权请律师，有权要求问话时律师在场。如果你没钱请律师，政府可免费为你提供一名。在任何问话过程中，你可随时决定行使这些权利，不回答任何问题，不作任何陈述。

nǐ yǒuquán bǎochí chénmò. rúguǒ nǐ fàngqì zhèxiàng quánlì, nǐ shuōde rènhé huà kě dàngzuò duì nǐ bùlìde gòngcí tíjiāo fǎtíng. nǐ yǒuquán qǐng lǜshī, yǒuquán yāoqiú wènhuà shí lǜshī zàichǎng. rúguǒ nǐ méi qián qǐng lǜshī, zhèngfǔ kě miǎnfèi wèi nǐ tígōng yīmíng. zài rènhé wènhuà guòchéng zhōng, nǐ kě suíshí juédìng xíngshǐ zhèxiē quánlì, bù huídá rènhé wèntí, bù zuò rènhé chénshù.

Appendix III
附录三

List of U.S. Immigration Forms
移民表格一览表

AR-11 Alien's Change of Address Card
外国人地址变更卡

AR-11 SR Alien's Change of Address Card, Special Registration
外国人地址变更卡简便版

G-14 Request for Additional Identifying Information
要求提供补充身份识别资料

G-28 Notice of Entry of Appearance as Attorney or Representative
指定律师或代理人通知书

G-325 Biographic Information
个人简历

G-639 Freedom of Information/Privacy Act Request
要求依据信息自由法/隐私法查阅资料

G-731 Inquiry About Status of I-551 Alien Registration Card
I-551外国人登记卡状况查询

G-845 Document Verification Request
要求核实证件

G-884 Request for the Return of Original Documents
要求归还原件

I-9 Employment Eligibility Verification
就业资格证明

I-86 Sponsor's Notice of Change of Address
担保人住址变更通知书

I-90 Application to Replace Permanent Residence Card
补发永久居民卡申请表

I-94 Arrival–Departure Card
入境/出境卡

I-102 Application for Replacement/Initial Nonimmigrant
　　Arrival–Departure Document
非移民入境/出境卡补发或颁发申请表

I-122 Notice to Alien Detained for Exclusion Hearing
在押外国人禁止入境听证会通知书

I-129 Petition for a Nonimmigrant Worker
非移民雇员申请表

I-129F Petition for Alien Fiancé(e)
外籍未婚夫 (妻) 移民申请表

I-129S Nonimmigrant Petition Based on Blanket L
　　Petition
L类签证非移民申请表

I-130 Petition for Alien Relative
外籍亲属移民申请表

I-131 Application for Travel Document
旅行证件申请表

I-140 Immigrant Petition for Alien Worker
外籍工人移民申请表 (又称职业移民申请表)

I-191 Application for Advance Permission to Return to Unrelinquished Domicile
提前允许返回未放弃住所申请表

I-192 Application for Advance Permission to Enter as Nonimmigrant
提前允许以非移民入境申请表

I-193 Application for Waiver of Passport and/or Visa
护照和/或签证豁免申请表

I-212 Application for Permission to Reapply for Admission into the United States after Deportation or Removal
被递解或驱逐后重新申请入境申请表

I-213 Record of Deportable / Inadmissible Alien—the INS arrest report
应递解出境 / 禁止入境外国人记录 (移民局逮捕记录)

I-286 Notice of Custody Determination
设定担保金额听证会通知书

I-290B Notice of Appeal to the Administrative Appeals Office (AAO)
向行政上诉办公室提出上诉的通知书

I-360 Petition for Amerasian, Widow(er) or Special Immigrant
亚裔、寡鳏或特别移民申请表

I -361 Affidavit of Financial Support and Intent to Petition for Legal Custody of P.L. 97-359 Amerasian
为97-359号公法亚裔提供经济担保和申请法律监护的意向表

I-485 Application to Register Permanent Residence or Adjust Status
永久居留登记或调整身份申请表

I-485 Supplement A Supplement A to Form I-485 Adjustment of Status Under Section 245(i)
I-485表补充A

I-485 Supplement B NACARA Supplement to Form I-485
I-485表补充B

I-485 Supplement C HRIFA Supplement to Form I-485
I-485表补充C

I-508 Waiver of Rights, Privileges, Exemptions and Immunities
放弃权利、特权、免除和豁免

I-526 Immigrant Petition by Alien Entrepreneur
外国企业家移民申请表 (又称投资移民申请表)

I-539 Application to Extend/Change Nonimmigrant Status
延长/改变非移民身份申请表

I-566 Interagency Record of Request –A, G or NATO Dependent Employment Authorization or Change/Adjustment to/from A, G or NATO Status
A、G、NATO 类家属申请工作许可或身份变更机构间记录

I-589 Application for Asylum and for Withholding of Removal
庇护和暂缓驱逐出境申请表

I-600 Petition to Classify Orphan as an Immediate Relative
孤儿移民申请表

I-600A Application for Advance Processing of Orphan Petition
孤儿移民提前受理申请表

移民表格一览表

I-601 Application for Waiver of Ground of Excludability
豁免禁止入境理由申请表

I-602 Application by Refugee for Waiver of Grounds of
Excludability
难民豁免禁止入境理由申请表

I-612 Application for Waiver of the Foreign Residence
Requirement of Section 212(e) of the Immigration
and Nationality Act, as amended
豁免回国居住要求申请表

I-643 Health and Human Services Statistical Data for
Refugee/Asylee Adjusting Status
卫生和公众服务部难民/受庇护人调整身份统计数据

I-687 Application for Status as a Temporary Resident Under
Section 245A of the Immigration and Nationality Act
依据移民法 Section 245A 申请临时居民身份表

I-690 Application for Waiver of Grounds of Excludability
Under Sections 245A or 210 of the Immigration and
Nationality Act
依据移民法 Sections 245A 或 210 豁免禁止入境理由
申请表

I-693 Medical Examination of Aliens Seeking Adjustment
of Status
外国人调整身份体检表

I-694 Notice of Appeal of Decision Under Sections 245A
or 210 of the Immigration and Nationality Act
依据移民法 Sections 245A 或 210 提出上诉通知书

I-698 Application to Adjust Status from Temporary to
Permanent Resident (Under Section 245A of Public
Law 99-603)
临时居民身份调整为永久居民身份申请表

I-730 Refugee/Asylee Relative Petition
难民/受庇护人亲属团聚申请表

I-751 Petition to Remove the Conditions on Residence
解除居留限制申请表

I-765 Application for Employment Authorization
工作许可申请表

I-817 Application for Family Unity Benefits
家庭团聚优待申请表

I-821 Application for Temporary Protected Status
临时保护身份申请表

I-824 Application for Action on an Approved Application
     or Petition
批件补发申请表

I-829 Petition by Entrepreneur to Remove Conditions
投资移民解除限制条件申请表

I-851 Notice of Intent to Issue a Final Administrative
     Deportation Order
签发最后递解出境行政命令的意向通知书

I-862 Notice to Appear (Notice to Deportable Alien)
出庭通知

I-863 Notice of Referral to Immigration Judge
移交移民法官的通知书

I-864 Affidavit of Support Under Section 213A of the Act
经济担保书

I-864A Contract Between Sponsor and Household
     Member
担保人和家庭成员协议

移民表格一览表

List of U.S. Immigration Forms

N-470 Application to Preserve Residence for Naturalization Purposes
为归化目的保留永久居民身份申请表

N-565 Application for Replacement Naturalization/ Citizenship Document
补发归化/公民证书申请表

N-600 Application for Certificate of Citizenship
公民证书申请表

N-600K Application for Citizenship and Issuance of Certificate under Section 322
子女公民身份和公民证书申请表

N-644 Application for Posthumous Citizenship
追认公民身份申请表

N-648 Medical Certification for Disability Exceptions
残疾免考医生证明

移民表格一览表